The Eye of Ra and the Promised Land.

Not to be confused with the eye of Horus. The Eye of Ra represents the power of the sun and the protection of Egyptian royalty. The symbol is used for this book to represent Egyptian suzerainty over the entire Promised Land for almost the entire 2nd Millennium BC.

After the Flood, lands were allocated amongst the sons of Noah – Africa to the descendants of Ham and the Fertile Crescent to the descendants of Shem. Canaan, one of Ham's sons, broke the rules by settling in land promised to Shem's family. Some 8,000 years later, the leading power, then under ecological and economic pressure, sent its crown prince with an elite squad of 600 naar to reconquer that promised land. 'Naar' means mounted on camels. Subsequent control was partial and fleeting – until nearly 4,000 years later, when those declaring themselves descendants of that crown prince finally established effective and lasting control in the mid 20th century.

I dedicate this book to Alberto Zancanaro, a dear friend, a congiunti with whom theological discourse has caused me to dig deeper and to think harder about what I discover.

The Truth Will Set You Free

THIRD EDITION

Part Two

The Promised Land 2000 BC to 1000 BC

The emergence of the Israelites within the Egyptian Empire

GLYN THOMAS

Quintology Publishing
www.quintologypublications.com

Copyright © 2024 by Glyn Thomas & Gregory Thomas

All rights reserved, including the right to reproduce this work in any form whatsoever, without permission in writing from the publisher except for brief passages in reviews or in citations and references.

Printed by Ingram Spark and affiliates – Lightning Source UK Ltd, Milton Keynes, United Kingdom (see inside back page)
Third Edition, published March 2024.

Earlier editions entitled:- *The Levant in the Second Millenium BC*

Paperback ISBN: 978-1-7384439-4-9
Ebook ISBN: 978-1-7384439-5-6

Typeset, layout and cover design by Gregory Thomas
www.gregthomas.design

Contents

Map	The Levant in the 2nd Millennium BC
1	Recap of Part One and introduction to Part Two
2	New theory for the Exodus from slavery in Egypt
3	Geo-political history of Palestine during the 2nd Millennium BC
4	Egyptian decline enables pre-monarchical Israel to emerge.
5	Conclusions reviewing Egyptian power during 2nd Millennium BC
6	Where do the Israelites fit into recorded history & archaeological findings?
7	Where did the Israelites originate from?
8	The Promised Land
9	The Table of Nations in Genesis chapter 10
10	The origin of The Shepherd
11	The Tower of Babel
12	Abraham's interactions with Hittites, Philistines & Arameans
13	The story of Joseph in Egypt & the cities of Pithom and Ramesses
14	The Book of Joshua
15	The United Monarchy – Saul, David & Solomon
16	The stunning implications of the name Elizabeth
17	Cyrus conquest of Babylon – aided by Yahweh or by Marduk?
18	Biblical Inerrancy
18 *bis*	New evidence concerning the destruction of Sodom & Gomorrah and Jericho
19	An alternative view of our creation
20	Conclusions
	Appendix: Key family members of the ancient 'gods'
	Index
	Biblical references
	Bibliography
	Books in this series
	Symbols used on covers in this series

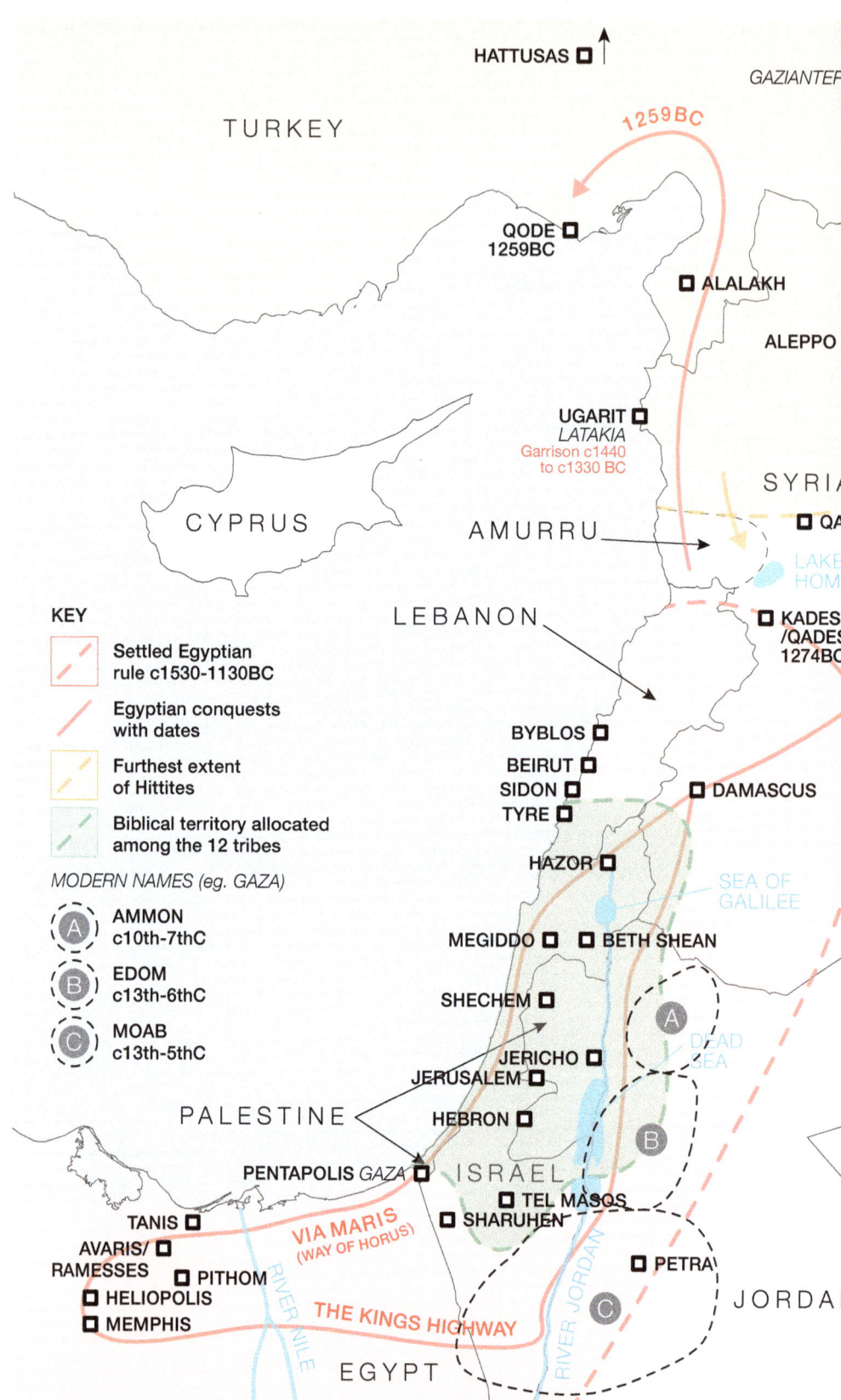

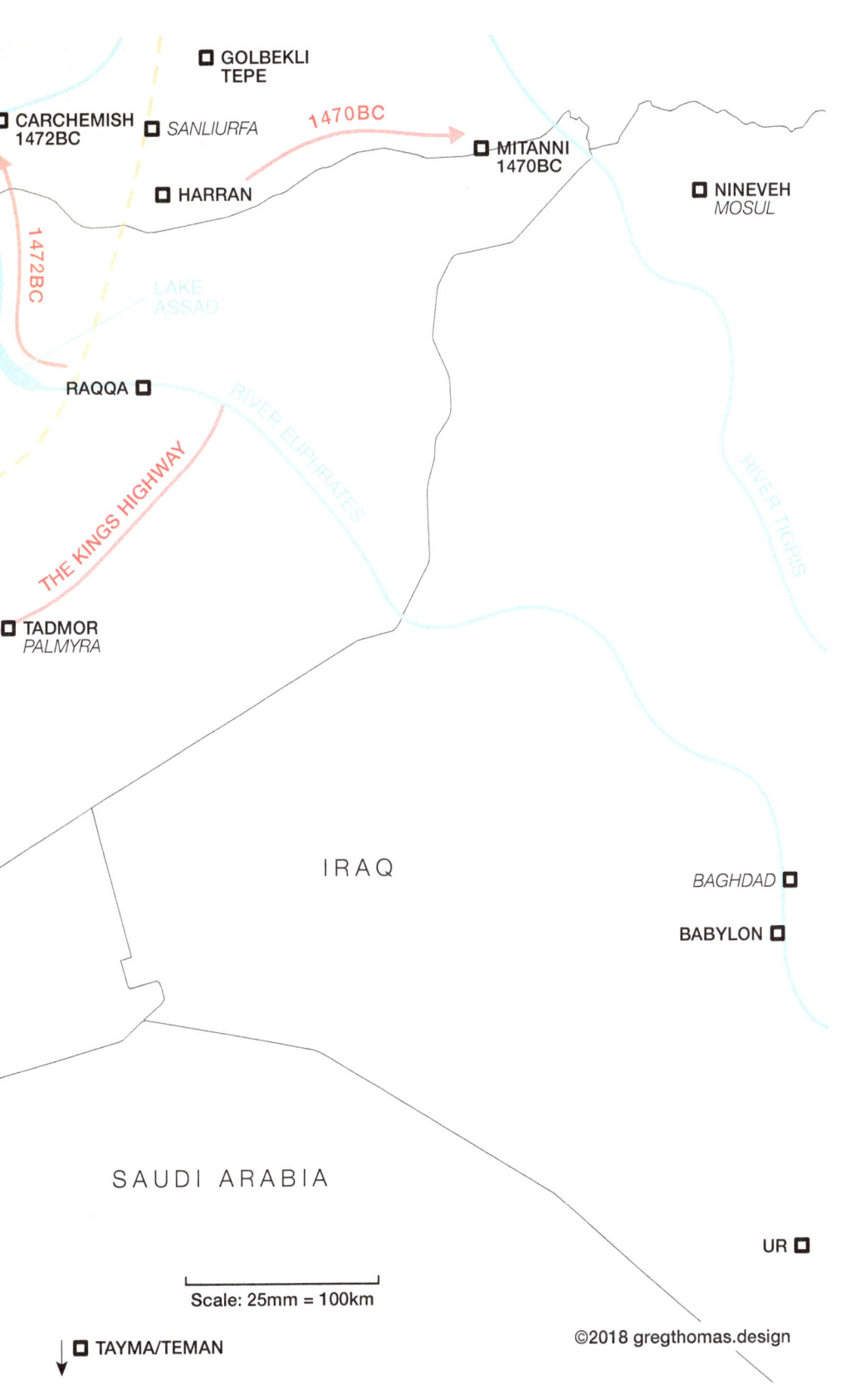

1

Recap of Part One and an introduction to Part Two

1.1 Firstly, a quick recap of Part One – "God, Enki, Ra/Marduk & Yahweh". The major imperative for the authorship of Part One was my 'discovery' of proof of the existence of unimaginable intelligence hard wired into the design of our Universe – specifically in the physical laws governing the atomic structures within the constituent members of the Table of Elements together with dozens of extremely finely tuned mathematical constants, from which often extremely tiny variations would have led either to an utterly inhospitable universe or to a very short lived event – far too short for any life form to have developed.

1.2 It also appears that the properties of compound elements, when subjected to heat and electrical impulses (such as lightening) are designed to fuse into complex compounds including amino acids. With amino acids being the building blocks of RNA and thence DNA – it seems life itself may be hard wired into the properties of the elements. From our human perspective, the unimaginable potential designed into the seemingly simple elements (hydrogen, carbon, oxygen, etc.) commonly existing in our universe containing the ability to combine in ways generating such profound abilities points to a designer with such an intelligence that it can only be described as God.

1.3 I then compared this awesome intelligence with the behaviour and character of Yahweh as described in the Old Testament and found that Yahweh, in many ways, represents the complete antithesis of Jesus. Moreover, even the Bible itself contains many clues that point to Yahweh

PART TWO: THE PROMISED LAND 2000 BC TO 1000 BC

being the Hebrew name for one of the many deities from ancient times we traditionally describe as 'pagan gods'. Again, the Bible itself describes extensive worship of many 'pagan' gods by the Hebrews, with Solomon accommodating many 'lesser gods' in niches when building the original Temple around 960BC.

1.4 Chronologically, strict monotheism amongst the Jews came only with the small minority who returned from exile in Babylon in 530BC – maybe influenced by the monotheism expressed by Cyrus, their Persian liberator following his occupation of Babylon. The release of the Israelites from Babylonian captivity even led the Prophet Isaiah to preach that Yahweh had anointed Cyrus as the prophesied Messiah (Isaiah 45:1).

1.5 Indeed, given the widespread assumption that the Jews were monotheistic at least after the return from Exile, it is amazing to learn that there still existed in Jesus time, a shrine in Bethlehem for Tammuz (a Sumerian king who ruled before the Flood, who because of his wise rule, came to be worshipped for millennia) – and that beliefs about Tammuz may have been weaved into one of the Gospels.

1.6 In assessing Yahweh, I examined the principal themes of the Torah – the first five books of the Old Testament. These books focus on four main topics – the Creation, the Flood, Abraham and Moses.

1.7 My findings were surprising: there is very strong evidence that the Creation story in Genesis is a blend of oral traditions, which must have originated from Abraham's education in Ur, documented by Levite priests in the 6th Century BC and of their review, whilst in Exile, of the original record from whence the story of creation originated. The original source being a Sumerian treatise now referred to as the 'Enuma Elish', fragments of which have been found dating back to 3800BC and large sections found dating back to around 2500BC. The Genesis version of creation constitutes an incomplete summary of the creation of our planet extracted from the Sumerian history of our solar system.

1.8 Alarmingly, most Christians have been led to believe Genesis is describing the creation of our entire universe!! Evidence suggests that during the Babylonian exile the Levite priests in Babylon had access to copies held in Nebuchadnezzar's library. Copying from the Enuma Elish by the Levites is evident by their mistakes in using Akkadian meanings for certain Sumerian words – as in attributing the creation of Eve to Adam's "rib".

Even worse, most Christian writers mistakenly refer to the Enuma Elish as Neo Babylonian, i.e. from only c600BC, based on the first example discovered that was translated in 1876, which was actually found in the Assyrian capital Nineveh and dates to two centuries earlier.

1.9 Noah emerges in a similar way, echoing Sumerian stories written thousands of years before the time of Abraham. In the Prequel to this series, I include material detailing recent geological work that enables us to precisely date and understand the event we refer to now as 'The Flood'. Other evidence has revealed that the Flood was not quite the mass extinction level event described biblically. However, a far earlier eruption of a mega volcano, Toba, around 75,000 years ago, came very close to making mankind extinct.

1.10 Biblical references to Abraham correlate with a real person about whose family extensive original documents (cuneiform tablets) have been uncovered which reveal he was the heir of a powerful family – and grandson of the High Priest of El Elyon and son of the High Priest of Sin. El Elyon being the Canaanite name for Enlil, the Lord Most High, and the name in Hebrew used to denote God in Genesis before the burning bush incident revealed the name Yahweh. Yahweh is also identified as one of the 70 descendants of Enlil's father – as described in Psalm 82. Another son of Enlil, Sin (associated with the Moon, whose symbol being a crescent moon turned 90 degrees and represented as a young bull), was known in Canaan as Ba'al. It is possible that Yahweh and Ba'al were different names for the same entity – for the second half of the second millennium BC, both Yahweh and Ba'al had a consort bearing the same name – Ashtoreth. Dozens of figurines of an entwined couple, 'Yahweh and his Ashtoreth', have been unearthed in excavations of pre-Exilic Israelite villages.

1.11 Just in case the cryptic note above, about Yahweh's parentage, sounds bizarre, I include the text of Deuteronomy 32:9 as translated from Hebrew and also from the Septuagint, clearly showing that the author of Deuteronomy saw Yahweh as one of many sons, or descendants or even emissaries of God:

Deut 32:9 – Hebrew "When El Elyon gave the nations as an inheritance, when he separated the sons of man, he set the boundaries of the peoples according to the number of the sons of God. For Yahweh's portion was his people; Jacob was the lot of his

PART TWO: THE PROMISED LAND 2000 BC TO 1000 BC

inheritance".

Deut 32:9 – LXX "When the Most High divided the nations, when he separated the sons of Adam, he set the boundaries of the nations according to the number of the emissaries of God. And his people Jacob became the portion of the Lord, Israel was the line of his inheritance".

1.12   Psalm 82 opens with Yahweh addressing the assembly of the 70 gods, the 'sons' of the Most High – *El Elyon* in Hebrew. Genesis 10 provides a list of the 70 nations between which the lands on earth were divinely allocated.

1.13   Moses, however, does not stand up to any examination – almost every aspect of the story of his life and events fails to pass any tests of logic or historical evidence – the entire saga being most accurately described as 'myth historicised'.

1.14   Since writing the first edition of Part One, I have come across far more evidence that the entire story of the Exodus is a confused work based on various tribal memories worked up into a confection to support a national foundation story bearing little regard to actual history. Much of the vocabulary and numerous references betray its origin as dating to the period during and after the Babylonian Exile – written a millennium or so after the time purported and without the benefit of access to reliable and accurate records of the period in which the story was set. Any germs of truth present in the story have been so diluted as to render the tale best treated as a work of fiction in its entirety.

1.15   We start this booklet by summarising the history of what is now Israel throughout the second millennium BC, and surprisingly we find the whole area under Egyptian control for almost the whole period, all except from 1655BC up to 1545BC and after 1120BC. This clearly has implications for biblical history. In Chapter 4, we see how although Egypt defeated the invading Sea Peoples (a federation of Greek tribes) who swept through what is now Turkey before turning south through Syria, Lebanon and Israel – and forced their defeated people to accept Egyptian suzerainty. However, the economic damage they had wrought – led inexorably to Egypt's decline. Shorn of its Hittite, Mycenae, Cypriot and Lebanese trading partners and particularly its suppliers of refined metals, Egypt's economic and military strength was badly hit. The cities of the Sea Peoples became the Philistines, who then spread out occupying the

RECAP OF PART ONE AND AN INTRODUCTION TO PART TWO

lowland areas of Israel until destroyed as an identifiable culture by the Babylonians.

1.16 In Chapter 5, we assess the evidence of the continuous Egyptian rule between 1550BC and 1120BC over what today is Israel, Lebanon and the western half of Syria and note the extent to which Biblical references can be found that reflect this.

1.17 In Chapter 6, we look at the evidence from historical records and archaeological findings to show the emergence of Israel and in Chapter 7 evidence of the sources of the nation of Israel.

1.18 Chapters 8 to 17 explore interesting subjects where new light can be shed on biblical events – in particular the reliance that may be placed upon the biblical texts describing the United Monarchy – the period of the kings Saul, David and Solomon.

1.19 A number of readers have suggested I should study the arguments put forward by "Inerrants", those believing that the Bible is the 'Word of God' and therefore cannot contain any errors. I have duly studied this point of view and include observations and conclusions as Chapter 18.

1.20 This new edition contains in new chapter 18*bis*, information on exciting new discoveries which show the destruction of both Sodom & Gomorrah and of Jericho were part of the same event. This explains both the mass migration into Lower Egypt and the consequent disruption in Egyptian culture.

1.21 Chapter 19 is dedicated to those who loved Chapter 1 of Part One – incorporating some mind-bending scientific suggestions concerning our origins!

1.22 I concluded Part One by noting that if Yahweh was not our Creator (which has serious implications for the books of the Old Testament) then two big issues arise – how should we view the numerous prophesies contained in the Old Testament which are interpreted as pointing to Jesus arrival on Earth and what to make of Jesus references to Jewish scripture recorded in the Gospels. These questions have fundamental implications but I concluded that this important subject fitted better into Part Three focused on Jesus than within the earlier historical focus of this book.

1.23   I have come to realize that Christian theology is long overdue a massive overhaul – to remedy numerous erroneous ideas adopted in the early centuries of the church but more importantly to recognise specific fundamental information about our universe and ourselves that has been revealed to us in the past few decades. These aspects are explored in Part Four.

RECAP OF PART ONE AND AN INTRODUCTION TO PART TWO

2

New theory for the Exodus from slavery in Egypt

2.1 Research undertaken for this booklet has led me to what I suspect is an entirely new explanation for Israelite memories of the Exodus and of slavery under Egyptian pharaohs. Despite wide reading, I have found no hint that anyone else has proposed the explanation set out herein – which makes it especially worthwhile to write for you.

2.2 In this section, I summarise the main issues that have led me to this new theory. Readers of the previous booklets were agreed that the breadth and depth of detail was helpful in understanding the issues addressed. Accordingly, you will not be disappointed by the wealth of historical evidence presented herein which leads to the novel conclusion.

2.3 The first issue involves trying to establish when the Old Testament books were first written and the extent to which they were edited by subsequent redaction and modification. Historically, the history as set out in biblical texts established primacy because from the Reformation onwards, when printing became mechanised (Gutenburg, 1440) and the volume of both books and readership soared – the history set out in the bible faced no competition. Classical scholars could understand Latin and Greek but any discrepancies between the historical detail in non-biblical records was scattered and inaccessible to all but a few scholars.

2.4 Total ignorance of pre-Greek history and languages prevailed until discovery of the trilingual Rosetta Stone in 1799 by Napoleon's troops. The Rosetta Stone provides a lengthy decree in Egyptian hieroglyphics, the contemporary Egyptian script of the Ptolemaic period (when carved in 196BC) and Ancient Greek. However, it was not until 1822 that the first translation of the hieroglyphics was published which allowed other inscriptions to then be translated.

2.5   Similarly, cuneiform text was deciphered by study of the Behistun Inscription, a trilingual text in Old Persian, Elamite and Babylonian cuneiform. Although first known to Europeans through reports of Robert Sherley in 1598, an Englishman retained as a diplomat by Austria, the Behistun Inscription defied easy translation due to its location. The inscription is located in a remote part of Iran near the top of a 100m high vertical limestone cliff on the ancient trade route from Babylon to Media. The inscription itself is vast: the Old Persian text contains 414 lines in five columns; the Elamite text includes 593 lines in eight columns, and the Babylonian Akkadian text is in 112 lines. The text covers an area of cliff face 15m by 25m. Next, a German surveyor, Carsten Niebuhr, visiting the area in 1764 representing King Frederick V of Denmark, copied the Old Persian text which he published in 1778 and which led to a general understanding of Old Persian. This facilitated the later translation of the Elamite and Babylonian Akkadian versions. This was enabled by Henry Rawlinson, a British army officer visiting the inscriptions in 1835, who returned in 1843 equipped with ropes and scaffolding to copy and make plaster casts of the cuneiform texts.

2.6   Having initially mastered Egyptian hieroglyphics and then Akkadian cuneiform during the 19th Century, archaeological expeditions from 1860's to the outbreak of WW1 fortunately yielded a treasure trove of original documents – mainly in the form of large baked clay tablets. It is estimated that museums in London, Berlin and Pennsylvania hold a few million. So many, that it is claimed that maybe only 10% have been translated so far.

2.7   The contribution of these early cuneiform tablets cannot be underestimated. Some have been dated back to the mid fourth millennium BC – i.e. around 3500BC. This compares with biblical texts, the oldest fragments being the Dead Sea scrolls from Qumran, with a few dating to around 300BC.

2.8   I have been delighted to discover that we now have an immensely detailed historical knowledge, derived from translation of a wealth of material, revealing the history of second millennium BC. Comparison with the biblical record reveals stark differences – hardly surprising given we are comparing original contemporary documents from the events in question with regularly recopied and evidently edited texts which cannot themselves have been in any written form during the millennium in question.

2.9 But surely, one may exclaim, the biblical record extends back before David (who captured Jerusalem in 1000BC), through Moses (c1500BC) to Abraham (c2000BC) and even further back to Noah and Adam?

2.10 In this booklet, we consider a wide range of historical physical evidence and identify many textual clues in the biblical texts that raise questions. Key questions include:

- When were the original texts of Jewish scripture written?

- In which language were they originally written?

- Is there evidence that the versions we have today have been altered – edited or redacted since the originals were written?

Much detailed evidence is provided in later chapters but let us just address language here – which provides a cut-off date for date of the earliest Hebrew texts.

2.11 Language is a good point to start. Original religious works were treasured and carefully guarded by the senior priests – the idea of translating the text to a different language or of redrafting sacred text into contemporary language would have been regarded as sacrilege. We have a very relevant example dating back centuries even before the claimed date of authorship of the first OT manuscripts and enduring right through the period when most conclude the bulk of the OT texts were written – and therefore illustrative of the prevailing cultural environment.

2.12 The High Priests (who included Abraham's father and grandfather) of the Lord Most High (Enlil, aka as El Elyon by both Canaanites and Israelites) never translated the original Sumerian texts regarded as sacred, such as the Enuma Elish (also referred to now as the Seven Tablets of Creation), into Akkadian, which was the lingua franca of the Middle East – but maintained the annual reading of their creation story in Sumerian for at least 1500 years after their demise – following the abandonment of Ur c2000BC through to Emperor Cyrus capture of Babylon in 539BC. This is a staggering achievement – indicative of the reverence and awe attached to these ancient texts. Perhaps we should study them more carefully?

2.13   We have the mysterious event, recorded in both 2 Kings 22:8 and 2 Chronicles 34, 35, describing Hilkiah, the High Priest of the year equating to 622BC, 'rediscovering' the Book of the Law hidden in a dusty crevice of the Temple. Why apparently the only copy of such a fundamental scripture for Judah should be so concealed is inexplicable. Scholars deduce it must have been part or all of what later became Deuteronomy because the versions of various laws that differ (from where the same laws are stated in Numbers and Leviticus) are the versions enacted under King Josiah's reforms. However, obviously written in Hebrew, the recovered document could not be much older than the Temple itself as the method of writing Hebrew only emerged around 1000BC from borrowing the then new Phoenician script.

2.14   If, as some believers insist, the Torah was written by Moses (maybe 1500BC) it could only have been written in Akkadian cuneiform or Egyptian hieroglyphics. The Ten Commandments, claimed originally to be written by Yahweh, were written in Hebrew? No, that is an invention from Hollywood. There was no written Hebrew at that time – so the tablets must have been written in Egyptian hieroglyphics. Actually, this would have been very logical as the inspiration for the Ten Commandments clearly comes from Chapter 125 of the Egyptian Book of the Dead – copies of which have been dated as far back as 2600BC – i.e. at least 1000 years prior to when most people place Moses.

2.15   So, imagine if the Ten Commandments had been written in Egyptian hieroglyphics, as dictated by Yahweh, surely no one would ever have dared to translate the official version into Hebrew and discard the originals. Oh, but of course, the Israelites "lost" the originals. Fundamentally, the priests would never dare to replace God's dictation with a translation into Hebrew and then use the result as the official version. Setting in a contemporary scene, today, people would be incredulous if it was suggested that a rendering of Shakespeare in modern English should be adopted as the official version of his works.

2.16 In fact, quite apart from numerous textual clues referring to events, practices and articles connected with the exile in Babylon, the greater part of both the Torah and the Prophets is written in Classical Hebrew – the language of the Jews when in exile in Babylon from 590BC. According to Persian census records nearly a million Jews remained in Babylon *after* Emperor Cyrus allowed them to return to Judah – despite providing a military escort to assist their return, a mere 40,000 bothered to do so. Indeed, Babylon remained the largest centre of Jewish culture until religious pressure from the Muslim rulers led to the rapid dispersion of the Jewish inhabitants of Babylon around AD1000.

2.17 To be fair, the Levite priests during the exile in Babylon faced an impossible task. Their flock believed Yahweh had abandoned them – most of the tribes had been carried away to Nineveh 150 years earlier and now the Temple was utterly destroyed and their leaders and the cream of their society were also torn away from Yahweh's promised land to dwell in Babylon. Developing the body of scripture must have seemed a worthwhile task to re-energise the devotion of the people. However, faced with an assortment of texts and oral traditions but without written history (and no internet to browse) – their tenuous knowledge of history is abundantly exposed. References elsewhere that are made to biblical accuracy with documented history invariably relate to the Monarchical period (1000BC to the exile in 596BC). This corresponds to the advent of Hebrew writing during the same period.

2.18 References to political facts prior to 1000BC suffer from the lack of any Jewish ability to record events prior to this date – so whilst texts supposedly recording earlier events refer to involvement of, for example, Egyptians, Hittites and Philistines – all the dates and places are hopelessly inaccurate.

2.19 As the next chapters explain, the most glaring historical facts are overlooked or misunderstood in the biblical texts placed in the pre-Monarchical period. The strongest anchor we have in the early period covered by the Bible is Abraham. Extensive details of his family have been uncovered – even the family home in Ur has apparently been identified and is now a tourist destination in Iraq! (It would be good to understand precisely how this attribution is evidenced.) However, the Bible omits to mention that when Abraham left his relocated family home in Harran, to journey to Canaan, he almost immediately went into lands under

PART TWO: THE PROMISED LAND 2000 BC TO 1000 BC

Egyptian suzerainty.

2.20 The map before chapter 1 (and downloadable from the website) shows the broad geographical extent of Egyptian rule in Asia from c2200BC through to c1030BC. The degree of control, occupation and exploitation waxed and waned during these 1200 years – but the only period when Egypt was weak was a short period of 110 years (1655BC to 1545BC) when Lower Egypt was occupied by originally nomadic peoples known as the Hyksos. However, after rising up and expelling the Hyksos, Egypt was at the pinnacle of its power for the succeeding four centuries – 1545BC to 1130BC. For almost all this period, records show Egypt exercising continuous control over all the currently populated areas of what today comprises Syria, Jordan, Lebanon and Israel. Egypt maintained garrisons along the key trade routes: the Way of Horus (along the coast) and the Kings Highway (along east bank of the Jordan) and in certain inland cities (including Jerusalem). Egypt maintained corvées (provision of seasonal labour by local population) to grow crops for the occupying military forces, extracting heavy taxation both in kind (minerals and foodstuffs) and in slave quotas.

2.21 Of all these matters, the biblical texts are strangely silent. But, actually the most likely explanation is just that memories based on oral traditions were hopelessly muddled.

2.22 From my research, the most plausible history places the Hyksos as the people referred to as enslaved Israelites in Egypt. Except that, in fact, the Hyksos were the slave-masters, controlling Lower Egypt (northern Egypt) and enslaving the Egyptians for over 100 years. Scattered memories of this role are even quoted in Exodus – where after crossing the 'Red Sea', the Israelites complain at the lack of food by reminiscing about life "with pots of meat, as much food as they could eat and lots of slaves" (Exodus 16:3) – clearly roles have been reversed in what is conventionally taught!

2.23 When the Egyptians expelled the Hyksos, they chased and repeatedly attacked their settlements in what would today be southern Israel. It is believed the surviving Hyksos settled to the east of the Jordan, some gradually filtered north and west to live a nomadic life in the Judean Highlands and possibly also Amurru. These peoples probably mixed with others such as the Arameans and Amorites around the northern and eastern fringes of Canaan. Those that stayed behind becoming the

NEW THEORY FOR THE EXODUS FROM SLAVERY IN EGYPT

People of 'Ad, later known as the Nabateans, with their capital at Petra.

2.24 My thesis is that Israelite memories of enslavement under Egypt actually relate to the 400 years after their remnants started to infiltrate Canaan whilst it was under Egyptian control and reflect enslavement as corvée and as slave quotas provided to Egyptian forces as part of annual tax levies. In addition, dozens of towns in 'Israel' were owned and run by Egyptian temples – the greatest being that of Thebes, each of which would have recruited hundreds of workers in what would have amounted to near slavery. In reality, this period of retained memory of enslavement took place mainly across Canaan – whilst Hebrew enslavement in Egypt would have originated from both annual tax tributes of slaves together with captives from military actions against roaming bands in the highlands regarded as bandits. The memories retained of a nightmare escape from Egypt was not from slavery but of being expelled by the Egyptians that the Israelites had enslaved.

2.25 Israelite memories of slavery under Egyptian control would have arisen from their experiences between c1400BC when we have references to nomadic bandits infiltrating into Canaan from the east – the Israelite slaves in Egypt never experienced an exodus. As slaves in Egypt, their families became assimilated as part of the underclass. The regular infusion of new batches of Israelite slaves would have continued until the demise of direct Egyptian rule over Canaan circa 1130BC. It was from this time that the Philistines spread out from the Pentapolis – the five walled cities built by Egypt in 1176BC for the defeated army of Greek tribes (aka the Sea Peoples). From the Pentapolis, modern day Gaza, the Philistines spread up the coast and across the lowlands surrounding the Judean Highlands and the area south of the Sea of Galilee.

2.26 In retrospect, it is easy to see how in Babylon circa 550BC, when heavily rewriting and working up the texts that became the Torah, these memories and folk tales of events which happened 600 to 1000 years earlier, in the period 1550BC to 1130BC, got somewhat mixed up.

2.27 The map shows just how far beyond the lands allocated to the 12 tribes that Egyptian power extended for the key period traditionally allocated to Joshua and Judges.

2.28 It has surprised me to discover that the Biblical books written during the monarchy (say 1000BC to 596BC) also contain many clues indicating a similarly loose connection with historical facts. Again, this points to texts either being written long after the events described (which is always quite helpful if one is adding in some prophesies) or having been heavily redacted during the many centuries prior to canonisation – the process that more or less permanently fixed the text of a scripture.

2.29 In Part One of this series, I noted substantial evidence supporting the existence and life of Abraham but the complete absence of any evidence of Moses existence. Subsequent research has reinforced both positions. However, I have been surprised to find that, historically, there is no evidence whatsoever directly supporting the existence of either David or Solomon. The sole piece of evidence found so far is a broken inscription found at Tel Dan in 1993 written by an Aramean king to commemorate his defeat and despatch of his two southern neighbours the "king of Israel" (Jehoram) and the "king of the House of David." (Ahaziah) in 842BC. There is even scholastic debate over whether the key, damaged, symbol can in fact be read as "House of David". Only from that title we can suppose David was a significant royal ancestor of king Ahaziah.

2.30 From the research undertaken, evidence indicates that Saul was probably a military leader but not king, that David probably was a king but maybe of far lesser stature and Solomon was also of far lesser stature than biblically drawn, assuming that he did exist. This could also mean that there may never have been a combined state of Israel and Judah – the lowland areas north of Jerusalem were controlled by heavily armed Philistines who may have prevented a contiguous Hebrew monarchy from ever being established. The development of two independent monarchies with separate religious traditions would explain why the hitherto 'forgotten' scroll was found by Hilkiah in 622BC. Maybe this scroll was brought to Jerusalem by refugees from Israel following its occupation by the Assyrians.

2.31 Moreover, the historical evidence of an emergent Israelite kingdom is meagre – what exists points to a small nomadic population emerging from the highlands, taking Jerusalem and, as recorded in biblical texts, constantly battling Philistine city states which occupied the lowlands – both coastal and around the Sea of Galilee. The idea of David carving out a large empire and Solomon enjoying a harem of a thousand or so women sounds delusional. Unfortunately, during the period after 1130BC, as Egypt lost control of what is now Israel and areas northward, very few records have survived from any of the powers in the region. However, it is challenging to believe the new monarchy under David would instantly create a competent body of scribes, exploiting the brand new written Hebrew language, adopted from Phoenician, needed to record the administrative duties of even his modest kingdom.

3

Geo-political history of Palestine during the 2nd Millennium BC

3.1 The more I research, the greater the discrepancy between our detailed evidenced based historical knowledge of this millennium (i.e. from 2000BC to 1000BC) and the pre-Monarchical history of Israel as recorded in the Bible. Egypt dominated during this millennium. The major phases were the 11th Dynasty (2125BC to 1991BC) with Menuhotep II reuniting Upper and Lower Egypt in 2050BC and campaigning as far as Lebanon, some years prior to Abraham's visit. During the next three Dynasties, known as the Middle Kingdom, there are records of campaigns to Ugarit (just south of the modern Turkish border), Qatna and Shechem – whilst sovereignty was claimed over the coast as far as Lebanon. When Abraham arrived in Canaan, he would have found it under Egyptian suzerainty – which is one reason he then decided to visit the Pharaoh. Then, a few centuries after Abraham, Egypt was racked by internal strife with weak Pharaoh's allowing the Hyksos to gain a foothold in Lower Egypt, forming the 15th Dynasty to rule for 110 years and even for a few years to rule some parts of Upper Egypt. After the Hyksos were expelled in 1550BC, came 400 years which saw the zenith of Egypt's power, with conquests into what is now southern Turkey and the extreme east of Syria. Throughout this period, Egypt ruled the whole of what is now Israel, Lebanon and the western half of Syria and all of Jordan. The arrival of the Sea People destroyed all the other 'great kingdoms' of the time (Mycenae, Cyprus and Hittite) – except Egypt. Egypt defeated the Sea Peoples militarily in 1177BC and then established their remnants in five new cities, the Pentapolis, (roughly today's Gaza) – these people later became known as the Philistines.

PART TWO: THE PROMISED LAND 2000 BC TO 1000 BC

3.2   Let us look at the historical record and see how credible the evidence is – first a summary of what we now understand as the historical events showing how, apart from a brief period between c1655BC and c1545BC when Lower Egypt was occupied and ruled by the Hyksos, Egypt enjoyed sovereignty over the whole of what today would be considered Israel and Lebanon and a swathe of lands east of the Jordan.

3.3   Firstly, I must acknowledge both Donald Redford's excellent work *"Egypt, Canaan and Israel in Ancient Times"* and Eric Cline's recent work *"1177BC, The year civilisation collapsed"*. These, in particular, gave me a very good grounding in the history of Egypt during the second millennium BC and its struggle for supremacy with Aryan and Amorite kingdoms over what is today Lebanon and Syria. The area allotted to the 12 tribes according to the Bible was never really in dispute – it was under continuous Egyptian control.

3.4   The principal learning was reinforcement of my earlier conclusion that the Exodus story was based on the experience of the Hyksos – but with the roles reversed, as the Hyksos were not Semite slaves who were freed by divine intervention – but the Hyksos themselves were ruling Egypt for a 100 years or so, and it was the partially enslaved Egyptians who rose up and expelled the West Semitic Hyksos!!

3.5   The Hyksos, the name given by the Egyptian historian Mantheo (c4th BC) to 'Asiatics', were also called the Shepherd Kings by the contemporary Egyptians. The Hyksos, who came from the east across Sinai, at first slowly, then as an invading army, have been difficult to firmly establish and separate out from various attributions during discoveries over the past century. Initially, references to their use of chariots was assumed to link the Hyksos to the Hittites and later the Hurrians – but both timeframes and ethnicity refute such assumptions. The Hittites migrated into north central Turkey, establishing their capital Hattusas, where nowadays Boghaz Keui is situated, and which has been extensively excavated. In the 17th century BC, the Hittites occupied a small area and moreover the Egyptians knew the Hittites well, consistently referring to them as 'Ht3'. The Hurrian people came slightly later and settled to the east of the Hittites gradually extending south east and down the Euphrates – there is no evidence of any significant presence of Hittite or Hurrian people as early as the Hyksos invasion of Egypt. Furthermore, the Hyksos were irrefutably Semitic whilst Hittites and Hurrians were Aryan, branches of the migrations of Aryans south east into Northern India. From linguistic analysis, the Hurrians appear to have migrated from Armenia and occupied an area similar to today's Kurds. The principal Hurrian kingdom was Mitanni where Hurrians blended with Amorites as an Aryan aristocracy but, by 1000BC, they seem to fade out as a distinct ethnicity.

3.6 The true identity of the Hyksos can now be established from archaeological and linguistic evidence. More recent excavations at Hyksos sites at Tel-ed-Dab'a and Tel el-Maskhuta reveal a culture whose ceramic and artifactual content is identical to the culture of contemporary Canaan and Phoenicia (i.e. Palestine and Lebanon). Contemporary Egyptian records call the invaders 'mw3' a term meaning West Semitic speakers. Whilst the Hyksos left no written inscriptions in their own language – probably as no written form existed, their personal names on seals and dedicatory inscriptions in Egyptian analysed syntactically and lexically all indicate West Semitic people, none equate to Hurrian.

3.7 The Hyksos pictorial depictions and their predilection for a mountain deity might suggest origins in the highlands of northern Palestine, Lebanon or western Syria and millennia later the references to these people giving rise to the 15th Dynasty, as recorded by the historian Mantheo (4th Century BC), as 'H3rw' – from whence 'Hebrew'? Surely an interesting pointer to the Hyksos being the origin of the exodus story?

3.8 As usual, the Bible does contain some clues if searched carefully: remember, Abraham's father had left the Sumerian capital city of Ur, taking his family to Harran, a very ancient centre of learning at the northern limit of the Sumerian empire. After some decades had passed, suddenly the Lord Most High (identified as Enlil/El Elyon) a person well known as the ultimate overlord of the Sumerian Empire, spoke to Abraham telling him to leave Harran and begin a journey to a new Promised Land of plenty.

3.9 Research of ancient Egyptian and Sumerian inscriptions and cuneiform tablets reveals the possible historical events which led to the Biblical story.

3.10 Let us start with Abraham. His original name was Abram. Abram (Ab. Ram) is a Sumerian name meaning 'father's beloved'. Abram's father, Terah, was High Priest to the Lord Most High, who according to the Bible was El Elyon. El Elyon is the Canaanite name of Enlil. Terah appears to have been born in Nippur, the Sumerian religious centre hosting the temple and shrines to the Lord Most High, Enlil.

3.11   An interesting clue lies in the name of Abraham's great grandfather, Eber, estimated to have been born in 2350BC. From Eber, the Hebrew root Ibri is recorded in the Bible, stemming from the root word meaning "to cross". The biblical suffix "i" when applied to a person meant "a native of", as in Gileadi meant a native of Gilead. Likewise "Ibri" meant a native of a place called "crossing" – precisely the Sumerian name for Nippur: Ni.ib.ru – the crossing place. The dropping of the leading "n" in transposing from Sumerian to Akkadian/Hebrew was a frequent practise. In stating that Abraham was an Ibri, the Bible simply meant that Abraham was a Ni.bi.ri, a native of Nippurian origin.

3.12   The Bible is full of enigmatic clues: The Lord Most High is unlikely to have chosen just anyone from the streets of Ur to be the foundation of his Chosen People. Back in 2000BC, the future descendants of the longest lasting civilisation the world had seen so far (Sumerian) would flow from this choice. The departure from the capital occurred at a key moment – which marked regime change and the beginning of a sharp and unremitting decline, just before the end of the Sumerian empire. So, who was chosen by the Lord Most High?

3.13   Clues lie in the names:

- Abraham's father, Terah, was thought to be a toponym (name signifying a place) but whilst the Akkadian sound "Tirhu" mean a vessel for magical purposes, in Sumerian the word meant "fate speaker/a pronouncer of oracles". Such priests, the Oracle Priest, was the only one allowed into the 'Holy of Holies' to hear directly from the deity.

- Terah's daughter, named Sarai – meaning Princess in Sumerian;

- Milkha the daughter of Abraham's brother Harran, meaning "queenly";

- The fact that Abraham married his sister (by another mother) – a practise followed by royalty to preserve their royal bloodline.

All point to a royal family, although not the first born sitting on the throne.

3.14 It was during the Third Dynasty of Ur that for the first time the kings of Ur were granted trusteeship over the Sumerian religious centre of Nippur – combining religious and secular affairs.

3.15 The Sumerian Empire comprised a series of cities where kingship passed between the cities according to the choice of the current ruling family. Ur, one of the oldest cities, had frequently been the seat of kingship. Its kings usually acted as high priest and they often appointed their sons and daughters to senior priestly positions as well. Records show that the kings of Ur cherished the title "pious Shepherd of Nippur" and performed priestly functions there, taking the title "Ur.Enlil" meaning "Enlil's foremost servant". It could have been during Ur Nammu's reign that Terah and his family moved from Nippur to Ur, maybe acting as a liaison between the throne and the temple. It would appear that Terah's second migration, to Harran, occurred in the year of Ur Nammu's death.

3.16 A family so closely associated with Nippur would naturally be remembered as Nippurians, i.e. Ibri, and later, Hebrews.

3.17 Another clue is the Hebrew calendar. Scholars have recognised that our present day calendars derive from the original Nippurian calendar system established soon after 4000BC. Uniquely, the Hebrew calendar appears directly linked to this first known calendar system. The Jewish calendar is based upon year 0 being 3760BC, with 21 September AD2027 being Rosh Hashana, Jewish New Year, for 5788. Some religious academics have suggested this count was from the "beginning of the world" but the actual formulation by Jewish sages is that this is "the number of years that have passed since the counting of years begun".

3.18 Other records tell of Abraham being well versed in astronomy and military tactics – suitable training for the first born son of a high ranking family. Josephus tells of Berossus (a Babylonian priest to Marduk and a historian who published three books 290BC to 278BC) describing Abraham as a righteous and great man excelling in astronomy. The biblical narrative describing the journey firstly to Canaan and thence to the Negev describes Abraham as having military allies and assisted by 'naar'. Naar has been translated as retainer or young man. However, studies of Hurrian texts equate naar with cavalry and Akkadian texts describe chariots and cavalry as "Lu.nar". 1 Samuel 30:17 uses the same term when describing David's attack on the Amelekite camp, the only ones to escape were "four hundred Ish.naar" – literally "nar-men" or Lu.nar" who were riding camels.

3.19 This background information from Sumerian cuneiform tablets provides useful insight to the background and role of Abraham – whom both Mantheo and Josephus indicate as the ancestor of the Hyksos.

3.20 Egyptian records demonstrate clearly the presence in Egypt of a sizable Asiatic population of servile status during the 12th and 13th dynasties (c1990BC until c1650BC) brought back partly as tribute and partly as booty from foreign wars. A partial inscription from what seems to be the daybook of one king's household provides insight to the Egyptian forays into Palestine during this period – seemingly to gather plunder and slaves rather than trade. In one year, the forces of Pharaoh Amenemhet II reigning 1914BC to 1879BC *(or 1877BC to 1843BC in an alternative chronology)* made at least four incursions. One excursion returned with 238 ingots of lead, 1554 'Asiatics' being prisoners of war; another excursion, to the Lebanese coast, included 10 ships being dispatched returning with 1665 units of silver, 4882 units of copper, 15961 units of [defaced] – certainly considerable plunder and no hint of trade having taken place. It is believed that these might have, in some instances, represented tribute recognising the suzerainty of Egypt and that 'Asiatics' returning with the expeditions may have been voluntary – part tribute of labour, part economic migrants to a Nile based economy where food of all kinds was plentiful by comparison with the dry desiccated lands of Palestine. These excursions took place between 100 and 150 years after Abraham's visit to Egypt – but where are the references in the biblical stories of Isaac and Jacob to Egyptian armies passing by?

3.21 The Egyptian state was weakened by internecine strife during the 13th and 14th dynasties. Over a period of only 125 years, the Turin List (itself dating to Ramesses era) records 120 to 130 pharaohs (depending how one counts co-regents) whilst Mantheo (4th century BC), who likely found the Turin List papyrus in better condition than we have now, lists 136 pharaohs. This gradual weakening of royal authority, allowing Egypt's eastern defences to decay, led to easy entry by nomadic transhumants from Sinai. The Asiatic population in the delta grew to outnumber the local Egyptians – shades of the Exodus story? Some speculation has linked the rise of the Hyksos in Egypt to the growing numbers of Asiatics. It has been suggested that successive waves of invading Hyksos turned the population balance and then with the new fast-moving horse drawn chariots overcame the Egyptian military.

3.22 However, the destruction wrought by the Hyksos, wholesale destruction of monuments throughout the Memphite region and their transport to Avaris does not seem to reflect the actions of a people culturally assimilated from long years of settlement to Egyptian life as suggested by Genesis – as others clearly had, such as Libyans and Nubians, but is more suggestive of aggressive recent invaders.

3.23 The multitude of very short lived reigns resulted in a paucity of commemorative buildings and a general lack of lasting inscriptions. The timing of the main Hyksos invasion has been linked to a pharaoh named 'Dd-nfr-r' or 'Dd-htp-r', referred to as Tutimaios by Mantheo. His inscriptions describe his own activities being confined to Upper Egypt and prominent references suggesting continuous military activity. The first listed Hyksos pharaoh of Lower Egypt, who probably led the invasion, was Sheshy/Salitis. A century later, Kamose describes the Hyksos as Asiatics who destroyed the land, led by a Syrian chief and that they had overrun the land of Egypt. Pharaoh Dedu-mose retreated far to the south, setting up his base at Thebes. At about the same time, the Nubian region to his south broke away setting up an independent kingdom based at Kerma, the third cataract.

3.24 The Hyksos established themselves in the Delta at Avaris before going on to occupy Lower Egypt and establish the 15th Dynasty – ruling from c1655BC to c1545BC. Evidence shows the Hyksos quickly established trade routes with the Nubians, initially using desert routes using way marks and settlements established during the 12th dynasty.

3.25 Excavations of Tel ed-Dab'a (Avaris) in 1966 revealed large areas with a purely Canaanite domestic and cultic character owing nothing to Egyptian culture being wholly of northern Levantine inspiration. Kamose inscriptions of his attacks on Lower Egypt indicate predominantly Hyksos population centres distinct from largely Egyptian towns albeit with large numbers of native Egyptian acting as servile workers. There are also numerous references to heavy taxes levied by the Hyksos. Virtually no Hyksos records survived as all Hyksos monuments appear to have been destroyed by vengeful Egyptians once the foreigners had been expelled.

3.26 The Hyksos appear to have assimilated much Egyptian administrative practise. Plentiful remains of scarab seals bearing royal names have been found, with Pharaonic names following the Egyptian practise of incorporating a resident god, usually Ra. In addition, Amorite traditions of a great King surrounded by lesser kings and many 'sons' which included courtesy offspring as well as genuine princes – "he who follows the lord", or in our terms a retainer/courtier.

3.27 In the Turin Canon there is a section of 32 names which defied interpretation for many years. It is now believed that these are garbled West Semitic names, constituting the family tree of the Hyksos pharaohs providing the pedigree of their royal ancestors. Many of these names are similar to far later Amorite names of Assyrian kings. Hyksos rule lasted only about a century, the king lists show six names and contemporary records from other countries confirm the duration. That the Hyksos, at least in part, evolved to become Amorite has echoes in the biblical assertion – "your father was an Amorite and your mother was a Hittite" (Ezekiel 16:3).

3.28 The penultimate Hyksos ruler, Apophis I, also known as Apepi (1615BC to 1575BC) marked the pinnacle of Hyksos rule. Apophis tried many times to subjugate Thebes, and his inscriptions claimed Thebes was administered by Kamose on his behalf but no clear proof of Hyksos rule over Thebes has yet been found. A blockstone unearthed at a fort at Gebelein, south of Thebes, bears Apophis name but may have arrived there as a result of looting.

3.29 Sequenenre Tao (Pharaoh of Upper Egypt from 1560BC) led the initial revolt against the Hyksos and his mummified head shows numerous fatal blows from weaponry typical of Hyksos warriors. Sequenenre was followed by his son Kamose, who despite initially signing a treaty with Apophis, governing trade promising safe conduct through each other's territory, soon resumed hostilities against Apophis (a change in prenoms has confused historians as to whether Apophis was succeeded by a son bearing the same name or just changed his pre-name). Kamose, who left detailed inscriptions of his campaigns, reigned for only 3 years and possibly died attacking Avaris.

3.30 Another son of Sequenenre, Ahmose I (1551BC – 1527BC), assumed kingship of Thebes and finally succeeded in driving the Hyksos out of Egypt around 110 years after their arrival. After chasing them out of

Egypt, Ahmose I attacked but failed to capture the Hyksos settlement of Sharuhen, near Gaza. Ahmose continued annual campaigns across Sinai and on the 3rd attempt succeeded in capturing and razing Sharuhen. Various Tel's around Gaza have been identified with Sharuhen, the most promising being Tel Heror. Sharuhen is mentioned in Joshua 19:6 as part of the land ascribed to Simeon. It would appear that despite evidence of successful trading with both Lebanon and Nubia to the south of Egypt, the Hyksos did not expand very far north beyond Joppa in Palestine – being blocked by the power based at Hazor in northern Palestine and the Golan. (see Yigael Yadin, *Hazor*)

3.31 Hazor was the principal Canaanite city from early C18th BC through until its destruction by intense fires c1200 BC – most likely by the Sea Peoples. Apart from the century during which the Hyksos ruled Lower Egypt, Hazor was an Egyptian vassal state with the kings of Hazor pledging allegiance to successive Pharaohs. Hazor lies just south of the modern border of Lebanon (see map). Hazor was a prominent trading centre but relatively few written records have been excavated. Yigael Yadin led one of the most extensive digs ever done in Israel, covering some 225 acres during 1950's and 1960's. One of the C14th Amarna texts writes of the King of Hazor joining with nomadic "Habiru" people and repudiating Egyptian suzerainty – a revolt quickly put down. In 2010, a cuneiform tablet dating from 17th or 18th century BC, was unearthed at Hazor, written in Akkadian, setting out a detailed legal code, very similar to Hammurabi's Code.

3.32 So, if blocked by Hazor from going northwards, where did the Hyksos go after expulsion from Egypt? A likely explanation, given their trading expertise, their familiarity with desert treks (e.g. trading with Nubia whilst avoiding Thebes) and across Sinai – is that they migrated across the Jordan and settled around Petra. Dan Gibson, in Quranic Geography, writes convincingly that the Hyksos formed the People of 'Ad, forerunners of the Nabateans – who went on to dominate the spice trade as near monopoly suppliers of spices and incense throughout both Greek and Roman empires.

3.33 Following the expulsion of the Hyksos around 1545BC there appears to be an absence of a servile community of aliens in Egypt for the next 50 years – whilst some Asiatics would have been captured in engagements or taken as booty, the vast majority must have been either killed or escaped towards Palestine.

3.34   The next 50 years (c1550 to c1500 BC) saw a transformation in the political structure of the Fertile Crescent. Little had changed in the political map during the Hyksos ascendancy in Egypt, Ahmose faced almost the same power structure of Amorite kingdoms as had been in place 100 years earlier. Babylon weakening, Assyria before its political rise, Yamkhad in Aleppo, Qatanum on the Orontes and Hazor on the upper Jordan dominating Galilee and Golan.

3.35   But the winds of change were blowing: the Kassites, migrating westwards from the Zagros mountains of Persia were beginning to squeeze Babylon. Whilst in the north, two Aryan peoples migrated into central Turkey (Hittites) and eastern Turkey (Hurrians). For Egypt, seaborne trade with Lebanon (Byblos) was augmented by trade with Cyprus and Crete.

3.36   The Hittites started trade with Egypt at the end of the Hyksos period and their first expansion southwards led by Hattusilis I, was to attack Alalakh, a dependency of the rich kingdom of Yamkhad centred in Aleppo. The same campaign captured Carchemish on the Euphrates. Four years later, Hattusilis attacked Aleppo but did not take it. Hatusilis successor, Mursilis I (c1556 to c1526 BC) succeeded in capturing Aleppo and terminating the Yamkhad kingdom. Later he led a c2000km campaign, and sweeping down the Euphrates to attack Babylon, it is thought in order to capture grain supplies due to the climatic changes wrought by the Thera eruption in the Aegean which ruined crops in Turkey. Mursilis made no attempt to garrison Babylon and maintaining control such a distance from his power base would have been impossible. His attack did destroy the Hammurabic dynasty and thereby allowed the Kassites to take over Babylon after he departed home.

3.37   Hittites and Hurrians were both seeking to expand and inevitably clashed, both tried to occupy Northern Syria and the Upper Euphrates. Around 1530BC a new Hurrian state of Mitanni emerged in Central Mesopotamia (covering the Upper Tigris and including Assyria). By 1450BC they formed a significant proportion of the population of what is now Northern Israel – analysis of name lists excavated at Tanaach (30km south west of the Sea of Galilee) show nearly 40% as Hurrian or Indo-Aryan. This again brings to mind Ezekiel 16:3 *"You are nothing but a Canaanite! Your father was an Amorite and your mother a Hittite."* This is an amazingly ignorant racial slur – Ezekiel is following the Abramaic slur against the descendants of Canaan, the son of Ham who trespassed by stopping off in modern day Lebanon when his family had been allocated Africa occupying land promised to Shem. But the claim that the party addressed by Ezekiel was nothing but a Canaanite – falls flat when one realises that supposed parents were Amorite (1st Babylonian empire) being of Shem and the Hittite was of Japhth.

3.38 Meanwhile, after expelling the Hyksos, Ahmose I went on to re-establish Egyptian sovereignty over Sinai and most of Canaan as well as lands to the south of Egypt. His descendants continued strengthening Egyptian rule over the coast of the Levant, which reached its greatest extent under Thutmose III.

3.39 Thutmose III waged 17 foreign campaigns during his reign, starting with attacks on Phoenician cities (modern Lebanon), he defeated Kadesh (which had previously controlled much of Canaan) at Mediggo in 1482BC. Despite all the local headmen pledging allegiance to Egypt, a number of the Canaanite cities fell behind on tributes and earned a return visitation. In 1476BC, Thutmose advanced beyond friendly Byblos (north of modern Beirut) to capture Ullaza and Ardata (near modern Tripoli). An Egyptian garrison was placed in Ullaza and the harbours of Lebanon were turned into depots stocked with food and military supplies. Records show huge quantities of copper, wine, fruit and timber, mostly raised as taxes, were shipped back to Egypt.

3.40 With the coast secure right up to the border of modern day Turkey, Thutmose concentrated on subduing what is now Syria. After repeated rebellions in Syria, Thutmose developed the idea of taking the children of city rulers to live in Egypt – thereby increasing the loyalty of vassal states. His 8th campaign, in 1472BC, ventured across the Euphrates as far as Mitanni – located at the extreme eastern corner of modern Syria. The logistics are impressive – Thutmose took his army by ship to Byblos, there manufactured pre-fabricated assault craft which were transported by cart across the Lebanese mountains towards Aleppo – where he met but overcame fierce resistance. Marching onwards they reached the Euphrates at Carchemish (close to modern day Diyarbakir, in Turkey) a distance of c800km north east from Byblos. There they assembled and launched their craft to sail south to Mitanni (today on the Syrian Turkish border). Thutmose victory here brought gifts and pledges of support from as far as Babylon and Assyria. However, Mitanni (a Hurrian people) rose again and Egypt struggled to maintain control despite a number of successful campaigns. To appreciate the scale of Tuthmose III adventures please refer to the map.

3.41 Eventually, Amenophis II (son of Thutmose III) tired of continued campaigns in Syria and signed a treaty with Mitanni, cemented by his son, Thutmose IV marrying a Mitanni princess – but no Egyptian princess was sent to Mitanni in exchange (qv later claims by Solomon). Peace then lasted until 1375BC, areas east of the Orontes were subject to Mitanni, whilst Kadesh, Damascus and other areas west of the Orontes were recognised as Egyptian and became referred to as Canaan.

3.42 The area west of the Lake of Homs as far as the coast became a sort of border zone, nominally part of Egyptian control but without any city. It came to be occupied by Amorites pressed west by Hurrian Mitanni and gained the name Amurru (simply meaning 'west' in Akkadian). Amurru grew into a warlike canton and came to the attention of various pharaohs as Canaanite cities appealed for assistance fighting off Cossack-like bands of outlaws known as Apiru (another name from which 'Hebrew' is believed to be derived). From the Amarna Letters it does not appear that Egypt took these skirmishes as particularly serious. The bigger political issue was the growing strength of the Hittites – who initially focused on taking over vassal states of the Mitanni. The Hittites also took over Amurru and Kadesh from Egyptian control – which did raise Egyptian attention.

3.43 After Tutankhamen, Egypt was ruled from 1356BC to 1321BC by three successive generals – Ay, Horemheb and Ramesses I. Egypt underwent internal reorganisation and greatly strengthened lines of communication with its possessions in western Asia by creating a string of fortified blockhouses along the key transit routes – the coastal Way of Horus (Via Maris) and the Kings Highway (the inland route running north south to the east of the Jordan valley). Thutmose III had deported so many of the hill people that the area around Jerusalem was largely depopulated – leaving it open to bands of Apiru and nomads from the Transjordan who occupied areas around Galilee. Records reveal stresses elsewhere caused by bands of Apiru – although the success of the Apiru in Northern Lebanon was not achieved by similar bands in Bashan (south of Damascus) or in the Judean Hills – who had to contend with an Egyptian military garrison. These nomads from the TransJordan could well have been descendants of the expelled Hyksos.

3.44 Pharaoh Seti (1290BC to 1279BC), son of Ramesses I, took decisive action in his second year, conquering Amurru and taking back Kadesh where he erected victory stelae. To humiliate the city chiefs, Seti required them to log timber themselves to build a new royal barque. In subsequent campaigns, Seti pushed further north into Hittite territory. The old Hittite king, Mursilis II, complained he had maintained the agreement with Egypt bequeathed by his father – and there are references to a new treaty between him and Seti confirming the status quo ante. Both Seti and Mursilis died soon after and it seems Kadesh had realigned with the Hittites who also took back control of Amurru. Seti's successor, Ramesses II, ruling from 1279BC to 1212BC, also favoured military expeditions to strengthen his empire, focusing his early years southwards in Nubia. The elder son of Mursilis II reigned briefly before his younger son Muwatallis took over, moving his headquarters south to oversee operations in the Levant.

3.45 Soon the Amurru triggered a new campaign by seceding from Muwatallis and offering themselves to Egypt. Ramesses II went north to receive his new vassal state and erect stelae. This triggered a response from Muwatallis leading to the battle of Kadesh – better documented than any battle prior to Marathon in 490BC. Muwatallis set spies to be captured and give false information to the Egyptians, who acting upon it fell into a trap with their forces split and strung out, Ramesses led a desperate fight to avoid total defeat. Both sides suffered heavy losses but ended with a healthy respect for each other – concluding that neither power had the strength to materially change the line of the frontier. Ramesses had to concede Amurru and Kadesh again, whilst the Canaanite cities had been shown Egypt could be beaten – whereupon in the wake of the retreating Egyptian army, all Canaan flared in rebellion.

3.46 Ramesses planned for 3 years and led a massive force northwards re-capturing all the major cities and this time penetrating well north into Hittite territory – with victory reliefs including Qode in Kizzuwadna – on the southern coast of Turkey, north of Cyprus, near Tarsus. The Egyptians were now threatening the Hittite heartlands when Muwatallis died. His successor, Hattusilis II faced with two militant adversaries Egypt and a growing threat from Assyria, which had largely absorbed the weakened

Mitanni, decided that negotiation would be wise. In 1258BC emissaries were sent to Ramesses proposing a peace treaty.

3.47 Surprisingly, Ramesses quickly agreed and to terms that gave up virtually all of his conquests – the northern line of Egyptian control retracted back south of Ugarit and Amurru to Kadesh. But all of Lebanon and the southern half of western Syria remained under Egyptian control. Drafts of the treaty have been found in Hittite and the final versions in Akkadian – the legal versions to which seals were attached – one with Ramesses seal deposited in Khatte and one with Hattusilis seal deposited before Ra in Heliopolis. The treaty covered a wide range of issues but its overriding concern was to establish a long-lasting peace – in that it was successful and for the remaining life of the Hittite kingdom the treaty was never broken.

3.48 The Late Bronze Age transition to the Iron Age brought traumatic disruption around the eastern Mediterranean coast with the destruction of many cities across the area and four of the five 'great kingdoms' of that time. Two primary causes have been identified which probably had a causal link – climate change and migrations bringing the 'Sea Peoples' to the eastern Mediterranean. The Sea Peoples, so called by the Egyptians as they came across the sea, ranged from armed incursions and later to mass migrations. The fighters came with new military equipment, iron long-swords, iron shields, helmets with plumes and iron body armour. Ramesses II first encountered the Sea People when a group of Viking-like sea raiders plundered the coast of the delta. Ramesses lured them into a trap and captured them. But he was so impressed by their fighting qualities and the arms that he pressed them into service as his personal elite bodyguard. These, from the Shardana clan, later excelled at the Battle of Kadesh in 1274BC.

3.49 The climate change theory is supported by a study in 2013 of data from coastal sites in Cyprus and Syria showed evidence that a 300-year drought began around the beginning of the twelfth century BC, coinciding with the Late Bronze Age collapse. Like the Hittite Empire, cities in Cyprus and Syria suffered destruction or decline in the same time period. A drought of this magnitude would have caused crop failures and widespread famine, as well as trade disruption across the Ancient Near East. The research in this study indicates that climate change precipitated an economic crisis at the end of the Late Bronze Age and caused population migrations as inhabitants moved to escape the drought affected areas.

3.50 Further evidence of the climate change was published in a study of pollen grains from sediment in the Dead Sea and Sea of Galilee that showed an increase in cultivation of dry-climate trees around the time of the Bronze Age collapse. Additional pollen data from Anatolia, Egypt, Cyprus, and Syria indicates broad changes in climate led to drought in those areas around the same time – for most of the period between 1250BC and 1100BC. In 2023, results of research by Professor Sturt Manning of Cornell University were published in Nature of tree ring analysis revealing drought conditions prevailing at the end of the 12th Century. Local juniper trees harvested to construct a burial chamber for a relative of Phrygia's King Midas around 748BC showed progressively drier conditions through the 13th Century BC and three straight years of very severe drought in 1198BC, 1197BC and 1196BC at the beginning of the 12th. Facing three consecutive years of complete crop failure, society would have crumbled. People may have had food reserves to tide over a single year in which crops failed but three consecutive years would have led to a collapse of the tax base and dissolution of the army. It is noteworthy that the capital, Hattusa, previously estimated to have been abandoned in 1200 was probably abandoned by the third year of drought. A large urban population survives on agricultural surpluses – if these cease for years, a city soon has to be abandoned.

3.51 There is written evidence that the Hittites were suffering from some type of famine in the mid-thirteenth century BC. In a letter from the Hittite queen Puduhepa to the Egyptian king Ramesses II, she states "I have no grain in my lands." Egypt traditionally enjoyed a superabundance of grain and records show that the Hittites were still importing food from Egypt during the reign of the pharaoh Merneptah from 1213BC to 1203BC. Famine could well have driven migration into Hittite lands, their capital appears to have been abandoned by the end of the three year drought from 1198BC to 1196BC prior to being destroyed a few years later.

3.52 References to famines suggest a weakening of the great kingdoms, exposing them to advances of warlike tribes exploiting their new iron weapons. The Hittites faced a rebellion in the 1240's BC from a confederation of 22 Ionian states along the western coast of Turkey. The Hittite king, Tudkhaliyas IV, managed to defeat the Confederacy but the

PART TWO: THE PROMISED LAND 2000 BC TO 1000 BC

western realms of the Hittites started to break away. However, Tudkhaliyas did manage to occupy Cyprus, thereby ending the first of the great kingdoms disappearing at the end of the Bronze Age. At the same time, southward migration by Thessalonian and Dorian Greeks created strife across Greece, during the 1250's and 1240's there is widespread evidence of cities being fortified. Then in the 1220's many Greek cities, including Mycenae, suffered violent destruction – marking the end of another of the great Bronze Age kingdoms.

3.53 When the aged Ramesses II passed away in 1212BC, he was succeeded by his 13th son (he had outlived the first 12) Merneptah – already aged and decrepit. To the west of Egypt, Cyrenaica had a mix of Libyan tribes and a growing population swelled by freebooting Greek seafarers – these formed a loose coalition and saw the chance to invade Egypt in Merneptah's 5th year. Merneptah recorded a great victory with over 9,000 attackers killed, but the following four Pharaohs were all short lived and weak rulers – allowing Libyan tribes to infiltrate the western delta and settle. It was 25 years before the next strong Pharaoh, Ramesses III (1186BC to 1155BC). Ramesses soon took action against the infiltrators, killing many and enslaving '10's of thousands'.

3.54 In the 8th year of Ramesses III reign something entirely new occurred. Egypt had become accustomed to raiding parties of well-armed warriors in a few longships bent on a quick raid and a quick getaway. What neither Palestine nor Egypt had seen before was an invasion force intent upon settlement. The invasion was first felt by the Hittites with their capital, Hattusa, destroyed in 1178BC. Ramesses records in his mortuary temple that a confederacy of Greek tribes (Peleset, Tjekka, Danyan, Weshesh and Shekelesh) had successively defeated and destroyed Hattusa, Qode, Carchemish and Cyprus. The Sea Peoples then attacked Ugarit – we have its last archives, in the oven for hardening as the city fell, which record its troops were away in Tarsus helping the Hittites and its fleet was away helping Lycia. The Sea People then made camp in Amurru (there are no Apiru records of this, as no Hebrew writing had been developed yet) before setting off southwards for Egypt.

3.55 Ramesses records his foreknowledge and his planning to destroy them in 'Asia' before they reached Egypt. Whilst the Egyptian reference is vague, tradition from 5th century writings place the battle at Ashkelon (just north of Gaza). The Egyptian record shows a formidable force was encountered, accompanied by women and children in oxcarts. Whilst certainly defeated, enough survived to grow into the Philistine state centred on Gaza and Ashkelon. Ramesses also prepared the delta area well and used archers to destroy the Sea People's fleet when it attacked.

4

Egyptian decline enables pre-monarchical Israel to emerge

4.1 After Ramesses III, the remaining Ramesside pharaohs ruled for another 80 years (Ramesses 4 through 11 spanning 1155BC to 1075BC) a period in which Egypt stagnated, weakened by internecine scheming and indulgent monarchs. The priestly records fall silent about new construction projects and deeds worthy of historical record. Egypt's power waned as the destruction of the Hittite Empire and the overrunning of the Levant terminated commerce and tribute flowing to Egypt, critically it cut off supplies of silver and iron for the treasury and armaments. The Nubian gold strata became exhausted and the turquoise mines in Sinai were abandoned. Frequent droughts caused a series of poor harvests with a bushel of wheat costing 1 copper deben at the end of Ramesses III reign soaring to 5 deben some 20 years later. Inflation and food scarcity are blamed for the start of tomb raiding which features prominently in records of the 11th century BC.

4.2 An outbreak of civil war led to Ramesses XI to appointing a military chief as high priest of Amun, Herihor, who rapidly consolidated power in Thebes and eventually proclaimed himself king. Herihor founded the 21st dynasty and established his capital at Tanis (30km north of Pi-Ramesses). In effect the Theban priesthood became sovereign. The wealth of the Amun priesthood was staggering – in 1155BC their records show ownership of 600,000 acres of land, 421,000 cattle, 433 gardens, 65 towns (although reduced to only 9 remaining in Canaan), 46 carpentry workshops and a fleet of 85 ships. Exclusive of priestly staff, 85,000 farmers laboured on their estates.

PART TWO: THE PROMISED LAND 2000 BC TO 1000 BC

4.3   Ramesses III claims to have settled enclaves of the defeated Sea Peoples in his territory binding them over to his service. His inscriptions state he settled them in fortresses, rebuilding Gaza and Ashkelon with gates emblazoned with his cartouche, providing clothing and provisions from tax receipts and his granaries. There are indications that Ramesses III also based a joint garrison of Sea People and Egyptians at Beth Shean (20km south of the Sea of Galilee).

4.4   However, less than 50 years after defeating the Sea Peoples, Egyptian control of its northern dependencies had been lost. By 1120BC, the Philistines had shaken off Egyptian control and begun to expand, taking over some of the Egyptian way stations along the Via Maris and moving inland along the valleys to the south east as well as along the Jordan Valley south from Beth Shean. By 1100BC, it would appear that the Philistines had spread to encircle the Judean highlands and around part of the Samarian highlands.

4.5   The Onomasticon of Amenemope, an administrative document of which 9 copies have been discovered, dates from around 1100BC, lists six cities Philistine cities – Ashkelon, Ashdod, Gaza, Yasur, Sabury and one name defaced and 3 Sea Peoples – Shaddana, Teukrians and Philistines. From these peoples emerged the Philistines and their Pentapolis recorded in the Old Testament at the time of the founding of the monarchy. 2 Samuel 31:10 suggests Philistine occupation of the area south of the Sea of Galilee was well established in the tenth century BC.

4.6   This has clear implications for the accuracy of the historical information set out in Judges and 1 Samuel.

4.7   Following the demise of Egyptian control over Palestine and Syria, various city states begun to emerge – in northern Syria these being: Samal, Cilicia, Gurgum, Carchemish and Hamath (replacing Ugarit and Aleppo) – all being regarded as 'Hittite' in racial complexion and choice of language. In southern Syria, the Aramaeans emerged – a Semitic people controlling Damascus and northern Palestine. Along the Mediterranean coast, enclaves of Philistines (including other Greek Sea Peoples, such as the Teukrians) encroached as far north as modern day Haifa – and, as the Egyptians before them, they tried to exert control over the Judean Highlands.

4.8   However, these Highlands begun to see the emergence of Israel from the various Hebrew tribes. Only north of Haifa did the original Canaanite population retain influence – maintaining the city states of Tyre, Sidon, Beirut and Byblos. Into this patchwork of states emerged Israel, according to biblical chronology becoming a monarchy around 1040BC under Saul, about 80 years after the demise of Egyptian suzerainty. However, there is no extra-biblical evidence of Saul and even Jewish sources suggest he may have been a military leader rather than a king. Certainly, the territory he could have controlled would have remained quite small, basically the Judean Highlands around Jerusalem – but excluding the citadel of Jerusalem itself. No archaeological evidence of any settlements from this period have been uncovered.

4.9 Unfortunately, the tenth century BC is one of the few periods from which virtually no written records have survived. The 21st Dynasty based at the new city of Tanis has left little record of any historical significance, earlier scribal traditions having suffered from the change of dynastic family, of administrative centre and from the decline of Amun Ra's estate at Thebes. Amun Ra revenues would have suffered from the loss of over 100 cities owned across Palestine. Neither have any useful contemporary inscriptions have been recovered from the city states across Palestine and Syria. The only source material available covering this century is the history of Tyre by Josephus (a first century Jewish historian) and from the Bible – the two books of Samuel and the early part of 1 Kings. Whilst probably reliable as a king list, as set out later, Samuel bears evidence of much later authorship and of extensive redaction prior to canonisation – rendering it somewhat unreliable as a historical record without any supporting evidence.

4.10 Given our conventional familiarity with the biblical stories of the kingships of David and Solomon, particularly of the empire and wealth accreted by Solomon, Solomon's wedding to a pharaoh's daughter and escapades with a visiting South Arabian queen – it comes as some surprise that no record of either reign nor any mention of either David or Solomon has been found anywhere in Egypt or Palestine.

4.11 There was great excitement in 2005 when an Israeli archaeologist, Eilat Mazar, uncovered in East Jerusalem what may be the fabled palace of the biblical King David. Some scholars are skeptical that the foundation walls discovered by the archaeologist are David's palace. But they acknowledge that what she has uncovered is rare and important: a major public building from around the 10th century BC, with pottery shards that date to the time of David and Solomon and a government seal of an official under King Zedekiah mentioned in the book of Jeremiah. The discovery reignited a major dispute in biblical archaeology: whether the kingdom of David was of some historical magnitude, or whether the kings were more like small tribal chieftains, reigning over a few dusty hilltops. Further findings have continued as excavation proceeds, reported as recently as January 2017 – but nothing specifically mentioning either David or Solomon has so far been recovered. Accordingly, for the time being, the massive walls uncovered are considered (by Eilat Mazar) as possibly being part of the Jebusite fortifications (the Fortress of Zion) dating before David's capture of Jerusalem and maybe of Egyptian origin; or part of David's palace (built by Phoenician craftsmen according to the Bible); or, part of fortifications constructed by Solomon.

4.12 Writing in *Bible History Daily*, Avraham Faust, opines: Eilat Mazar's excavation and archaeology methods are beyond reproach, but her recent claim to have discovered King David's palace at her Jerusalem dig site has met with harsh criticism from other scholars in the field. In the September 2012 issue of *Biblical Archaeology Review*, senior archaeologist Avraham Faust reviewed evidence to show why he agrees—and disagrees—with her theory. The narrow ridge, still known as the City of David, lies south of Jerusalem's Temple Mount. It is the location of the most ancient settlement of Jerusalem. Mazar's decision to dig was informed by the Biblical text and by the excavations that preceded hers. Based on earlier finds, Mazar thought she knew where David's palace should be located. When she uncovered a complex structure that she named the Large Stone Structure, she proposed it to be built by King David as his palace. Within this Large Stone Structure were layers of Iron Age I remains, showing that it must have been built no later than the Iron Age I (i.e. of Jebusite origin). Avraham Faust argues that the archaeological evidence indicates a construction date before David's time but David may have used the structure as his palace. Anyway, so far, we still lack any definite evidence of David, or of Solomon.

4.13 Biblical texts uniquely refer to Jerusalem prior to its capture by David as 'Jebus' and its inhabitants as Jebusites – as referred to in the two paragraphs above. However, despite Israeli government adoption of this term, there is no extrabiblical support for these terms. Jerusalem was established and known as Uru-salem to the Sumerians for at least a millennium before David. The Amarna Letters, Egyptian administrative documents dating from around 1330BC, include six letters from the ruler of the Egyptian city state of Uru-salem, Abdi-Heba, pleading for additional military support (specifically archers) to deal with marauding bands of Habiru – proto-Israelites who came to settle in small villages in the Judean Highlands. Later correspondence during the reigns of Seti (1290BC to 1279BC) and Ramesses II (1279BC to 1213BC) refer to large scale construction and fortification works at Uru-salem. Maybe this is what Eilat Mazar has discovered?

4.14   Redford argues that historians relying solely on biblical sources for their assessment of the early monarchy tend to justify such decision on two bases – both rather weak: firstly, that the 'Story of David's Succession' (second half of 2 Samuel and first two chapters of 1 Kings) is a stunningly good prose composition and must be regarded as the earliest specimen of ancient Israelite history. However, rating the quality of the prose as equating to its veracity is a non-sequitur. Secondly, that monarchical states in antiquity, exercising hegemony over large territories depended upon a cadre of scribes to record and manage details of resources, staff, tax assessments and collections, etc. Therefore, such a cadre would be available to record the biblical texts. However, the counter argument is that David, almost definitely, was in fact the first monarch and probably did not inherit any scribes at all. David had to carve out an empire whilst recruiting, training and developing a scribal tradition – indeed, it was only from this period that Hebrew writing emerged, borrowing the then new Phoenician alphabet.

4.15   Moreover, Samuel and 1 Kings (describing events between c1075BC and c925BC) are full of anachronisms pointing to a much later authorship. Again, from Redford, with added details:

- Reference to coined money – 1 Samuel 13:21, when the earliest coins date from 500 years later, during Persian rule c 500BC

- Armour of a much later period – 1 Samuel 17:4-7, 17:38-39; 25:13

- Use of camels – 1 Samuel 30:17 when the first use of camels in Palestine was around 930BC – brought by Arab tribes (biblical Amelikites) when developing copper smelting in the northern Negev

- References to cavalry (as distinct from chariots) when first use

PART TWO: THE PROMISED LAND 2000 BC TO 1000 BC

c865BC by Assyrians deploying mounted archers riding in pairs – in 1 Samuel 13:5; 2 Samuel 1:6

- Sophisticated siege techniques developed by the Assyrians – 2 Samuel 20:15

4.16 The core Succession Narrative (2 Samuel 9-20 and 1 Kings 1-2) also includes various anachronisms – including a reference to an army runner as 'the Kushite'. This term seems to refer to the Nubians (Kushites) prowess in running as demonstrated by the Kushites in the Egyptian army operating in Palestine in an alliance with Judah under the Kushite pharaoh Taharqa (690BC to 664BC). This reference in Samuel only makes sense when Kushites had been in evidence in Palestine.

4.17 One might ask, so what? If these books were written long after the events described rather than being contemporary – why does this matter? Certainly, the passage of time must detract from historical accuracy, the numerous statements quoted as words spoken by individuals cannot be assumed accurate if only written hundreds of years later whilst the theological value of prophesies made on the basis of hindsight must be questionable.

5

Conclusions reviewing Egyptian power during 2nd Millennium BC

5.1 For over 400 years following the expulsion of the Hyksos (1550BC to 1120BC), Egypt ruled the entire area of modern Israel, Lebanon and the western half of Syria. The complete absence of any reference to Egyptian occupation and sovereignty throughout Israel anywhere in the story of the Exodus, 40 years in the Wilderness, the capture of the Promised Land and the period of the Judges strongly indicates these books were written much later than their contemporary setting and, at best, reflect very selective memory.

5.2 From the start of the 18th Dynasty, with Ahmose expelling the Hyksos and subjugating Canaan, Egyptian references to Canaan (and Nubia) changed from designating these areas 'foreign lands' to being Egyptian possessions. In Canaan and Transjordan, two main highways had existed from antiquity (some settlements along these routes date back to 8000BC) – the Way of Horus coastal route and the Kings Highway along the ridge running east of the River Jordan. Under Egyptian control, both routes became important trade routes bringing tax levies and commerce from Canaan and Syria back to Egypt. Over time, both routes became fortified with regular blockhouses and small garrisons. Garrisons were maintained in the key ports all along the Mediterranean coast as far as Ugarit, later lost to the Hittites, and inland the main garrisons in Israel were in Jerusalem and at Beth Shean (just south of the Sea of Galilee), Sumar, Kumadi (in the Bekaa valley, Lebanon) and Megiddo.

5.3 Egypt deployed a sizeable police force in Canaan, largely of Nubians

PART TWO: THE PROMISED LAND 2000 BC TO 1000 BC

from the Medjay tribe – so many, that in Canaan the term Medjay became synonymous with policeman.

5.4 The Egyptian tax system in Canaan involved annual assigned quotas for the salaries of the Egyptian administrators and for the upkeep of temples and garrisons. 'Benevolences' were due every New Year's Day as well as a portion of the 'products of their labour'. Taxes could be brought to Pharaoh himself when he was on a tour of inspection but more frequently the locals had to arrange transport to deliver their taxes to Egypt. Taxes were levied in resources Egypt lacked – including silver, copper, lapis lazuli and glass, Lebanese timber was important, wines, oils and fruit. The sheer quantity extracted by Egypt was surprising.

5.5 The scale of the impact on the Egyptian economy of the conquests made by the Sea People can be seen from the fortunes of the leading temples. From the earliest Asian conquests, selected areas of land and whole towns were confiscated and made the property of Egyptian temples – by the 20th Dynasty (starting 1189BC) the temple of Ptah had accumulated ownership of 56 Canaanite towns and the temple of Amun Ra owned 103 Canaanite towns. This may have been the peak of temple wealth as by 1155BC, only 34 years later, we see the extent of Egypt's loss of sovereignty over Canaan reducing Amun's tally of Canaanite cities to a mere handful of 9 (see section 4.2 above). This rapid change reflected the emergence of the Philistines (former Sea People's) from the cities of the Pentapolis to take over much of the lowland areas of Canaan.

5.6 Canaanite cities were also required to harvest barley, wheat and vegetables to stock military stores in the coastal cities in anticipation of future campaigns. A corvée operated to provide the labour to work the land to provide these crops.

5.7 Each campaign brought large numbers of captives back to Egypt, some from battles, some as a form of quota. In addition, many Canaanite cities provided slaves from their own populations. Upon arrival in Egypt, the name, family and place of origin were registered by a special department and the individual branded with the name of the king or god he was to serve. Then he was placed into one of the state institutions – temple, government department, king's house, army, etc. Work was allocated based on skill and training, and indeed some reached high rank.

5.8 Egypt exploited the trade routes from Mesopotamia and Arabia that came to the northern Mediterranean coast, offering products to exchange with Mycenae, Crete and Cyprus as well as Egypt. The sheer range of merchandise traded between these centres may be appreciated by checking the cargo found from a shipwreck dated to 1302BC off the coast of southern Turkey – referred to as the Ulun Buru, the nearest landfall.

5.9 But do we have contemporary evidence of the Egyptian occupation of the Promised Land during this period? Yes, extensive records from both Egyptian sources and from local Canaanite, Hittite and Hurrian records – but complete silence in the biblical record.

5.10 We have extensive written evidence of Egyptian occupation and administration of, what is today, Israel, Lebanon and western Syria, supported by archaeological evidence in towns across these territories – throughout the 18th, 19th and 20th Dynasties – from 1550BC to 1120BC. Archaeologists label this period the Late Bronze Age. This covers the entire period from the expulsion of the Hyksos until after the defeat of the invading 'Sea Peoples' by Egypt in 1177BC.

5.11 Egyptian administration of 'foreign lands' in the 2nd millennium BC started as military occupation focused on suppression of resistance and protection of commerce – the sea route from Lebanese and northern Palestinian cities predominated but the land route was also used by caravans particularly from Mesopotamia. Egyptian references to territory beyond Sinai are either to Canaan or just to 'foreign lands' – at this point no structure of separate administrative provinces was set up.

5.12 Initially, the titles were a resurrection of Old Kingdom (2613BC to 2181BC) names such as "Overseer of Foreign Lands", but gradually a series of other titles appeared – supervisor, counsellor, governor. In the 19th Dynasty a regularised state department became established and from voluminous records of the 19th and 20th Dynasties the head administrator was primarily a courier, personally carrying the pharaoh's orders to the administrative centres. The "King's messenger to every foreign land" became a romantic type widely eulogised in society and literature of Ramesside Egypt. From a 13th century papyrus, the courier's qualifications are listed as "a choice scribe" and an able serviceman, a leader of troops, a good charioteer and archer. In particular, the candidate would be tested on his detailed knowledge of the defensive qualities of Canaanite cities, its roads and overnight stopping places.

5.13 After the period covered by the Amarna Letters (1405BC to 1340BC) references to governors appear, as in correspondence between Ramesses II and Hattusilis III (the Hittite king) which refers to the Pharaoh's governor in the land of Upe (Damascus). In excavations of various Canaanite cities relating to this period, Tel Fara, Beth Shean, Tel Sera, Tel Masos, Tel Hesi, Tel Jemmah, Apek and others, a house type has been detected with a layout differing markedly from the contemporary Canaanite house plan. The unusual layout does recall plans of contemporary, upper middle class residences in Egypt. Current scholars interpret such buildings as residences and offices erected by and for the pharaonic administrators. The presence of such buildings in most cities excavated from this period supports the presence of officials managing collection and transport of taxes (which being in the form of produce and resources required transport to Egypt), supervision of temple holdings and garrison duty probably required the presence of numerous petty officials and soldiers whose details have not come down to us.

5.14 Although the sea route was preferred, the Egyptians considered the land route from the Delta through Gaza the most important transit corridor – and it was dotted with about a dozen way stations. Texts and artistic depictions refer to these and indicate usually administered by a bailiff or a battalion commander. These way stations comprised small fortified keeps with water reservoirs, two have been excavated and confirm the descriptions in the texts.

5.15 The occupation by Egyptian troops of Canaanite towns is well detailed in Egyptian inscriptions and in the Amarna Letters. The distribution of garrisons seems to have been strategic: from early in the 18th Dynasty, Sharuhen was garrisoned; and references to other garrisons at Tyre, Byblos, another as yet undetermined "on the sea shore of Lebanon", Ullaza and Ugarit. Inland garrisons were fewer but reflect concern the routes through sparsely populated areas that might fall prey to banditry – Jerusalem had a garrison to monitor the surrounding highlands, as did Beth Shean on the southern edge of the Sea of Galilee and Deir 'Allah (level with modern Nablus) on the King's Highway on the eastern side of the Jordan to monitor the crossing.

5.16 Evidence of Egyptian rule over the whole of Israel, Lebanon and the western half of Syria is extensive and comes from a wealth of primary source material. Over this period, we have both Egyptian and cuneiform texts providing contemporary records but also from opposing vantage points for the same period and sometimes for the same events.

5.17   Whilst 'Annals', the year books recording major events and data necessary for future generations appear to have died out after the end of the Old Kingdom, similar 'Journals' proliferated. From the Middle Kingdom come the genre of "the Daybook of" such and such institution, a compilation of major events, memoranda, income and expenditures, organised in calendar form by day, month and year. Temples, departments of government and the palace all kept such Journals. Most important for historians, the Daybook of the King's House recorded not only the King's activities day by day, but also receipts and expenditures of the royal household. On campaign, the Daybook became a war diary. Whilst no complete Daybook of the King's House has survived intact, large tracts were frequently carved on stelae that have been recovered.

5.18   During the Late Bronze Age period (1550BC to 1177BC) international correspondence of a diplomatic variety was conducted between the major states. Pharaohs retained a staff of Akkadian cuneiform scribes to translate his letters from Egyptian to Akkadian and to translate responses received. The Amarna Letters contain numerous such letters from the reigns of three pharaohs – Amenophis III, Akhenaten and Tutankhamun, whilst correspondence from Ramesses II has been found in the excavations of Hattusas, the Hittite capital – together with the Hittite copy of the Treaty with Egypt signed by Ramesses II.

5.19   Other secondary sources include stelae recording battle triumphs and elaborate reliefs of battles and booty recovered, lengthy songs recording heroic deeds and private biographical statements by those committing themselves to destiny by inscribing their achievements on the walls of their tombs.

5.20   Extensive caches of state records have been recovered from the Hittite city of Alalakh (some 250 cuneiform tablets in Akkadian from the palace archives dating to the C15th BC; many thousands of tablets from Ugarit (Canaanite capital) covering the period 1425BC until its destruction by Sea Peoples in 1179BC and at Hattusas (the Hittite capital) plus lesser caches from a number of other excavations dating to this period.

5.21 This wealth of historical evidence makes it very difficult to fit the story of the Exodus and the Israelite conquest of Canaan into the timeline of detailed archaeological evidence.

CONCLUSIONS REVIEWING EGYPTIAN POWER DURING 2ND MILLENNIUM BC

6

Where do the Israelites fit into recorded history & archaeological findings?

6.1 How does the historical evidence of the history of the lands described in the Bible as the Promised Land and occupied by the 12 tribes compare with the Biblical record in Joshua, Judges and Samuel – covering the period from the Exodus to the establishment of the Israelite Monarchy under Saul or David?

6.2 I have already written extensively, in Part One of this series, analysing the story of Moses as told in the Torah and concluded it has no credibility, neither is there any shred of evidence outside of the Bible to support it. The extensive and detailed written evidence we now have provides no support for any part of the biblical narrative of either captivity in Egypt, the Exodus or the capture of the Promised Land. The most likely origin of the story of Moses and the Exodus was tribal memory of the expulsion of the Hyksos overlords from Egypt around 1550BC and their flight, which is suggested ended with settlement in the TransJordan where they became known as the People of 'Ad. Later, these former Hyksos infiltrated into the area surrounding Galilee and the Judean Highlands around Jerusalem being referred to by the Egyptians as 'Apiru' – wandering bandits. The disposition of the '12 tribes' may also have included the region of Amurru north of Lebanon (which may have been shared between the notional tribes of Asher and Naphtali). However, historical evidence suggests the inhabitants were more likely to have been Amorite. The Amorites had grown to control most of modern Syria from c2000BC, taking over some Akkadian and Sumerian cities following the decline of Ur, and ruling the First Babylonian Empire from 1894BC. Weakened by the Hittite capture of Babylon in 1595BC, the Kassites then took over Babylon pushing the Amorites back to the area of Syria – whence they begun filtering west across Canaan to occupy an area that became known as Amurru. Again the reference by Ezekiel (16:3) provides an echo: *"You are nothing but a Canaanite! Your father was an Amorite and your mother a Hittite."*

6.3 Genesis and Exodus find the Philistines already in Palestine in Abraham's time (800 years earlier than they actually arrived). Of the great Egyptian dynasties, Amenophids, Thutmosids and Ramessides that controlled the entire 'Promised Land' from 1550BC to 1177BC there is no mention in the Bible. No Egyptian armies going forth across the land, no punitive taxes, no rounding up of locals to meet slave quotas, no rough handling by infamous Medjay police, no corvée – none of the issues which would have loomed large in daily life in Palestine during these 400 years are mentioned at all.

6.4 A few Egyptian names occur as echoes – the Hyksos 'Sheshy' gives his name to a Canaanite giant (Numbers 13:22); 'Ssy-r', a name of Ramesses II is given to a Canaanite general (Judges 5). Errors persist into later periods, the Egyptian king expected to help Hoshea (2 Kings 17:4) finds his city used as his name. Pharaoh Shabtake/Sabteca (697BC to 690BC) turns up in the Table of Nations (Genesis 10:7) as a Nubian tribe. Clearly, the writers of Jewish scripture had a very shaky knowledge of the periods they wrote about. This makes claims of Biblical inerrancy risible. The pre-Monarchical books boldly present a precise chronology through the entire millennium between Abraham and Saul which actually reveals near total ignorance.

6.5 According to 1 Kings 6:1, 480 years had elapsed between the Exodus and the dedication of Solomon's Temple. The Biblical chronology dates the period of the Judges from 1456BC to 1080BC – pretty much the period that saw the greatest extent of the Egyptian empire. Yet our Egyptian sources are completely silent on the Patriarchs, Israel in Egypt, Joshua or any of his successors – whilst the Bible is blissfully unaware that the Promised Land was entirely under Egyptian rule throughout the period.

6.6 According to the scriptural record, Joshua is credited with assuming leadership of the Israelite host of some 2 million following the death of Moses and leading them to make the conquest of Canaan in a tide of destruction. Using biblical references, working back from the date of

Solomon's temple, it is argued that Joshua lived from 1355BC to die in 1245BC at the age of 110 (Joshua 24:29). However, there are many problems with this proposition – not least that this would have occurred during the reign of powerful Pharaohs (Seti and Ramesses II) whose domain extended far beyond area claimed to have been conquered by Joshua (please refer to the map). The list of cities destroyed by Joshua also has problems: a number of Canaanite cities were destroyed around 1300BC but few that the Bible associates with Joshua. Joshua refers to Hazor and Lachish but documentary evidence from Egyptian, Canaanite and Hittite sources attributes these destructions to Egyptian forces under Ramesses II that attacked these cities in 1250BC. Other cities linked to Joshua such as Ai and Jericho show little or no sign of even being occupied at that time.

6.7 Israel Finkelstein, a leading Israeli archaeologist, has gathered extensive pottery remains across the Judean Highlands and used the collection to help estimate the growth of Israelite settlements in the 200 years leading up to the monarchy. His work estimates around 25 Israelite settlements in 1200BC with a combined population of between 3,000 and 5,000. Two hundred years later, the number of settlements is estimated to have grown to around 250 with a combined population of around 45,000. From the pottery collected, which is uniformly simple in form, mostly unglazed and mostly unpainted, and of designs identical to those from the poorer Canaanite cities. This rapid growth in the Israelite settlements is most likely to be attributable to people fleeing the destruction wrought by the Sea Peoples sweeping down through Canaan in 1178BC.

6.8 Using the population estimates of Israel Finkelstein, we have an estimated 41,000 Israelite population at the time David captures the citadel of Jerusalem, generally assessed as 1000BC, +/-3 years. Paula McNutt also corroborates this estimate. I have not been able to find any estimates of the contemporaneous Philistine population but from the establishment by the Egyptians of their original five cities , the Pentapolis (in today's Gaza), soon after 1177BC, the Philistines had taken advantage of the weakening Egyptian hold over Levant to start spreading around the lowlands surrounding the Judean hills and across the plain of Galilee. Almost certainly the Philistines significantly outnumbered the Israelites occupying the highlands. In his *The River Nile: Geology, Hydrology and Utilization*, Rushdi Said estimates the population of Egypt grew from an estimated 2 million 2000BC to around 3 million by 1000BC. This data puts a few issues into perspective.

6.9 The biblical record of the books of Kings and Samuel is full of references to troublesome Philistines — they plainly caused the Israelites many problems. With Egyptian control over its Asiatic possessions weakened and the rise of Assyria still a century in the future, the new Davidic monarchy was surrounded by relatively modest kingdoms which may have helped it emerge as an independent state. The scale of its resources and its modest population was far too limited to justify the tales of fabulous wealth and power related in the biblical texts. Maybe the lack of contemporary records in other cultures just reflects the insignificance of the new Israelite kingdom. Centuries later, stories were written up in periods of national crisis to invent a glorious past — e.g. Solomon married to 700 royal princesses, etc.

6.10 The contest between the Bible and the Truth is unequal — the pre-monarchical period (pre 1000BC) covers the time (i) before Hebrew first became a written language and (ii) mostly before the Israelites first appeared — apart from references to the Shasu and Apiru, the first mention of Israel is by Merneptah c1209BC. By comparison, our historical records are derived from vast numbers of *original* records currently available today — baked clay tablets of cuneiform and monumental inscriptions in a huge array of buildings. Indeed, far from being 'inerrant', only a few references in the first eight books of the Old Testament appear to record anything close to factual truth.

6.11 There is a general consensus amongst theological academics that the Joshua traditions in the Pentateuch are secondary additions. E. Meyer and G. Hoelscher deny Joshua's existence as a historical reality and conclude that he is the legendary hero of a Josephite clan. Carolyn Pressler, in her 2002 commentary for the Westminster Bible Companion series, suggests that readers of the Book of Joshua should give priority to its theological message ("what passages teach about God") and be aware of what these would have meant to audiences in the 7th and 6th centuries BC. Richard Nelson explains, in his History of Israel, "The needs of the centralized monarchy favoured a single story of origins combining old traditions of an exodus from Egypt, belief in a national god as a 'divine warrior', and explanations for ruined cities, social stratification and ethnic groups, and contemporary tribes."

6.12 Authorship of the biblical Joshua narrative is ascribed to Joshua himself in the Talmud and by early Christian tradition, but in 1943 Martin Noth published an argument that behind Joshua and other books was a unified "Deuteronomistic history", composed in the early part of the Babylonian captivity (6th century BC). Most scholars today believe in some such composite, containing the epic history of the pre-monarchical period. Internal evidence of the book of Joshua, and the repeated use of the phrase 'to this day' all suggest that it records events long after they took place.

6.13 The conclusion by most scholars is that the Book of Joshua holds little historical value. The story of the conquest represents the nationalist propaganda of the 8th century kings of Judah and their claims to the territory of the Kingdom of Israel incorporated into an early form of Joshua written late in the reign of king Josiah (640 – 609BC). The book was revised and completed after the fall of Jerusalem to the Babylonians in 586BC, and possibly after the return from the Exile in 538BC.

6.14 Errors abound in Judges and Samuel robbing these books of credence – including:

(i) iron is common for chariots and implements (Judges 1:19; 4:3; 13; and 1 Samuel 13:19-21) although historically it did not replace bronze until well into the monarchy;

(ii) camels are frequently mentioned, the plot in the story of Gideon depends on camels (Judges 6:5; 7:12; 8:21-26) – but camels did not appear in the area as domesticated beasts of burden until the 9th Century BC;

(iii) the writer knows of kings in Moab (Judges 2:12-30; 11:25) and Ammon (Judges 11:13) long before we have historical knowledge of these forming kingdoms;

(iv) many references to Amalekites, whose only extra Biblical reference does place them geographically where the Bible indicates – but only migrating into the area after 975BC;

(v) there are frequent references to Sidon, to the exclusion of Tyre, as a strong city able to provide protection, a clear reflection not of the Iron Age when Tyre dominated but to the period when Sidon

PART TWO: THE PROMISED LAND 2000 BC TO 1000 BC

enjoyed hegemony – under the Persian empire, between 600 to 800 years later.

6.15   The story of the Judges seems to be of successive individuals, each from a different tribe of Israel, chosen by Yahweh to rescue the people from their enemies and establish justice and the practice of the Torah amongst the Hebrews. This is most unlikely to be the case, as if all the figures given in Judges (years of oppression, years the judges led Israel, years of peace achieved by the judges) are treated as consecutive, then the total duration of the events described in Judges is 410 years. If we accept a date of 1000BC for the beginning of David's reign over all Israel, which puts the beginning of Eli's leadership of Israel at about 1100BC, then the Judges period would begin no later than 1510BC—impossible even for those who date the conquest to the fifteenth century BC.

6.16   The archaeological and written evidence indicates Egyptian control of the Levant coastlands, valleys and the Kings Highway east of the Jordan by the Egyptians until circa 1130BC. Yet, the collective memory of the Israelites in their formative years retains no recollection of Egyptian occupation. It seems clear that the evolution of Israel as a political entity post-dated the Ramesses age and happened in the Judean Highlands remote from Egyptian imperial control.

6.17   The earliest factual link to Egypt given in the Bible is 1 Kings 14:26, describing Sheshonq I (reigning 943BC to 922BC) seizing all the gold shields of the royal guard made by Solomon, which Rehoboam (931BC to 913BC) then had to replace with bronze shields. From Egyptian records we see Sheshonq campaigning across Israel, Judah and Philistria, listing 154 towns that he defeated and sacked. 1 Kings places the campaign in the 5th year of Rehoboam's reign, 926BC, noting that during the attack on Jerusalem, Sheshonq "took away the treasures of the House of Yahweh and the treasures of the royal palace. He took everything including all the gold shields Solomon had made. So, Rehoboam made bronze shields to replace them". And, finally, we have an event where Egyptian historical records are matched by the Bible!

6.18   A closing thought for this chapter – if the Ten Commandments were written around 1550BC when the Hyksos were expelled from Egypt, the writing could only have been in Egyptian hieroglyphics (or possibly Akkadian cuneiform) – as Hebrew writing would not be invented for at least another 500 years. The Hyksos ancestors of the later Israelites certainly appear to have retained memories from their time in Egypt, as evidenced by:

(i) The Ten Commandments, which appear to have been inspired by Chapter 125 of the Egyptian Book of the Dead, of which copies have been dated to around 2500BC;

(ii) the salutation of 'Amen' at the end of every prayer – the Egyptian dedication of prayers to the great god Ra, who having left Egypt to dwell in Babylon around 1850BC, had become the hidden Ra – i.e. Amun Ra or Amen Ra; and,

(iii) dietary laws. I have found a few references to very long-established dietary laws established by the priests of Amun from Thebes but no details of what these laws were – as it would be very illuminating to compare with the Mosaic laws. They existed during the Old Kingdom (i.e. starting from 2613BC) and remained extant until as late as the 8th century BC. The Kushites (a Nubian kingdom formed from an earlier Egyptian colony established in the 16th century BC), took control of Egypt in 760BC forming the 25th dynasty. The Kushites restored a more fundamentalist worship of Amen, they recorded their horror at the previous Libyan dynasty showing no reverence for the dietary laws. The second Kushite pharaoh, Piankhy despatched his sister to Thebes to serve as co-regent of the 'Divine Adoratress', the queen of the Thebes estate. So, Egyptian dietary laws were very long standing and of a religious origin.

6.19 Comparing the theology of Egypt and the Hebrews throughout the second millennium BC, we see Egypt always ruled by a son of the ruling line of the gods – Ptah, Ra, Osiris and Thoth as denoted by the Pharaoh's name invariably incorporating one of these. The Pharaoh owed his authority to his father and he alone had the relationship with god, who dwelt above – "heaven is thy temple". By comparison, the polytheistic Hebrews believed Yahweh dwelt in a portable tent – and until the return from Exile in 538BC, Yahweh was always one of many gods.

7

Where did the Israelites originate from?

7.1 The Bible traces the Israelites as descendants of the Sumerian Abraham. As set out in Part One, we have good contemporary, extra biblical, source records explaining Abraham's family and his status as the heir apparent to the High Priesthood of Enlil (El Elyon in Hebrew per Genesis, same name as used by the Canaanites) in the temple city of Nippur and to the Governorship of the city of Ur, the capital province of the Sumerian Empire.

7.2 After the family moved to the ancient city of Harran (now just inside Turkey), Abraham was asked to go to Canaan, accompanied by 600 "naar" (armed cavalry). After this there are few extra biblical references of his visit to Egypt or to the later migration of his descendants to Egypt. However, we are certain that West Semitic people increasingly occupied the Delta area from around 1750BC and identified as the 'Shepherd Kings' (Hyksos) they ruled Lower Egypt from 1655BC to 1545BC. Pharaoh Ahmose expelled the Hyksos in 1545BC, giving chase and, after three attempts, destroying their new settlement at Sharuhen, near present day Gaza.

7.3 Afterwards the record of the Hyksos grows cold – to the north they were blocked by the Kingdom of Hazor which dominated Canaan at that time and to the east by the Negev desert. A likely explanation, given their trading expertise and their familiarity with desert treks – is that they migrated across the Jordan River and settled in areas which became known as Edom and Moab. Dan Gibson, in Quranic Geography, writes convincingly that the Hyksos formed the People of 'Ad, forerunners of the Nabateans with their capital at Petra. As we saw in Part One, the biblical exodus to Sinai described an journey to settle in Northern Arabia, around Teman, to the south east of Edom and Moab.

7.4 Josephus, writing late 1st century AD, in a work rebutting an anti-Jewish Egyptian writer, Apion, in *"Contra Apionem"* 1.74, 91, speaking as a Jew, refers to the Hyksos as "our ancestors".

7.5 The pattern of migration from references in Egyptian, Canaanite (from Ugarit) and Hittite records indicates a pastoral, transhumant, people migrating westward from about 1350BC from Transjordan (later to become Moab and Edom) into four main areas: –

(i) the area of the Judean highlands around Jerusalem;

(ii) the northern highlands around Shechem;

(iii) the highlands both to the east and to the west of the Sea of Galilee;

(iv) and possibly also into what became the buffer state of Amurru (a no man's land in northern Lebanon between the Egyptian and Hittite spheres of influence) – although it seems more likely these were Amorites who maybe got adopted into the Israelite tribal structure;

The Egyptian records show these highland areas were seen as staging areas for renegades and therefore an imperial presence was necessary to protect the valleys and coastlands from marauders – and hence both areas were garrisoned by the Egyptians.

7.6 A further clue to the origin of the Israelites lies in another term used by the Egyptians for 'lawless plunderers' – Shasu (S^3sw) used from the 18th Dynasty onwards. The Egyptians identified six tribes of Shasu concentrated in southern TransJordan – Se'ir (Moab), Laban (probably Libona, south of Amman), Sam'ath (a clan of Kenites, 1 Chronicles 2:55) and Wrbr (probably linked to Wadi Hasa) and Pysps. Other texts throughout the 19th and 20th Dynasties (1292BC to 1064BC) also link S3sw to Edom and Moab. Most significantly, biblical text records Yahweh as "coming forth from Se'ir" and "originating in Edom" (Deuteronomy 33:2, Judges 5:4).

WHERE DID THE ISRAELITES ORIGINATE FROM?

7.7 Egyptian records during the 60 year period 1320BC to 1260BC refer to the Shasu continuing to foment trouble in the steppe and as pressing westwards through the Negev towards major towns along the Via Maris.

7.8 The first record of the name 'Israel' occurs in the Merneptah stele, erected for Egyptian Pharaoh Merneptah c1209 BC, it states that "Israel is laid waste and his seed is not". William Dever sees this "Israel" in the central highlands as a cultural and probably political entity, well enough established to be perceived by the Egyptians as a possible challenge to their hegemony. The number of villages in the highlands increased to more than 300, with the settled population rising from 20,000 in the twelfth century to 40,000 in the eleventh. (McNutt, 1999)

7.9 In the biblical narrative, the Moabites were relatives of the Israelites, sharing a common ancestor, Terah, the father of the brothers Abraham and Haran. Haran was the father of Lot, who was the father of Moab and Ammon. Intermarriage between Israelites and Moabites was not forbidden as it was with Canaanite tribes, but children of mixed marriages with Moabites or Ammonites were considered *mamzers*, meaning that they could not enter fully into the "congregation" of Israel until the tenth generation. This rule, however, must belong to a later time, for Israel's most pious king, David, was of Moabite descent with only three generations intervening.

7.10 The Moabites had apparently close ties to the clans of Jacob's sons Reuben and Gad, which settled in the Transjordan region of Moab, together with part of the tribe of Manasseh. Some scholars hold that elements of Reuben and Gad may have remained in Moab while the other Israelites migrated to Egypt, or even that they were Moabite clans who were later adopted into the Israelite federation. This would explain why these tribes asked to remain east of the Jordan rather than entering Canaan with the other Israelites.

7.11 David himself committed his parents to the protection of the king of Moab (who may have been his kinsman), when hard pressed by Saul. David went to Mizpah in Moab and said to the king of Moab, "Would you let my father and mother come and stay with you until I learn what God will do for me?" So, he left them with the king of Moab. (1 Samuel 22:3-4)

7.12 Later, however, David made war against Moab and forced the Moabites to be his tributary (2 Samuel 8:2 and 1 Chronicles 18:2). In this campaign he reportedly killed two out of every three Moabite men left alive after their surrender, possibly a fulfillment of Balaam's earlier prophecy. David also plundered sacred items of the Moabites and dedicated them to Yahweh. Moab was apparently under the rule of an Israelite governor during the following period (1 Chronicles 4:22). However, a stele recovered from Moab, the Mesha stele, dating to 840BC, gives a diametrically opposite account – that the Moab forces under Mehsa completely defeated the Israelites and taking Yahweh's sacred ornaments, dedicated these to Chemosh. Given the Mesha stele is contemporary and the biblical text was written centuries later, one might believe the stele, indeed despite the devastation described in Chronicles, the Moabites later fought with Nebuchadnezzar against Judah. So, the veracity of the biblical account is dubious.

7.13   The 'House of Joseph' ensconced on Mount Ephraim, around Shechem (today's Nablus) appears connected with the clans of Machir and Gilead in Transjordan, possibly reflecting the original path of entry. On the Josephites southern flank, the tribe of Benjamin (in tribal lore descended from the same mother, Rachel) occupied the highlands north of Jerusalem. The Book of Judges pays lip service to Judges representative of all 12 tribes but in fact all the detailed legends focus on the Houses of Joseph and Benjamin, reflecting the dominance of Jerusalem in the selection process leading to the recorded canon.

7.14   With early references to the Apiru (from c1350BC) migrating westwards south of the Sea of Galilee and reports of Shasu in the Judean Highlands (from c1260BC) leading up to the reference to 'Israel' in the Merneptah stele of 1209BC, there are strong indications that Israel initially emerged in this Judean Highland area – growing as Egyptian control weakened during the 12th century BC. However, other emerging powers quickly replaced Egyptians power – the Philistines occupying the coastal plains to the west and the valleys on the south of the Judean Highlands and the former Canaanite towns of Tyre, Sidon, Beirut and Byblos emerged as the Phoenician state.

7.15   Worthy of note is the Phoenician invention of the alphabet, which emerged around 1050BC and within 100 years had been adapted by the Israelites to develop the first written Hebrew. To the north of the emergent Israelites, northern Syria saw various city states referred to as Hittite because they used the Hittite script but probably of mixed racial groupings, whilst southern Syria, including Damascus, came under the aegis of the Aramaeans.

7.16 According to Finkelstein, writing in *The Archaeology of the Israelite Settlement*, other regions harbouring tribes traditionally held to be part of the 12 tribe federation were added somewhat later. The archaeological and textual record suggests 1100BC to 900BC for settlement by the four Galilean tribes, followed by later incorporation into the monarchy,. To the south of Jerusalem, the picture seems more complicated – with no evidence of settlement by the Kenites, Yerahmeelites, Calebites, Othnielites and others constituting the population of the rugged Har Yehudah prior to the monarchical period. Both Dan and Simeon remain absent from all bodies of evidence, however some have speculated that Dan may be linked to a component of the Sea Peoples known as the Danune.

7.17 Some confusion appears to have been created by Immanuel Velikovsky trying to understand history by examining the biblical texts. Velikovsky developed a theory that the biblical Amalekites were in fact the Hyksos, who he describes as invading Egypt after the Exodus and later, following their expulsion by the Egyptians, becoming those described in the Bible as Amalekites. Thus, many biblical writers now link the Amalekites with the Hyksos. Analysis of Velikovsky's theory shows some key problems – the Exodus he puts as early as 1660BC – leaving the Israelites quiescent for 450 years before the first evidence of them on the Merneptah stele. There is no evidence of the Egyptian society in ruins after plagues, etc., only a series of weak Pharaohs allowing gradual encroachment by the Hyksos. Following the Egyptian ejection of the Hyksos, Velikovsky, based upon biblical references, has them assume the role of a continuing irritant to Israel up to and including the early Monarchy. However, we know from extensive historical records that the Egyptians ruled the entire area of what is now Israel, Jordan, Lebanon and western half of Syria.

7.18 There is no extra biblical reference to Amalekites in the second millennium BC. However, there is some reference to the name Amalek at the Tel Masos site in the Negev. Again, Egyptian records refer to tribes from Arabah (Arabia) infiltrating north-westwards across the Negev early in the first millennium BC and founding a settlement based on copper smelting around Kh en-Nahas (now referred to as Tel Masos). Tel Masos has been extensively excavated, with carbon dating providing dates of occupation between 975BC to 845BC. Pharaoh Sheshonq I recorded an attack on Tel Masos in 926BC, the same campaign that saw him erect a stele at Megiddo. Tel Masos is in the same area as biblical references always place the Amalekites – this appears to be another case of biblical text written long after the event confusing the chronology.

7.19 William G. Dever, Distinguished Professor of Near Eastern Archaeology at Lycoming College in Pennsylvania, has directed a number of excavations revealing extensive archaeological evidence from a range of Israelite sites, largely dated between the 12th and the 8th centuries BC. Dever was Director of the Harvard digs at Gezer in 1966–71, 1984 and 1990; Director of the dig at Khirbet el-Kôm and Jebel Qaaqir (West Bank) 1967–71; and Principal Investigator at Tell el-Hayyat excavations (Jordan) 1981–85 amongst other excavations.

7.20 Dever used his background in Near Eastern archaeology to argue, in *Did God Have a Wife? Archaeology and Folk Religion in Ancient Israel* (2005), for the persistence of the worship of Asherah in the everyday religion of 'ordinary people' in ancient Israel and Judah. Asherah (derived from Sumerian & Akkadian goddess Inanna/Ishtar) was viewed as the consort of El/Baal and later Yahweh. Dever argued that this folk religion, with its local altars and cultic objects, amulets and votive offerings, was representative of the outlook of the majority of the population, and that the 'book religion' of the Deuteronomist circle set out in the Bible was only ever the preserve of a Jerusalem based elite, a 'largely impractical' religious ideal.

7.21 Dever's conclusions concerning the worship of Asherah are based on inscriptions at Khirbet el-Qom, Kuntillet Ajrud and Taanach. This is corroborated by other archaeologists as well as thousands of Asherah figurines found in various locations in Israel.

7.22 In retirement, Dever has been critical of 'Biblical minimalists' who deny any historical value to the biblical accounts, on the other hand, he is far from being a supporter of biblical literalism. Instead he views the biblical narratives as 'stories,' often fictional and almost always propagandistic, but that here and there they contain some valid historical information. Some things described there really did happen, but others did not. The biblical narratives about Abraham, Moses, Joshua and Solomon probably reflect some historical memories of people and places, but the 'larger than life' portraits of the Bible are unrealistic and contradicted by the archaeological evidence.

7.23   K.A. Kitchen, in "Ancient Orient & Old Testament", writing over 50 years ago, provides a detailed analysis of treaty structures written during the period 1500BC to 500BC in which he sees a trend towards simpler and more fluid forms. Older treaties conformed to a standard structure of a historical introduction, undertaking, blessings and curses (if adhered to or if broken) and witness by respective gods of the parties. Later treaties generally missed the introduction and varied the sequence, often placing the witnessing prior to the blessings and curses. Kitchen then argues that because the Sinai covenants Yahweh made with the Israelites followed the early form – they must have been genuinely 'written' following the Exodus and around the conventional timing by biblical scholars – 14th century BC.

7.24   However, there are numerous objections that can be made against Kitchen's argument:

(i)   the central assumption of a clear pattern is very weak as there are very few examples of treaties between parties that have so far been recovered, thus the assertion of a strict pattern is unconvincing – the most famous treaty, because we have full copies of both sides executed copies in Akkadian, as well as drafts in Hittite, is the Egyptian Hittite Treaty of 1258BC;

(ii) the Israelites enjoyed neither writing nor a scribal class until the monarchical period starting around 1000BC – so any record of any older covenant would be solely oral tradition;

(iii) the biblical record of the covenants are descriptive without formal signature points – so any issue about the sequence indicating where the parties signed does not apply anyway;

(iv) as we learned from the Egyptian Hittite Treaty of 1258BC, the witnesses were not the parties respective gods but the same gods shown with both their local names and their original Sumerian names. Thus, we now realise the same 'gods' acted as witnesses for both parties. This is key to understanding the entire pantheon of ancient pagan gods were actually a single family of related 'gods' revered across all ancient civilisations which led to local variations of the names of the individual gods. Our initial assumption that each civilisation had its own unique set of pagan gods is clearly erroneous. It is also noteworthy that neither king, nor any of their descendants ever broke the terms of the 1258BC Treaty.

7.25 Whilst reading Kitchen's work one also finds the common mistake of biblical apologists reliance on the Late Babylonian (Chaldean) versions of the Enuma Elish (the 7 tablet Story of Creation) to claim the version in Genesis is older and the inclusion of numerous references to Marduk (senior god of Babylon) indicates a different derivation. Again, these assumptions ignore key facts:

(i) The age of the Enuma Elish. Like most biblical academics, Kitchen only seems aware of the Chaldean versions of the Enuma Elish (it is true that the very first copy was translated by George Smith, curator of the British Museum, in 1876) from a copy, dating at least 200 years earlier, found in the Library of Ashurbanipal (the Assyrian king) so not even Chaldean. Subsequent excavations have found whole and partial copies dating back as far as 3800BC – 1800 years before Abraham!

(ii) The references to Marduk were added by the Babylonians, reflecting the fact he had become their senior god, inheriting the role from his uncle, Enlil (whom the Canaanites and the early Israelites called El Elyon).

(iii) Whilst we have original written documents (cuneiform tablets) dating back to 3800BC for the Enuma Elish, there is no record of written Hebrew before 1000BC – and the alphabet it uses came from Phoenician which itself dates back only to around 1050BC. So it is little wonder that remote tribes of Shasu and Apiru, passing down oral traditions, overlooked certain details but they did remember that the name of the supreme god was El Elyon!! El Elyon (originally Enlil in Sumerian) is the Hebrew name used for God in Genesis prior to the burning bush incident and the god for whom Abraham's grandfather was high priest in Nippur.

7.26 Another example from Kitchen's book again confirms highly selective and arbitrary arguments put forward – in this case dismissing possible Babylonian origin of any Hebrew festivals:

"Some Old Testament scholars (notably Mowinckel) insist that such a festival, on a

Babylonian model, was celebrated at New Year in ancient Israel, reflecting a supposedly widespread Near Eastern usage. But there is no proper (i.e., explicit) evidence in the Old Testament for this at all. No such major festival features among the feasts and rituals of the Pentateuchal writings; the historical books know of passovers and renewals of covenant on significant occasions, but not of Enthronement or New Year celebrations. It is indeed conceivable that during the monarchy there was a New Year feast associated with the temple at Jerusalem which ended with the monarchy, copied, like that monarchy, in some measure from 'the nations round about' and not revived by post-exilic orthodoxy. But this remains purely a speculation, and so is of no value at present.

Mowinckel's festival is principally based on the highly questionable use of supposed allusions in the Psalms, and on a scheme inspired by supposed Babylonian models (through Canaanite intermediaries). The phrase "YHWH mdldk" in certain Psalms, despite assertions to the contrary, means simply 'YHWH reigns' (or, '...exercises kingship'), and not 'YHWH has become king' (implying enthronement) as partisans of the theory have held. No adequate reason has been offered why Israel should import and celebrate an entirely alien type of festival from distant Babylonia, and so far Canaan has failed to yield indisputable evidence for assumed intermediary forms."

7.27 However, Kitchen ignores the glaring examples which clearly indicate Hebrew adoption of "Babylonian" festivals:

(i) The Sabbath, derived from the Sumerian 'shabbatu' was originally the Sumerian monthly day of rest (obviously celebrated by Abraham's family), but by the era of the Babylonian exile had become a weekly festival. Funny how the Pentateuch reflects the Exilic period of weekly occurrence – if authentic, the Mosaic assumption would surely have been monthly!!

(ii) The Feast of Tabernacles, celebrating the grape harvest in honour of Dionysus (originally a Sumerian god, later known to the Romans as Bacchus).

(iii) The monthly celebration of the new moon, in adoration of the god Sin – the city god of the ancient cities of both Harran and Ur.

7.28 To enable the reader to consider the "Promised Land" in the context of the political situation of the second half of the second millennium BC – the map, shown immediately after the Contents page, seeks to provide perspective of the area governed by the Egyptians during the height of their power, from 1550BC to 1130BC to be precise, which embraced the entire Promised Land and far beyond. The dates are highly significant – covering the 420 years from the re-establishment of Egyptian power following the expulsion of the Hyksos until the Philistines started to throw off the Egyptian yoke in 1130BC. This period covers the centuries in which almost all biblical historians place the Exodus, the wandering in Sinai, the conquest of Canaan and the period of the Judges. Yet none of these writings ever mention unchallenged Egyptian rule over the entire area that the Israelites supposedly conquered.

7.29 Over the three millennia before Christ, Egyptian power ebbed and flowed – the dotted red line shows the largely settled area governed between 1550BC and 1130BC. Cities such as Hazor and Kadesh, the sites of famous battles between Hittites and Egyptians did change hands a few times but the settled northern boundary during this period was near the Lake of Homs – equivalent to the northern boundary of Lebanon today. An area between the Lake of Homs and the Mediterranean long formed a buffer zone between Egyptians and Hittites. The area became known as Amurru, and the occupants, who are recorded as wild bands of vagabonds were referred to as 'Apiru' – from whence some argue 'Hebrew' might have originated.

7.30 However, from time to time, Egyptian power was projected far further north than Amurru. In the 1470's Egyptian forces dis-assembled ships and carried them along the King's Highway as far as the Euphrates. Once reassembled, the ships were used to carry the Egyptian forces as far as Carchemesh (now just over the Turkish border) and by land far to the east to Mitanni (also now a Turkish border town). Two hundred years later, the Egyptians had pushed the Hittites as far as Qode, well inside modern Turkey and almost opposite the north coast of Cyprus.

7.31 There is evidence that Egypt held suzerainty over most of Canaan for centuries before Abraham's arrival and centuries afterwards before succumbing to the Hyksos. Once Egypt was unified to constitute more or less it's present state, it also occupied much of what is today Sudan and eastern Libya.

7.32 The two major highways used as land corridors by the Egyptians, the Way of Horus (known mainly by its Roman name, Via Maris) and the King's Highway, are shown as red lines on the map. The Way of Horus provided a land route along the coast. References to the King's Highway seem almost impossibly old – up to 6,000 years ago. The highway ran from Memphis on the Nile, across Sinai, thence north along the crest of the hills along the eastern side of the Jordan Valley before turning to Damascus and then via Tadmor (better known today by its Roman name of Palmyra) and on to the River Euphrates. Both roads were dotted with fortified Egyptian blockhouses. Both roads continue in use today as part of state highway networks.

7.33   The King's Highway appears to be the world's oldest continuously used road, serving as the primary connection between the civilisations in Mesopotamia, as far back as the Sumerians, and the Egyptians. Its route went through, or close to, many ancient cities – including Damascus, Palmyra, Petra, Jericho and Tell el-Hamman (the current name for the site of the most likely candidate for what the Israelites named Sodom & Gomorrah – see chapter 18*bis*). I may not have identified the earliest references to the use of the King's Highway but Damascus has been settled from a very early date. Tell Ramad, on the outskirts of Damascus, indicates settlement since c6300BC whilst evidence across the Barada basin gives dates back to 9000BC. Note that Damascus is less than 50km south of the Baalbek Terrace and around 600km from Göbekli Tepe - which also shows evidence of occupation around 9600BC and recently other nearby Tepe indicate occupation for millennia earlier than that.

7.34   Ancient references to use of the King's Highway abound, linking Bashan, Giliad, Ammon with Moab, Edom, Paran and Midian. The Highway gets a number of references in Hebrew scripture, used by Abraham and Moses. Abraham would have used the King's Highway to journey from Harran to Canaan when originally despatched to recover the Promised Land, the battle of the four kings verses the five kings in Genesis 14 would have used the King's Highway. Moses asked the King of Edom if his people could use the King's Highway to traverse through Edom to travel to Canaan but was famously refused.

7.35   From 1550BC, following the expulsion of the Hyksos and the reestablishment of Egyptian suzerainty over the Levant, both the Way of Horus and the King's Highway were progressively fortified with manned Egyptian blockhouses. Long sections of the King's Highway eventually formed the eastern boundary of the Roman Empire, and the Romans duly referred to it as Via Regia. The importance of the road for Roman trade and military purposes was confirmed by Emperor Trajan, AD98 to 117, who rebuilt long sections and renamed it Via Trajana Nova. Both roads continue in use today as part of state highway networks.

7.36   The 'Promised Land', using the detailed biblical definition, is shown by the pale green area, and looks relatively small within the greater area of Egyptian control.

7.37   For reference, I have also added Harran and indicated the position of Ur – two of Abraham's home towns. I have also added Göbekli Tepe, of which only a tiny percentage has yet been excavated but which appears to date back to around 9600BC – hopefully, once peace prevails in the area, we may learn far more from this amazing site. Intriguingly, Harran, which some evidence suggests dates back as far as 8000BC is tantalizingly close to Göbekli Tepe.

7.38   To help readers find places on modern maps, I have shown current political boundaries of Israel, Lebanon, Syria, Turkey, Jordan and Iraq. I have also shown the modern cities of Gaziantep and Sanliurfa in Turkey to enable readers to locate Harran and Göbekli Tepe. In addition, Mosul and Baghdad are shown to facilitate appreciation of where Nineveh and Babylon were located.

7.39   One is left wondering why, despite the entire area supposedly settled by the Israelite descendants from the Exodus actually lying deep within the Egyptian Empire, biblical writers make no reference to their Egyptian overlords, heavy taxes and compulsory work levies. The most plausible explanation lies in the advent of Hebrew writing only emerging around the time of David's reputed kingship. Gradually a priestly scribal class would have emerged which started to develop a catalogue of texts recording oral traditions over the subsequent centuries. The evidence in this booklet strongly indicates much was written and rewritten hundreds of years after the events recorded. Therefore, it is entirely possible that the story of the Exodus is a melange of muddled memories of the expulsion from Egypt as Hyksos (around 1550BC) and centuries of repression during the period 1450BC to 1130BC as the remnants drifted west across the Jordan, back into Egyptian controlled territories.

WHERE DID THE ISRAELITES ORIGINATE FROM?

7.40 The previous six chapters have looked at the sweep of the historical evidence from the second millennium BC and compared detailed archeological evidence with the record from the Bible. I now turn to focus on some sections of the biblical record to search for the historical foundations. Tracing the potential origins of some of the obscure statements in the Old Testament reveals some intriguing details.

8

The Promised Land

8.1 At some point in your life you must have stopped and wondered – why were the Israelites "Chosen" and why was ancient Canaan specified as the "Promised Land"? Well firstly, it was not the Israelites that were chosen – but Abraham, a high ranking Sumerian prince.

8.2 A clue as to why the Promised Land, Canaan, was identified for Abraham to take over lies in the Biblical story of the descendants of Noah. According to the Table of Nations laid out in Genesis 10, the descendants of Noah are identified with lands supposedly allocated to them. Grouped under each of Noah's three sons, the lands allocated fit neatly with the spheres of influence of the leading gods of the Sumerian pantheon. Japheth (the fair one) was allocated the highlands of Asia Minor and across the Zagros mountains, spreading into the Indus and northern India – broadly equivalent with the original disposition of the fair skinned Aryan peoples. The early cities of Harappa and Mohenjo-Daro in the Indus Valley, which exhibit strong similarities with Sumerian urban designs, were under the control of Inanna (Akkadian: *Ishtar*). The descendants of Ham (the dark hued one) were allocated Africa, Enki's domain, whilst the descendants of Shem (the sky chamber) were allocated the Fertile Crescent, Enlil's domain.

8.3 Genesis (9:25-26) singles out Canaan, named after the fourth and youngest son of Ham, for special rebuke and curses the descendants of Canaan to be servants to the descendants of Shem. The improbable excuse for this treatment was that Ham (not even Canaan) had seen the naked genitals of his father Noah. This apparently justified placing a curse upon Noah's grandson, Canaan: *"Cursed be Canaan! The lowest of slaves will he be to his brothers. Praise be to the Lord [El Elyon], the God of Shem. May Canaan be the slave of Shem"*. This is puzzling, if the father transgressed why is the son punished and why is the punishment to be a slave to the god of another son? The text clearly indicates familiarity with the allocation of lands under different gods – Shem's descendants are El Elyon's inheritance, whilst Ham's descendants are Enki/Ptah's inheritance. The curse predicts the Canaanites will become slaves to the Sumerian Abraham's descendants. But why?

8.4 The answer lies in the Book of Jubilees (Ch 10), where the real transgression is explained – the illegal occupation by Ham's son of land allocated to the descendants of Shem. Jubilees states that when Ham and his family journeyed south from the grounding of the Ark at Mount Ararat (in Turkey, 25km from the border with Armenia) towards their allotted lands in Africa, "Canaan saw the land of Lebanon all the way to the River of Egypt, that it was very good." And so, he changed his mind: "He went not into the land of his inheritance to the west of the sea (Red Sea); he dwelt instead in the land of Lebanon, eastward and westward of the Jordan."

8.5 Canaan's father and brothers tried to dissuade him from the illegal act: "And Ham his father, and Cush and Mizraim his brothers, said to him: You have settled in a land which is not yours, and which did not fall to us by lot. Do not do this! If you do, you and your sons will be fallen in the land and be accursed through sedition; for by sedition you have settled, and by sedition will your children fall, and you shall be rooted out forever. Dwell not in the dwelling place of Shem, for to Shem and his sons did it fall by lot." They pointed out that illegal occupation would bring a curse upon Canaan: "You are cursed, and you will be more cursed than all the sons of Noah, by that curse with which we bound ourselves by oath in the presence of the sacred judge, and in the presence of Noah our father. But Canaan did not listen to them".

8.6 Studies have indicated that much of the content of the Pentateuch was derived from ancient Sumerian era history and their scientific knowledge. The Genesis creation story, Adam, Noah and the Flood, and Abraham's ancestors – some of the knowledge undoubtedly taught to Abraham, we also now have from original cuneiform tablets. During the wanderings after leaving Harran for the Promised Land and for the next 1000 or so years, writing skills seem to have been forgotten – and no records have been found. Tribal history would have been passed down orally and gradually embellished and modified. So, one can imagine the utter delight felt by the Levites upon discovering copies of the Enuma Elish in Nebuchadnezzar's library – probably contributing to their decision to assemble a written record of their oral traditions which ended up as the Torah.

8.7 As the Jewish tradition relies so much on Sumerian history and legends dating back many millennia before the Old Testament scriptures were actually written down, it might be instructive to consider the Sumerian view of their deities and what they understood their deities sought from mankind.

8.8 The Sumerian records of their deities described interactions with and between quite human deities. The Sumerian deities were not immortal, they did die but unless killed in battle they lived extraordinary long lives. They designed temples – giving detailed instructions on how these were to be built – just as Solomon was given. The temples were built for them to enjoy as their abode. Even the term used in Sumerian to describe a home, the abode where someone lives, "E" is similarly applied to all temples – but our historians have translated as "temple" rather than "house" of each god. All these gods liked having meals cooked to proscribed recipes, as set out in Exodus, the meat had to be properly butchered, fat drained off, causing aromas of roasting meat pleasing to the Lord, bread baked in a particular way, etc. These gods appear to have had a clear moral code, breaches of which made individual gods subject to strong punishment.

8.9 Territory was allocated amongst the gods, as reflected in the concept of the table of nations in Genesis 10 – and Yahweh got the issue of Abraham: *Deuteronomy 32:9 "When El Elyon gave the nations as an inheritance, when he separated the sons of man, he set the boundaries of the peoples according to the number of the sons of God. For Yahweh's portion was his people; Jacob was the lot of his inheritance"*. Once territory was allocated to a deity, encroachment by another was frowned upon. Hence, Canaan's occupation of the eponymous area set himself up for trouble – that land was allocated to Enlil to dispose amongst the sons of Shem – hence it was 'promised land'. Thus Enlil, aka El Elyon, aka the Lord Most High, instructed Abraham, the heir to the governorship of Ur, to take his naar (armed cavalry) and go to recover Canaan.

8.10 Maybe resulting from incredibly long lives, senior deities enjoyed multiple wives but the severest punishment was for rape – even the son of the ultimate god was judged and sentenced to death for rape, although he was later reprieved when they agreed to marry. One quirk in their code appears to have been ultimately responsible for many of the wars between early civilisations. Succession amongst the deity passed to the firstborn of the highest ranking consort – who was defined as the sister by a different mother – a rule seemingly designed to protect the purity of the bloodline. The son birthed by your half-sister took precedence over progeny of your official wife and any other wives. But, under the Sumerian code, marriage to a full sister was forbidden. We see this aspect of their legal code laid the foundations for millennia of strife and is known to have been copied by other leading families – e.g. most Pharaohs, and even Abraham, married their half-sisters!

8.11 As we saw in the Prequel to this series, there is strong evidence of a relatively advanced human culture existing prior to the meteor impact that triggered the climatic changes referred to as the Younger Dryas Period (c10765BC to c9620BC). There is also widespread evidence of small groups of survivors of this calamity who brought "civilisation-in-a-box" to areas such as the Nile, Euphrates and Göbekli Tepe. Is it just coincidence that the earliest conventionally recognised ancient civilisations all seem to share very similar stories of wise and benevolent visitors?

8.12 Some writers have concluded that these survivors were extra-terrestrial visitors, colonising our planet and fashioning humankind as hybrid manual workers. Whilst some authors, such as Zecharia Sitchin, have developed well researched and argued descriptions of early civilisations led by such aliens and their offspring – the biggest problem with these theories lies in DNA. If humanity is a hybrid creation combining on and off planet DNA it is amazing that fertile unions between 'gods' and men took place and in turn spawned fertile offspring. The more difficult question to answer is why human DNA is so impossibly closely related to the DNA of all other lifeforms on this planet.

8.13 I conclude that, despite many puzzling aspects, there must have been an earlier advanced human civilisation prior to the 10765BC meteor impact and a few survivors who managed to kick start new cultures after the devastation. These intelligent survivors easily assumed leadership positions, were seen as heroes in their new communities, served by grateful supporters whose attention became seen as worship and whose interlocutors became identified as priests. Naturally inter-marriage occurred and mixed offspring identified 'demi-gods'.

8.14 The key remaining puzzle for me are the numerous references to the 'gods' and 'demi-gods' amazing longevity. However, for the purely hunter gatherer societies these civilised survivors had initially chanced upon, lives would have generally have been brutish and short – survival beyond say 25 would not have been the norm. By contrast, for those who had long mastered cooking food, using a range of recipes and with knowledge of medicines and a mastery of surgical techniques – lifespans would have been much longer. Note: the skills just noted above are all skills credited to the arriving survivors. We can only speculate as to actual lifespans, but if the 'gods' lived to say 100, when ordinary folk only managed around say 25 – then early myths and fables could have resulted in the exaggerated ages we find credited to these heroes.

8.15 Sumerian history texts have been interpreted as describing arriving survivors being subjects of a remote kingdom – which is entirely logical. These texts record the firstborn of the visitors' ultimate ruler, Enki, being leader of the first team. However, his performance fell short of expectations and his sibling Enlil, the official heir, was despatched as overlord. Enlil became titled the Lord Most High, his brother, Enki, was known as the Lord of the Underworld (which may have meant the southern hemisphere). Enlil's character seems harsh and brutal (threatening, cajoling, punishing with abandon) maybe becoming the role model of Yahweh. By contrast, his brother Enki seems to have been more of a scientist and a medic.

8.16 According to some interpretations of the Sumerian records, the visitors toiling to build the new infrastructure rebelled at the continuous hard labour, Enki had the bright idea of developing a primitive worker species. Enki collaborated with his half-sister, Ninharsag, a biologist, to develop a genetically improved version of early humans – and after many failures, finally Ninharsag is recorded as herself bringing to term a hybrid which was judged to be a capable worker – whom they named 'Adamu'. It appears this was an infertile hybrid of human and visitor genetic material.

Only later were fertile hybrids created and a female Eve developed to improve 'production efficiency'. Maybe this is an interpretation designed to perpetuate the subordinate role of primitive peoples to the few advanced survivors seeking to perpetuate their overlordship.

8.17 This version of history explains evolutionary puzzles and odd statements in the Bible:

- Why homo sapiens suddenly developed from primitive hunter gatherers to farmers developing sophisticated cities in an incredibly short period. The earliest cities in Mesopotamia dating from around 4000BC, Eridu, Ur, Nippur, Erech, etc were well laid out with large civic buildings, extensive docks, granaries, generously proportioned private houses, etc. Similarly, the earliest cities on the Nile and the Indus, dating to around 3000BC were equally incredible "first" cities.

- Biologists are puzzled why from primitive humans, homo sapiens, shed virtually all their hair in an evolutionary blink of an eye.

- The Biblical narrative of Nefilim, descending from heaven and taking the daughters of men for their wives and having children. This might tell of the visitors developing relations with the erstwhile primitive workers – indicating they shared a very close genetic makeup. How on earth could that have occurred??

8.18 Having had the idea and led the project to create the Adamu, Enki was always seen as sympathetic to humans. His insignia, the intertwined double snake, suggestive of a double helix, remains today the global sign for medicine – used by doctors and hospitals worldwide. Enki was the inspiration for the wise serpent in the Garden, bestowing knowledge on the primitive workers and showing them how to make clothes.

8.19 It is noteworthy that the most ancient Sumerian and Egyptian depictions of deities and their workers always show the deities clothed but the workers and servants naked !!

8.20 It has been suggested that much of the history between the Flood and the last of the Jewish scriptures records the long epoch of a titanic struggle for hegemony on Earth between the two brothers Enlil and Enki, together with their descendants and human nations faithful to their respective geographical 'deities'. Records throughout the centuries from

3000BC to at least 400BC repeatedly tell of kings 'instructed' by their deity to go to war; led in battle by their deity; and the forces of their enemies being smote by their deity. Conventional history dismisses all such nonsense as "pagan myths" but maybe some of these myths grew from real events.

8.21 The visitors' ultimate ruler, Anu (the sky god), the father of Enlil and Enki, is described in various records (including Psalm 82) as having divided up the habitable territory on Earth between 70 descendants, collectively known as the 'assembly of the gods'. After some millennia of struggles, Enlil, whose main residence was Nippur, is recorded as being absent for long periods – leaving Enki to scheme. Enki had managed to seduce his half-sister, Ninharsag, and the resulting son carrying the purest bloodline, Ra (aka Marduk) became favoured by his grandfather. Confident in support from father and grandfather, Marduk became more and more adventurous, he played a role in the downfall of Sumer and later, basing himself in Babylon, he was the senior deity under the Babylonian, Hurrian, Assyrian and Chaldean empires.

8.22 It is noteworthy that Cyrus, the Persian emperor who defeated the Chaldeans and released the Hebrew captives, also praised Marduk – not as a deity but as a valuable advisor and teacher. There are descriptions of Cyrus Persian army marching on Babylon in 539BC which describe it being led by Marduk – who had despaired of the weak rulers of the Babylonian empire and whose army capitulated in front of the city without a fight. There are numerous references to Marduk in the Old Testament.

8.23 With Ra, Enki's foremost son, being complicit in the downfall of Sumer, it is logical that Enlil would select a righteous, knowledgeable and skilled military leader who was also a royal scion to carry the line forward of his beloved civilisation. It also explains why the line of Levite priests to Abraham's descendants would characterise Enki, the wise serpent, as the wicked devil.

8.24 And, another puzzle about Abraham. From original cuneiform tablets recovered from Ur, we understand he was the heir apparent to the Governorship of Ur, the capital province of the 2000+ year old Sumerian Empire. Abraham would have received the best education and military training (e.g. references to him leading 600 armed cavalry when he entered Canaan) for his future role. In this role, the cultural imperative would have made one of his objectives to produce at least an heir and a spare, probably more. In such a wealthy household, he would have been surrounded with buxom wenches and able to enjoy his pick of the servant girls – so the claim in Genesis that he had reached the ripe old age of 99 without any offspring is just not credible. Unless, perhaps, he suffered from phimosis (an inability to retract foreskin) – which explains why he became a father immediately following his circumcision.

8.25 Even the choice of Harran as the family home after Ur was highly significant – already inhabited for around 6,000 years when Abraham's family arrived and renowned for its priest-astronomers (later known as the Sabians), it was a second centre of worship of Sin, for whom a new temple was built and dedicated by Nebuchadnezzar around 1,500 years later.

THE PROMISED LAND

PART TWO: THE PROMISED LAND 2000 BC TO 1000 BC

9

The Table of Nations in Genesis chapter 10

9.1 Having seen how non-canonical books can help explain obscure references, let us take a closer look at the Table of Nations in Genesis 10 and see what else can be gleaned.

9.2 Genesis chapter 10 attempts to provide a genealogy of humanity in tabular form – again when first studied post Reformation, it was seen as a reliable historical record of how the early nations had descended from the handful of humans surviving the Flood. For hundreds of years there was no contrary evidence available to question its accuracy. Gradually, we learned how to translate ancient languages and extensive evidence has emerged to help identify the various names and races referred to in Genesis 10. What we now know is that the identifiers used in Genesis 10 enable us to link its authorship to the period immediately prior to the Exile with a few pointers to post Exilic editing. We can see it has little grasp of history even at the dawn of the first millennium BC; its coverage relates to little more than the Fertile Crescent and it conflates ethnicity with geographic labels and kings.

9.3 The basic structure enumerates the progeny of each son identified followed by a geographical reference and a summation. The descendants of Japheth and Shem are taken to the 3rd generation from Noah whilst Ham is taken to the fourth. There are huge gaps and the focus is very patchy – on the Scythians (offspring of Gomer, i.e. the Cimmerians, the eastern Greeks, the Aramaeans). The narrative similarly only covers a few of the progeny – families of only two of the Hamitic races (Misrayim and Canaan) and one of Shem (Arphacsad) whilst Japheth descendants are ignored.

9.4 The table strangely omits the line of Israel, even when dealing with the progeny of Shem the writer avoids the descent from Peleg. However, Peleg's brother Joktan is credited with 13 sons. Chapter 10 seems to be setting the scene for the descent from Abraham set out in Chapter 11, attempting to place Israel within the broader context of the foreign peoples the author was familiar with. So, what does the tabulation reveal about its date of creation? The Japhethites appear as an arc from the Ionian Greeks in the west to the Medes of Iran in the east – taking in the Caucasus and Asia Minor. The names included indicate a mid 6th century authorship – the inclusion of the incipient Medes and Persians, included in Yawan's sons are Kittim (Cyprus) and Ridanim (Rhodes) – names given to Greeks first settling on these islands from c700BC. The Hebrews first encountered the Greeks after returning from the Exile. Heading the sons of Japheth is Gomer, the ancestor of the Cimmerians – who according to Assyrian sources first appeared when migrating southwards from the Caucasus they attacked Urartu in 714BC. In 705BC the Cimmerians killed the Assyrian king Sargon II in battle and continued to harry parts of the Assyrian empire until heavily defeated by Esarhaddon and Ashurbanipal. The Cimmerians also attacked and briefly controlled Lydia (the western half of Turkey) c650BC to 630BC and also raided the Ionian islands – thereafter they were defeated by the Scythians and disappeared from history. In Genesis, Gomer is the father to Ashkenaz (the Scythians) – the writer of Genesis 10 knew that the Scythians succeeded to the lands of the Cimmerians, describing conquest as a father-son relationship!! This gem limits authorship of Genesis chapter 10 to around 630BC at the earliest.

9.5 A similar conclusion may be drawn from the listing of the sons of Ham – Kush, Misrayim, Libya (Put) and Canaan. This sequence is not geographical but political – the precedence of Kush reflects the conquest of Egypt by Kush (Napata) from 711BC until defeat by Psammetichos II in 593BC. Libya is in third place, the Libyan supremacy of the 22nd and 23rd dynasties (920BC to 720BC) being a distant memory. Last comes Canaan, a faint memory of Egyptian rule until overrun by the Sea Peoples in 1177BC. The writer identifies the geographies by using the eponymous names of the peoples as the identity of their founder. One of the sons of Kush, Sabtecah, has been identified as the Kushite pharaoh

Shabtaka (ruling 697BC to 690BC).

9.6 The sons of Shem also point to a similar date range. The inclusion of Elam points to recent memory. Elam (now part of western Iran) was conquered by Ashurbanipal in 640BC and their leading citizens deported to Samaria. The inclusion of Ashur, Assyria, reflects its empire (destroyed in 612BC) and Arphacsad is regarded as a reference to Babylon whose absence would be inexplicable.

9.7 The reference to "Heth" is not regarded as meaning the Hittites of the second millennium but to Khatte, a name given to the states within modern Syria by both Assyrians and Babylonians in the 9th to 6th centuries BC. Finally, that Sidon be listed as the firstborn of Canaan instead of Tyre (which is not even mentioned) points to a period when Tyre's fortunes were at a low ebb and Sidon was the leading city of Phoenicia. This recognition of Sidon dates authorship between Nebuchadnezzar's destruction of Tyre in 586BC following a 13 year siege and the Tennes rebellion in 385BC. This places authorship of Genesis 10 firmly in Babylon during the Exile.

9.8 In summary, the political and ethnic distribution of the table of nations seems to reflect a plausible last glimpse the Judeans, as an independent nation, had of the world prior to their Exile, slightly modified by their descendants returning from the Exile.

9.9 It is curious that the Biblical authors clearly believed that they were writing datable history and provide genealogical material to facilitate dating. Each author thinks it is possible to locate the events on the ground and packs his narrative with topographical details. Research concerning Exodus chapters 1 through 14 can now, according to Radford, speak of unanimity of evidence. Whoever supplied the geographical information in Exodus had no information earlier than the Saite period – 664BC to 332BC. The eastern Delta and Sinai described are those of the 26th Dynasty and early Persian overlords. The author knows of Goshen of the Qedarite Arabs and a legendary Ramesses II but he cannot locate the Egyptian court other than to Tanis – the largest and most famous city in his day. Tanis was the royal residence from 1070BC until 725BC. The author presses into service the reed lake adjacent to Tanis as the 'Reed Sea' of the miraculous escape and then has the Israelites traverse the same route as the canal of Necho II (610BC to 594BC) from Bubastis to the Bitter Lakes. The post-exilic compiler of Exodus had no genuinely ancient details and had to use contemporary knowledge – significantly he used several places where Judean mercenaries engaged by Egypt had resided in the 6th and 5th centuries.

9.10 Other details from the exodus tale also indicate garbled folk memories written many centuries after the original events. Egyptian captives were traditionally used in quarrying and heavy stone construction not brick-making. Brickmaking was a common task for captives of the Assyrian Empire. The reference to store cities also suggests a Mesopotamian setting rather than Egyptian.

THE TABLE OF NATIONS IN GENESIS CHAPTER 10

10

The origin of The Shepherd

10.1 It is interesting to consider the ancient origin of 'the shepherd' in human affairs. Jesus references to a shepherd appeared to some to echo the origin of King David, picked from obscurity as a young shepherd. But in turn the story of David and his son's instructions for the building of Solomon's Temple, themselves echo a far earlier tale – the story of Etana.

10.2 Etana features in the Sumerian King Lists as the 13th king after the Flood, the first 12 being gods or demi gods – ***exactly*** as in Egypt. The immediate predecessors of the fully human Pharaohs are described as demi gods, the offspring of gods and humans, whilst the very earliest kings were gods. In Sumeria, the change from gods to demi gods happened after the Flood which, in the Prequel, we determined occurred around 10765BC. According to the Sumerian records, after the Flood had subsided and the valleys had been drained, the original cities were rebuilt exactly where they had previously been, but Kish was designed as a new city – the first city of men. Kish was founded as the new capital of Sumer and after the first twelve rulers being demi gods, the gods decided it was time to appoint a man to rule – from Etana the Sumerian King List adds the title EN.SI (Lordly Shepherd) as a prefix to each king.

10.3 The Tale of Etana describes Enlil (our Biblical El Elyon) asking Inanna (his granddaughter) to identify a suitable candidate to be appointed as king-priest, build a new ziggurat temple and rule the city. Inanna recommended a humble shepherd, Etana, who was taken up '4 beru' (either 4 leagues or 8 hours) above the Earth to 'heaven' and to be vetted and approved by Enlil. Archeological evidence has identified Etana, dating him to around 3760BC.

10.4 The Tale of Etana describes Kish and its ziggurat as being planned, orientated and inaugurated by 'seven gods' – the gods had counterparts amongst the planets and it is believed that the orientation was based upon astronomical events and the investiture timed for a propitious alignment event.

10.5 All of the above is obviously mythological... except, consider the supposed origins of the Hebrew calendar (2028AD being counted as year 5788) the starting point for which is understood in the Jewish faith to be the date of creation, **NOT** the creation of the world, but the start of the counting of years from the creation of kingship and priesthood – *"when kingship was lowered from heaven"*. The Christian equivalent date of the Hebrew year 1 is 3760BC – a plausible date for the crowning of Etana !!

10.6 Nearly **3,000** years after the installation of Etana, we read of interesting parallels in the selection of another humble shepherd to assume kingship and responsibility to build a new temple. David, originally only a leader of the tribe of Judah, was called by the Lord "You shall shepherd my people Israel and shall be a *Nagid* over Israel" (2 Samuel 5:2). Biblical translators have variously translated *Nagid* as Captain or Prince – only Zecharia Sitchin identified the word as a Sumerian loan word, in Sumerian meaning "herdsman"!

10.7 A key objective for the Israelites c1000BC was to find a home for the Ark of the Covenant – somewhere permanent and also safe – rather than continue to cart it around on a wheeled carriage. Inlaid with gold inside and out, with gold plated cherubim, each time Yahweh communicated, he did so from between the two cherubim with outstretched wings. Very likely the Ark was a communications device and electrically powered – as attested to by the few who dared to touch it.

10.8 The major assignment for the newly appointed Shepherd King was to establish a new national capital (by capturing Jerusalem) and therein to build a permanent home for the Ark in the "House of the Lord". David was to establish a place for the "*Name* of the Lord", *Name* being the word our translators have used for *'shem'* – another Sumerian loanword meaning *'ship'* or *'vessel'*.

10.9 It is intriguing to note that around 500 years prior to David capturing Jerusalem, the idea of God deciding the location for 'parking' his *shem* was already mooted. In Deuteronomy 12:11, sometime after the Egyptians had expelled the Hyksos from Lower Egypt, El Elyon states that once the Israelites have crossed into the Promised Land "the Lord shall choose a place for his Name to dwell, where you shall bring all I command, your offerings, sacrifices, tithes, contributions and votive offerings." Is it a coincidence that when recently excavating along the Wailing Wall, that huge ashlars weighing hundreds of tons were discovered forming the base of the Temple Mount – approaching the dimensions of the trilithons at Baalbek and unmatched anywhere else in the Fertile Crescent. Such a solid base might be necessary for housing an aerial craft – Yahweh's *shem*.

10.10 In the battle for supremacy between Nannar (aka Sin) and Ra (aka Marduk) the foremost sons of Enlil and Enki respectively, Ra was becoming ascendant. Nannar's main base, the Ziggurat at Ur had been destroyed around 1960BC, followed by his High Priest, Terah taking his family (including his son Abraham) north to the secondary cultic seat of Nannar at Harran. Abraham was then dispatched to occupy what is now Lebanon and Israel which had been occupied by the offspring of Canaan and ruled by Egypt under the oversight of Ra. Maybe this expedition was also intended to capture Baalbek – a great base for one's *shem*.

10.11 The gigantic trilithons and ashlars used in building the Baalbek platform and the Temple Mount in Jerusalem point to a common (pre-Abrahamic) culture behind both constructions. This culture had the skills and resources to quarry and position huge blocks weighing many hundreds of tons – an achievement beyond even the Romans. As we researched in the Prequel to this series, one is forced to consider a culture dating back before the Flood or one benefiting from the knowledge of some survivors.

10.12 Instead of focusing on Lebanon, Abraham and his seed ended up infiltrating Egypt, and set up a dynasty to rule Lower Egypt. However, the Hyksos regime was unstable and efforts to conquer Upper Egypt failed and ended with the resurgent Egyptians expelling the Hyksos. The Hyksos fled back to lands under Nannar around Tayma in Northern Arabia (the true location of Sinai, meaning land allocated to Sin). After this it would appear that Nannar tried to use the Israelites to capture Jerusalem – what is now the Temple Mount being the second-best landing site in the entire region.

10.13 If the last four paragraphs sound a bit fanciful, then consider this. If, like me, you have concluded that Yahweh was not God, then who was he? Clearly, he was powerful and made a big impression – at least on the Israelites. Looking at the evidence, Abraham had strong ties to Nannar/Sin – being the son of the High Priest at the Ziggurat, who accompanied his family to the second base in Harran. When the Israelites flee Egypt, they build a golden calf, the symbol of Nannar/Sin. They hold special festivals every New Moon – the original Sumerian shabbatu – the Moon being the celestial symbol of Nannar/Sin. And they end up spending a generation based in the land of Sin around Tayma in northern Arabia.

10.14 The Tale of Etana and 1 Kings 3 similarly provide very detailed instructions on the temple construction, specifying precise east west orientation (identifying both as equinoctial temples) and both replete with numerous references to the number 7. We are told Solomon's Temple was completed in the eight month – but left undedicated for 11 months – so that the dedication could take place on the festival in the seventh month – the Israelites New Year festival. By this time (c1000BC), a thousand years after Abraham had left Sumeria and power had long since passed to Babylon and Assyria, the people of Mesopotamia still continued to celebrate the spring equinox as the New Year. However, the Israelites were commanded to celebrate the New Year in the seventh month – the autumnal equinox – but the Bible does not explain why. A clue might lie in the Hebrew name for the seventh month, unlike for most months of the year, the Hebrews do not use the Akkadian name 'Tishrei' but name the seventh month 'Etanim' – surely a pointer to Etana? A German theologian of the 19th century who studied rabbinical writings cited similarities between Mesopotamian "portrait of the heavens" and rabbinical references to "the seven heavenly bodies that indicate time – Sun, Mercury, Venus, Moon, Mars, Jupiter and Saturn".

10.15 The design of the temple atop the ziggurat of Kish, later Sumerian temples and Solomon's temple all incorporate the same tripartite layout – a rectangular anteroom, an elongated ritual hall and a square 'holy of holies'. The entrance to each were flanked by two pillars. Solomon's temple calls the anteroom 'Ulam', its ritual hall 'Hekhal' and the inner sanctum 'Dvir' – the first two names have been identified as stemming from Sumerian: 'ulammu' and 'E-gal'.

10.16 The parallels between Etana and David increase when, as reviewed earlier in this booklet, it appears that Saul was not a king but a military leader – so Israelite kingship was lowered to David as their first king.

10.17 David was told (through the prophet Nathan) the time was not right for him to build the Temple, possibly the delay was to enable construction ready for dedication on a timely basis when the planets were suitably aligned?

10.18 The implication of both the construction with a precise east west alignment and the delay in dedication until the day of the autumn equinox is that Solomon's Temple was designed to provide a precise annual calendar – the date of each equinox measures precisely the start (but not the precise duration) of semi-annual periods. Equinoctial temples were perfect for marking off each half year – but not for celestial time measurement which would be affected by the waxing and waning of the Earth's tilt and by precession – such astronomical detail as addressed at Göbekli Tepe (near Harran) and at Stonehenge.

10.19 The very earliest reference to a Shepherd King goes back much further. Dumuzid the **Shepherd** King, was the fourth king of Sumer *prior* to the Flood(*) (c10765BC) when Sumerian kingship was based in Bad-tibira. Dumuzid was still being worshipped in Solomon's Temple (as Tammuz) according to Ezekiel 8:14-15 writing c600BC – that's a truly staggering longevity for anyone's reputation!! P.S. Not to be confused with Dumuzid, the *fisherman king*, when the kingship of Sumer was based in Uruk c 2600BC.

* There is now very strong evidence of what event caused the catastrophic rise in sea levels as well as precisely where and when it occurred. This topic is covered in detail in the Prequel of this series.

10.20 And, how did the Israelites maintain a counting of the years throughout the sojourn in Canaan, the Hyksos period and later infiltration into the Judean Highlands before the monarchy? How did they maintain records starting with Abraham using Sumerian cuneiform c2000BC, switching at some point to hieroglyphics whilst in Egypt and adopting the Phoenician alphabet to develop written Hebrew only after 1000BC? How did they maintain accurate records throughout the second millennium? Perhaps the link is in Harran.

10.21   Harran is the city Abraham's family migrated to from Ur. Intriguingly, Harran is only 56 kms south of Göbekli Tepe, where dozens of monoliths with incredibly detailed carvings are being excavated that indicate a vast astronomical observatory existed as early as 10000BC. Harran itself was known for its very ancient astrologer priesthood, the Sabians, who are recorded as regular visitors to key temples in both Egypt and along the Tigris and Euphrates and were renown throughout the Middle East. The Sabians not only maintained their existence from a period well before Abraham's arrival but endured the rise and fall of countless states and empires around them – right through to AD1032.

10.22   The reputation and status of the Sabians in 530BC is reflected by Isaiah 45:14. After Yahweh is reported by Isaiah as appointing the Persian Emperor Cyrus as Messiah, Yahweh singles out three treasures he will deliver to Cyrus: (i) the products of Egypt; (ii) merchandise of Cush (Sudan & Ethiopia) and (iii) the Sabeans, men of stature. As all three will be delivered in chains it implies the conquest of the entire Egyptian empire – but note: the astrologer priests of the observatory in Harran are singled out for special mention in the same verse – as men of stature.

10.23   Surviving until the advent of Islam, the Sabians were defined by Mohammed as one of the Peoples of the Book – to be offered protection along with Jews and Christians. Sadly, the Sabians came to an unfortunate end when massacred by an impoverished and long unpaid Muslim militia in AD1032.

THE ORIGIN OF THE SHEPHERD

11

The Tower of Babel

11.1 According to our tradition, the destruction of the Tower of Babel (situated on the Plain of Shinar – i.e. in Sumer) by the Most High (El Elyon in Hebrew, aka Enlil in Sumerian) was supposedly accompanied by the deity acting to confuse humanity by henceforth making us speak many languages. However, the historical facts deny the popular myth – the whole of the civilized world continued to use the same language for the next ***two millennia*** – Akkadian.

11.2 Paul Seely writing in the Westminster Theological Journal 63 (2001) pps15-38 gives a studious explanation of the possible date range for the Tower of Babel – placing it between 3500BC and 2400BC. He suggests that the reference to language change may have reflected the change from use of Sumerian to Akkadian as the common language of daily life. The Akkadians, a Semitic people, entered the area of the Sumerian civilization from around 3000BC and became dominant from 2400BC, although later, Sumerian rule was reestablished. Sumerian rule endured until their final demise in 1960BC – attributed to a combination of rising seawaters inundating farmlands around the top of the Gulf and invading Elamites from what later became Persia. The Sumerians and Akkadians seem to have co-existed for many centuries, the Sumerian language became restricted to use for religion, history and science whilst Akkadian was used as the everyday language.

11.3 Cuneiform Akkadian remained the lingua franca of the whole Fertile Crescent area and was also used by the Egyptian government and traders. Akkadian declined as the Assyrians adopted a new cursive script, Aramaic, which progressively replaced Akkadian from around 800BC, although Akkadian continued in use with tablets found dated as late as 100AD.

THE TOWER OF BABEL

12

Abraham's interactions with Hittites, Philistines & Arameans

12.1 Whilst analysis (see chapter 9 herein) of the Table of Nations set out in Genesis 10 requires a very detailed familiarity with ancient history, knowledge generally beyond that of most of us, some of the errors in the story of Abraham and Isaac should raise many eyebrows.

12.2 The composition of the Table of Nations points to the author having detailed knowledge of the 8th and 7th centuries BC. The nations referred to in Genesis 10 either emerged only in this period or disappeared from history during this period. However, the references to be examined here in the story of Abraham indicate uncertainty of both when and where the Hittites, Philistines and Arameans settled – knowledge which indicates authorship no earlier than the 10th century BC – but the biblical story purports frequent direct quotes of individuals (and God) dating at least a millennium further back in time. What credibility can be given to direct quotations when evidence indicates they were not written down for at least 1000 years after the purported events?

12.3 Three elements of Abraham's story stand out: his purchase of land from a group of Hittites; the interactions with the Philistines, primarily over wives and grazing rights; and, the racial implications of Abraham's choice of wife for his son Isaac and Isaac's similar instructions to Jacob.

Abraham's purchase of land from Hittites

12.4 Genesis 23 tells of Sarah's death and of her husband Abraham's purchase of a plot at Hebron for her burial. It states that the location, known today as the Cave of the Patriarch, lies at Kiriath Arba, in Hebron.

12.5 As we saw in section 3.1, at this time Canaan was under the control of the Egyptians: "Menuhotep II reuniting Upper and Lower Egypt in 2050BC and campaigning as far as Lebanon, some years prior to Abraham's visit. During the next three Dynasties, known as the Middle Kingdom, there are records of campaigns to Ugarit, Qatna and Shechem whilst sovereignty was claimed over the coast as far north as Lebanon."

12.6 Egyptian occupation may explain why, after responding to El Elyon's request to move to Canaan, Abraham having got there and finding all of Canaan under Egyptian control – Abraham then decided to go to see the Pharaoh.

12.7 Chapter 23 of Genesis, telling of Sarah's death, makes no mention of Egyptians in Hebron but instead makes numerous references to groups of Hittites gathering outside the city, owning the plot of land, etc. However, Hebron lies south of Jerusalem, in the southern part of the Judean Highlands – in the same latitude as Gaza. (Please refer to the map.) These references to Hittites throughout Genesis 23 are clearly erroneous.

12.8 Firstly, at the time Sarah died, most likely between 1980BC and 1960BC, the Hittites had barely begun to transit from the Pontic Steppe (now Ukraine) through the Caucasus into northern Turkey. The Hittites assimilated the pre-existing Hatti tribe and developed as the Old Assyrian empire, which extended into Anatolia but collapsed between 1800BC and 1750BC. Hittite expansion south of Turkey only occurred after 1600BC. Under Suppiluliuma (1350BC to 1322BC) the Hittite Empire reached its greatest extent, extending as far south as Kadesh and later the historical Egyptian Hittite battle occurred at Kadesh in 1274BC. The Hittites, even at the height of their power never came near the Sea of Galilee – let alone as far south as Gaza – nor would they have ventured into the barren and then depopulated heart of the Judean Highlands where Hebron developed.

12.9 Secondly, there is no record of Hittites ever settling anywhere near Hebron, and any merchants would have used sea borne routes or at least the Via Maris – along the coast. Thirdly, there were no cities or even small villages in these Highlands until the 13th Century BC. Prior to that there were only a few tent dwelling transhumants who got regularly clobbered by the Egyptians whenever they caused trouble – usually rounding them up for use as slaves, to such an extent that these highlands were regarded as unpopulated until bands of Apiru started appearing in the 15th Century BC. In such circumstances, one must wonder about whether there is any factual basis for burial plot purchase story of Genesis chapter 23 – wandering transhumants in the wild unpopulated highlands would not think in terms of land titles anyway – the textual reference to 400 shekels of silver for the plot speaks to a much later period, maybe 800 years later, when a settlement had arisen in that location.

12.10   Given that Menuhotep II had recently established Egyptian sovereignty as far north as Ugarit and Qatna (far to the north of Hebron – see map), it is highly unlikely Abraham would have purchased land from a Hittite, more likely a Canaanite or even an occupying Egyptian. The reference to a Hittite in Genesis again betrays the books much later authorship – memories of a powerful trading empire generally extending southwards but only as far as northern Syria. There is no record of Hittites ever controlling anywhere as far south as Shechem (near present day Nablus halfway between the Sea of Galilee and Jerusalem) which is also sometimes referred to as a Patriarchal burying place, and certainly never as far as Hebron mentioned in Genesis 23. It is theoretically possible that a Hittite individual had purchased land in Hebron or Shechem, but this would have only occurred during the peaceful coexistence between of the Hittite and Egyptian empires – many centuries after Abraham. The already waning Hittite empire was destroyed by the invading Sea Peoples in 1178BC. But, certainly most of the period from 1550BC to 1177BC, Shechem was under Egyptian administration and even the site of an Egyptian garrison for many years.

12.11   Abraham clearly did not meet a village full of Hittites in Hebron in the 20th century BC, neither did his grandson Esau based in Beersheba, even further south, meet and marry two Hittite girls in the 19th century BC (Genesis 26:34). The furthest south that the Hittites expanded was to Kadesh, close to the northern border of Lebanon, in the 14th Century BC.

Abraham and Isaac's interaction with the Philistines

12.12   Genesis 20 tells of Abraham's interaction with Abimelek, described as the king of the Philistines, whilst Abraham was staying near modern

Gaza. The chapter tells of the Abraham again describing Sarah as his sister (culturally, a more senior title than merely a wife) with the baffling intervention of 'God' to advise the Philistine king that he was 'interfering' with a married woman – whom the bible claims is now around 100 years old! El Elyon's extraordinary intervention leaves the king fearing his entire nation will be destroyed – so he gives Abraham many sheep, goats, female slaves and 1000 shekels of silver. Nothing about this event sounds at all credible!

12.13 Genesis 26 is fundamentally a repeat of chapter 20. We are told Abraham's son, Isaac, repeats the same events with the same Abimelek with similar results. Admittedly, Isaac's wife is not his sister and is also much younger than Sarah but it is odd that the story is essentially a repeat. Some suggest that Abimelek is a Hebrew title given to Philistine kings – but its meaning is 'father of the king' – surely a person who would normally have already been dead? At the close of chapter 26, we are told that Esau, Isaac's brother, marries two Hittite girls – something that is extremely unlikely if not impossible at such an early date.

12.14 The two stories about the early Israelites interactions with the Philistines do occur in the right geographical area – the Gerar valley (which extends inland towards Beersheba) was an area that the Philistines originally settled – at the direction of the Egyptian forces. But the Philistines did not arrive in that area, from Greece, until 1177BC. The interactions with the Philistines are recorded in Genesis as occurring around 700 years earlier!

Isaac and Jacob's interactions with the Arameans

12.15 The fact that Abraham originally lived in Ur is recorded in Genesis – but the identity of the empire into which Abraham was born and whose male ancestors held high office was unknown to the authors of Genesis. Abraham is laughably described as coming from "Ur of the Chaldeans" (Genesis 11:31 and 15:7). Assyrian and Neo Babylonian records refer to the Chaldeans as a tribe which emerged in the 9th century BC from the Arabian plain west of Ur – which had by then lain in ruins for 1,000 years. These Chaldeans gradually migrated north, becoming the initial ruling family of the Second or Neo Babylonian Empire. Nebuchadnezzar was a Chaldean.

12.16 Genesis records Abraham's father migrating the family to Harran, the northern capital of the Sumerian Empire. Later in Genesis, Abraham decides that his heir, Isaac, should marry from amongst his blood relations to preserve the purity of the bloodline and avoid local Canaanite girls who might worship 'pagan' gods. Surprisingly, when a girl is selected, Rebekah, and her brother Laban, are described as Aramean (Genesis 25:20). Similarly, when Isaac's chosen heir Jacob comes round to marrying, he is also packed off back to Harran to find a daughter from the family clan – and again the prospective girls are described as Aramean (Genesis 28:5).

12.17 The Arameans were a people basically occupying modern Syria, they were centred around Damascus from c1300BC to 700BC – but again the biblical dates are hopelessly wrong – Isaac would have married around 1900BC. Fundamentally, one must also question what the difference was under Judaism between Isaac marrying an Aramean verses a Canaanite? Historical evidence indicates that Abraham's family, the Canaanites and the Arameans did in fact all worship the same gods – El Elyon (Enlil), his sons Sin (Nannar) and Ishkur (Adad).

12.18 The references in Genesis to Arameans tell us two things. Firstly, the author of these chapters is presumably a different person to that wrote of the journey from Ur, as the family have been transformed from Chaldeans to Arameans. Secondly, the author knows of the historical location of the Arameans and assumes that because they occupied the area roughly the northern half of Syria and around Harran – Abraham's family must have been Aramean.

12.19 Unfortunately for Biblical Inerrants, neither Isaac nor Jacob could have married Aramean girls as these people only emerged six centuries later – in the 13th Century BC and were finally absorbed into the Assyrian empire in the 7th Century BC. The biblical writers in Babylon in the 6th Century BC did at least know of the Arameans and also the geographical area they had earlier inhabited.

12.20 The Arameans had emerged as a distinct culture as the Middle Assyrian Empire (1365BC to 1050BC) declined and the upheaval and mass migrations triggered by the Sea Peoples destruction of various Bronze Age cultures in the 12th Century BC left a vacuum in the northern Levant. The Arameans expanded across modern Syria and western Iraq, creating a number of small kingdoms. However, the growth of the Neo Assyrian empire from 911BC was largely at the expense of the Aramean kingdoms. With the fall of Damascus in 732BC and their last kingdom, the Assyrian policy of mass deportation of conquered peoples effectively removed the Arameans from history. However, one aspect of their culture endured far longer – their language, Aramaic, spread across the new Assyrian and later Neo Babylonian empires. Aramaic replaced Akkadian as the lingua franca and endured as a regional language until displaced by Arabic 14 centuries later.

How the Israelites became Semitic

12.21   Everyone is familiar with the label 'anti-Semitism', a term meaning hostility to, prejudice or discrimination against Jews. This term had always puzzled me as the 'Father of the Nation', Abraham was not a Semite – but Sumerian. The Semitic peoples of biblical times comprise the other inhabitants of Mesopotamia and Arabia – the Arabs, Arameans, Amorites, Akkadians, Canaanites and Phoenicians but not the Sumerians, Hittites or Egyptians.

12.22   The common understanding of the term Semite is as a definition of an ethnic and language grouping. Many theological writers use a biblical definition of Semite as being a descendant of Seth, one of Noah's three sons. However, the world view of the authors of Genesis, as tabulated in Genesis 10, embraced only about 10% of Earth's landmass – whilst showing total ignorance of arguably the world's greatest empire that had existed in their backyard – the Sumerians. Genesis also seems to assume that the Hittites, who had disappeared almost 6 centuries before most of Genesis was written, were Semites – when even Genesis allocates them to Japheth. Today we understand the Hittites were a branch of the migrating Aryan peoples and not Semitic.

12.23   The information in Genesis contradicts itself and history. According to Genesis, Abraham was likely pure Sumerian but his wife's mother was Egyptian so Sarah was 50/50. Therefore, Abraham's son's ethnicity (daughters are never mentioned) was: Isaac being 75% Sumerian and 25% Egyptian (assuming he was not from a union between Sarah and Senusret); Ishmael being 50/50 Sumerian and Egyptian. Genesis is silent concerning the ethnicity of Abrahams' later wife Keturah. However, both Midrash (ancient rabbinic interpretation) and Aggadah (Jewish Babylonian Talmud) indicate that Keturah was in fact Hagar. In Genesis 25:6 English translations state "wife and concubines" but in Hebrew the word used for 'concubine' is singular – suggestive of 25:6 referring specifically to Hagar – being his wife and former concubine. Moreover, these Midrash and Talmud references date from periods contemporary with the time Genesis was mostly written in its current form and therefore may be just as reliable as the biblical text.

12.24 Therefore according to Genesis:

(i) the peoples of Arabia are descendants of Ishmael – with no Semitic bloodline;

(ii) the descendants of Abraham and Keturah were all sent off eastwards over the River Jordan also populating parts of modern Jordan. If Keturah was in fact Hagar, all her descendants would also be 50/50 Sumerian and Egyptian – which would again mean no Semitic bloodline;

(iii) According to Genesis, Isaac (being 75% Sumerian and 25% Egyptian) married an Aramean but if she was a descendant of Abraham's brothers' she was more likely pure Sumerian. Isaac had two sons, Jacob and Esau – who were therefore 87% Sumerian and 13% Egyptian.

(iv) Esau married two Hittites and went off to found Edom, the heart of today's Jordan. Those descended from Esau would have started as 50% Hittite, 44% Sumerian and 6% Egyptian – again no Semitic bloodline. According to Genesis 28:9, Esau then married Mahalath, described as a daughter of Ishmael – supposedly to spite his father Isaac who only wanted his sons to marry from the family. (Yes, I know that makes no sense!) However, if the author of chapter 28 had read the earlier chapters he would have realized that daughters of Ishmael would be a Sumerian/Egyptian mix – again no Semitic bloodline.

(v) That only leaves Jacob whose descendants could become Semitic – but again although he started by marrying two Arameans, these were more likely to be Sumerian – so the offspring of Leah and Rachel would have been 94% Sumerian and 6% Egyptian – no Semitic bloodline

12.25 My conclusion on all this is that there was no Semitic blood amongst the early Patriarchs at all. However, the one author of Genesis writing in from Babylon in the 6th century BC, mistook Abraham as Chaldean (and Semitic) whilst another author, presumably unaware of the parts referring to "Ur of the Chaldeans", assumed Abraham and his brothers must have been Aramean. This assumption presumably on the basis that, after Abraham left Harran, the rest of the family stayed in land remembered as Aramean. Why do we know both these writers of different portions of Genesis wrote in Babylon – because the Arameans only emerged in the 12 century BC and the Chaldeans in the 9th century BC. If Isaac and Jacob had indeed married Arameans then they would have progressively changed the bloodline into majority Semite.

12.26 The modern label of anti-Semitic to describe discrimination against Jews therefore seems nonsensical – particularly when applied to criticism by Palestinians and Arabs in general. If derived from the ancient biblical groupings of the descendants of Ham verses the descendants of Shem, then one might claim the Palestinians and Lebanese today are descendants of Ham – but all of Abraham's sons had mixed blood as his wives were wholly or partly Egyptian and descended from Ham. This also makes Abraham's efforts to find wives who were not Canaanite a bit moot. According to Genesis, all the Arabian tribes were also descended from Abraham – and therefore 50% Hamite. Historical evidence indicates that Abraham's descendants who, when filtering into Egypt, were labelled as the Hyksos were by them definitely Western Semitic in language and culture – and indistinguishable from the Canaanites.

A defence of "Ur of the Chaldeans" by a Jewish theologian

12.27 Given the challenge of defending biblical references to Abraham, as coming from 'Ur of the Chaldeans', one interesting theory has been formulated by a Judaic source – www.thetorah.com . An article tagged as 'ur-kasdim-where-is-abrahams-birthplace' tries to solve the problem by claiming the Chaldeans lived in a very different area – land north of Harran, further into modern Turkey, in a city which happened to also have 'Ur' in its name. The claimed solution is supported by poorly thought through arguments but is worth explaining as it illustrates the pitfalls of a non-holistic approach. The article suggests that references to Abraham's family having originating in Ur, the capital of the Sumerian empire, resulted from Charles Woolley. Woolley was the archaeologist who excavated the ruins of Ur during 1922 to 1934, and who made headlines by announcing that the rich and sophisticated urban area that he had uncovered had a biblical connection as the birthplace of Abraham.

12.28 The article claims that, based on references in Joshua 24:2-3 of a place 'beyond the river', that Abraham's family had lived in 'Ur Kasdim' a place 44km north of Harran first referenced in cuneiform tablets recovered from Ugarit dating to the 14th Century BC as Ura and described then as a Hittite town. Today, the town is known as Urfa. The article overcomes the inconvenience of Assyrian and Babylonian records identifying the Chaldeans as coming from the northern Arabian plains by quoting a Greek historian, Xenophon (431BC to 354BC) who places the Chaldeans as a people occupying lands between western Turkey and Armenia, who in their past had occupied northern Syria. Xenophon linked the Chaldeans to the Carduchi, precursors of the Kurds. Whilst Xenophon lived during the rise of the Macedonian Greeks, he died 20 years before Alexander the Great crossed the Hellespont – so it is unclear how accurate his knowledge of the ancient Chaldeans might have been. Almost certainly, Xenophon would have known of the Chaldeans as the former ruling family of Babylon defeated by the Persians.

12.29 The article further claims the four ancestors of Abraham named in Genesis can be linked to the names of four cities in the area north of Harran – but we have recovered original cuneiform tablets from Ur that also mention Abraham's ancestors as dynastic governors of the province of Ur. The article also notes the existence of an ancient Christian community in the area known as the Chaldean Christians. But their use of this label seems to be derived from the original Christian community of Baghdad, who when adopting Latin rites were prohibited from using their previous title of Nestorian Christians (regarded by Rome as heretics) and hence adopted an ancient ethnicity associated with Babylon (now situated in a suburb of Baghdad).

Did Moses originate in the Northern Kingdom, not Judah?

12.30 As a generalization, our assessment of the Old Testament texts needs to treat almost each book independently. The books describing the pre-Monarchical period rest entirely upon ancient oral traditions, with a substantial part appearing linguistically to have been drawn together during the exile. It is noteworthy that despite the centricity of Moses to the Hebrew religion, he barely gets a mention prior to the time of Josiah, king of Judah (640 to 609BC) during whose reign 'a book of the law was found in the Temple'. 2 Kings 22:8 says, "The high priest Hilkiah said to Shaphan the secretary, 'I have found the book of the law in the house of the Lord.'" This is referenced to the 18th year of his reign – so 622BC.

12.31 There has been long debate over exactly what was found – generally now believed to be text that later became the core of Deuteronomy although some believe it was the complete book or even the complete Torah – which for a host of reasons is highly unlikely. How could Judah have simply forgotten about Moses? It seems unimaginable, but the very few references to Moses after Samuel only occur after the 'discovery' of 622BC. Differences between festivals and laws comparing Leviticus and Deuteronomy have led some to suggest Deuteronomy was an updated version suitable for the period of Josiah's religious reforms.

12.32 The prophet Isaiah, active in Jerusalem about a century before Josiah, makes no mention of the Exodus, covenants with God, or disobedience to God's laws. However, in stark contrast, Isaiah's contemporary Hosea, active in the northern kingdom of Israel, makes frequent reference to the Exodus, the wilderness wanderings, a covenant, the danger of foreign gods and the need to worship Yahweh alone. This puzzle has led scholars to see the traditions behind Deuteronomy as Samaritan in origin. In the late 8th century both Judah and Israel were vassals of Assyria. Israel rebelled, and was destroyed c.722BC. Refugees fleeing to Judah brought with them a number of traditions new to Judah. Fundamental was the idea that Yahweh, already worshiped in Judah, was not merely the most important of the gods, but the only god who should be served. This view influenced the elite of Judah, who seized the discovery of the Deuteronomic text as requiring sweeping religious reform.

12.33 The discovery in 622BC spurred an independence movement exploiting the rapid decline of Assyrian power. This movement expressed itself as a state theology loyal to Yahweh as the sole god of Israel. Josiah launched a major reform of worship based on an early version of Deuteronomy 5–26, which takes the form of a covenant (i.e. treaty) between Judah and Yahweh to replace that between Judah and Assyria.

12.34 The next stage took place during the Babylonian captivity. The destruction of the Kingdom of Judah by Babylon in 586BC and the end of kingship was the occasion of much reflection and theological speculation among the elite of Judah, now in exile. They explained the disaster as Yahweh's punishment of their failure to follow the law, and created a history of Israel (the books of Torah, Joshua through Kings) to illustrate this.

12.35 If Judah was unaware of Moses, perhaps the written Pentateuch may have originated in the northern kingdom during its separate existence between 930BC and 722BC. Indeed, writing in this period, the author may have assumed memories of a powerful former empire lying to their north had indeed occupied Samaria – in which Shechem is centrally located. Careful comparison of the extant Torah with the Samaritan bible (comprising only their version of the five books of the Torah) may reveal what the Torah contained prior to the Exile and therefore the extent of redaction carried during and after the Exile. Analysts have identified over 6,000 textual variations between the two versions.

12.36 Finally, given the evidence of extensive redaction in most Old Testament books and the fact that no texts were canonized (their text locked) until after the return from the Exile, the general absence of references to Moses from Joshua to Hosea (a period from say 1500BC as a proxy for the supposed Exodus, until Hosea in say 700BC) is all the more surprising.

12.37 It is also very noteworthy that Psalm 78, attributed to David, seems to provide an executive summary of the Exodus but is also silent regarding Moses, attributing all to Yahweh. Taken together, it would seem that (i) Psalm 78 was a major contributor to the legend of Moses and the Exodus, and (ii) that this legend was created in the Northern Kingdom during the period of angst as the threat from Assyria was growing. Again, the Samaritan bible should be quite illuminating as regards the earliest version of the legend.

13

The story of Joseph in Egypt & the cities of Pithom and Ramesses

13.1　The story of Joseph marks an abrupt change in style from the preceding disjointed sections dealing with Abraham, Isaac and Jacob. Genesis 37 to 46 stands out as a composition, a beautifully turned and symmetrical plot displaying unity and integrity indicating a single author. Literary assessment concludes these 9 chapters contain a composition rather than a record and the tale is viewed by many academics as a novella. Whilst there are a few acknowledgements to divine providence, Yahweh and his angels are absent from this story.

13.2　The 'poor fit' of the Joseph story extends to factual details – in Genesis 45:11 the movement of Jacob and his family was a temporary measure to seek relief from famine but elsewhere the clear purpose was to settle in Egypt where all the sons of Jacob live out their lives. In part, this contradicts the traditions of the individual tribes in later times in which their ancestors live, marry raise families and die in Canaan: in Genesis 46:12 Perez (Judah's son borne by his daughter-in-law) and Perez son, Hezron, travel to Egypt with Judah but Hezron's grandson, Jair, controlled 23 towns in Gilead (1 Chronicles 2:21-22); Simeon marries a Canaanite; Ephraim dies in Palestine; Manasseh married an Aramean (1 Chronicles 7:14) – although the first historical attestation of Arameans as a people appears much later (maybe 700 years later) than the supposed time of Joseph, namely in the inscriptions of Tiglath Pileser I, c1100BC.

13.3　Four Egyptian names appear in the Joseph story – Saphnathpane'ah, Asenath, Potiphar and Potipherah (itself a variant of Potiphar). The use of these names indicates authorship during the Kushite-Saite period – 760BC to 525BC. Saphnathpane'ah is a type of name which appeared in the 21st dynasty (1069BC to 945BC) and became very common during the 9th to 7th centuries. Asenath was common in Greco-Roman times but known throughout the first millennium whilst Potiphar has been found as far back as the 21st dynasty but was far more common during the Kushite and Saite dynasties.

13.4 Some titles used in the Joseph story also indicate late authorship. The term "overseer" in Genesis 41:34, the officials whom Joseph advises pharaoh to appoint, is an Aramaic title common in the Egyptian administration during the Persian period (525BC to 410BC). The word 'saris' of Genesis 37:36 rendered as either 'officer' or 'eunuch' is recognized as 'sa resi' a common Akkadian title of the Assyrian administration – it was only used in Egypt during the Persian period, applied to high ranking governors.

13.5 Joseph's accusation that his brothers are "spies" come "to see the weakness of the land" (Gen. 42:9) whilst obviously trumped up, employs a word used of intelligence agents sent out ahead of an invasion. Since the brothers have already said they came from Canaan (42:7) such an accusation makes no sense – there was no hostile power in Canaan during the second millennium until 1177BC when the Sea People invaded from the north. Apart from the Hyksos period, Canaan was under, more or less, continuous Egyptian tutelage throughout the second millennium. However, it makes absolute sense during the Kushite-Saite period with threats from Assyria, Babylon and lastly Persia. This again indicates that the author was writing at least 1000 years after the purported events.

13.6 And a final clincher – Genesis 47:11 referring to the land at Goshen allocated by Pharaoh to Jacob's family of shepherds upon their arrival in Egypt, is described as being "in the district of Ramesses". However, the earliest Ramesses only ruled 1294BC to 1292BC but the reputation of his son, Ramesses II, probably the most illustrious pharaoh of all, has meant the name has always endured – certainly such a description would have been understood in the Kushite and Saite periods. However, Jacob, Abraham's grandson would have arrived in Egypt many centuries earlier. Original records from Ur referring to Abraham's father and grandfather indicate Abraham was likely born in the last quarter of the 20th century BC. Even using the extraordinary ages given in Genesis, whereby Abraham fathered Isaac when he was 100; Isaac fathered Jacob when he was 60 and Jacob arrived in Egypt when he was 130 years old – the latest date for the discussion granting land in the district of Ramesses could only have occurred around 1750BC.

13.7 According to Exodus 1:11, the cities of Pithom and Ramesses were built as store cities by the Israelites in bondage. This has caused many biblical historians to place the Exodus in the reign of Ramesses II – a thankless task as he was the longest reigning and most powerful pharaoh of all, controlling the Egyptian empire at its largest extent. The location of Pithom has also been discovered, with foundations clearly dating to Necho II, constructed between 609BC and 606BC midway along the canal he built along the Wadi Tumilat, the fortified trading port was named The House of Atum, "pr-itm" which became known in Hebrew as Pithom. At the time, Judah was a vassal of Egypt and Judean mercenaries were deployed to a number of frontier forts, including Pithom. One can see how an Exilic author could hear of Israelites 'working' in Pithom and weave it into the story.

13.8 Thus one has to conclude from the use of place names, official titles and references to ethnicities that the story of Joseph in Egypt was definitely embroidered during the Exile in Babylon more than 1000 years after the events were purported to have taken place.

14

The Book of Joshua

14.1 Analysis of the language and various terms used in the text indicates that Joshua was written in Babylon sometime between 580BC and 540BC. The intention of the author was to try to give spiritual strength to the Jews taken there in captivity after seeing their Temple in Jerusalem destroyed. The Jews feared their defeat and the destruction of Jerusalem had resulted in the death of their god Yahweh. Given various pieces of evidence now available – such a possibility must be considered. As we have explored in Part One and this booklet, Yahweh displayed many very human attributes and human weaknesses – and not much righteousness – and that's just what the Israelites recorded in their scripture!

14.2 In those days, what we now call pagan gods were known to have long lives but were not seen as immortal – they aged and could be killed in battle. If Yahweh had been in Jerusalem, it is possible that he had been killed and his priests knew as much. Fearing the demise of their cult and thereby their livelihood, the Jewish priests would naturally develop a different explanation for Yahweh's disappearance. The fallback scenario was that their god was loving, faithful and mighty – it was only because the Jews had sinned that their god had deserted them. They only needed to repent and pray long enough and Yahweh would return and help them. When Babylon was captured by the Persian Emperor, Cyrus, it is recorded that Marduk marched at the head of the Persian army. Isaiah decided that this Marduk was either Yahweh himself returning or someone acting at Yahweh's behest and wrote that Cyrus had been appointed a Messiah by Yahweh (Isaiah 45:1).

14.3   However, whilst the conventional understanding is that Cyrus freed the Jews from captivity and they returned to eventually rebuild the Temple and continue life in the Promised Land the facts are quite different. Persian census data indicate that only about 4% of the Jews in Babylon returned to Jerusalem. Between roughly 600BC and 300BC, Babylon was the largest city in the world and remained the centre of Jewish life for a very long time. The Babylonian Talmud became the highest source of rabbinical rulings and the Babylon community were relied upon to determine the dates of the festivals and holy days for another 1000 years after the Exile ended. Babylon continued under Sassanid Persian rule until the conquest by Muslim armies around AD650 after which the city progressively declined until abandoned cAD1000.

Concept of the Promised Land

14.4   Joshua refers to "Hatti-Land" as being part of the "Promised Land" – by "Hatti Land" they meant the Hittites (who at their strongest c1400BC to c1200BC) had occupied all of modern Turkey. Joshua not only contradicts Genesis definition of the Promised Land but later "Hatti-Land" is completely forgotten in Joshua's conquests.

14.5   The origin of the idea of a Promised Land was referred to above in chapter 8 but is reviewed here in the context of the Book of Joshua. Genesis includes a half-baked story that because Ham saw his father, Noah's, genitals, one of Ham's sons, Canaan and his issue would be cursed. No attempt is made to explain this weird curse. The original explanation of the "Promised Land" is hidden from modern bibles – it is set out in Chapter 10 of the Book of Jubilees. There it explains that, after the flood, the gods divided the lands between the sons of Noah – Ham, Shem and Japheth. Ham was awarded Africa; Shem was awarded Mesopotamia and the Levant (modern Saudi, Iraq, Syria, Jordan, Lebanon and Israel); whilst Japheth was awarded modern Turkey, Iran and the Indian sub-continent. As Ham journeyed south from Mount Ararat in Turkey, through Syria, Lebanon and Israel towards Egypt, one of his sons, Canaan, saw the cedars of Lebanon and the northern plains of Israel and coveted them. Canaan decided to cut loose from the convoy and settle in what became known as Canaan. Canaan's father and brothers warned Canaan that the land he was settling in was Promised Land – promised to the descendants of Shem – and that much trouble would follow.

14.6 The earliest civilisation in the lands awarded to Shem was the Sumerian – dating from at least 4000BC. And, around 1960BC, the god whom Abraham's grandfather was high priest to (Nannar, foremost son of Enlil – aka El Elyon) approached Abraham and told him to go forth from Harran (the northern capital of the Sumerian empire) to take back and occupy the Promised Land, i.e. land promised by the gods to the descendants of Shem but which had been occupied by Canaan.

When was Joshua's attack on Canaan?

14.7 Biblical records give no real clues as to when the occupation of the Promised Land took place. Biblical academics date the exodus anywhere from 1550BC to 1200BC. However, the historical facts show that throughout this period, the whole of modern Israel, Jordan, Lebanon and most of Syria were firmly part of the Egyptian empire. Incredibly, Joshua never mentions the Egyptians, his Israelites never come into contact with the Egyptian army or their numerous garrisons! The Egyptians controlled the area through two main roads – known today as the Kings Highway (from Aqaba north to Damascus, running east of the River Jordan) and the Via Maris (along the Mediterranean coast).

14.8 Joshua is hopelessly confused – he writes of battles against the Hittites and of confronting the Pentapolis (the five original cities of the Philistines – in modern Gaza). The facts are that a mass armed migration (by forces which are nowadays referred to as the Sea Peoples) emanated from what is now Greece, armed with lethal new iron weapons, passing through modern Turkey, destroying the Hittite kingdom in 1179BC. It is possible that the trigger was not just a desire for conquest but evidence indicates a long period of drought which had caused widespread famine. In the decades prior to 1179BC, the Hittites had become very dependent upon grain supplies from Egypt. Perhaps the Sea Peoples found that the Hittites were mainly reliant on imports and decided to continue towards the source. The Sea Peoples swept south all along the coast of modern Israel destroying all opposing forces. Their conquest was abruptly stopped by the Egyptians forces, near Gaza in 1177BC. The Pharaoh made peace, absorbing them into his realm and magnanimously built five cities for the remaining Sea People to live in – which became known as the Pentapolis – with the Pharaoh's cartouche on their city gates.

14.9 So, it is impossible for Joshua to confront both Hittites who disappeared

PART TWO: THE PROMISED LAND 2000 BC TO 1000 BC

in 1179BC and the Philistines from the Pentapolis who were only given the Pentapolis cities in 1177BC. Joshua 13.2 refers to the Philistines and Joshua 11.3 names the Pentapolis – yet Joshua's campaign is supposed to have taken place sometime between 1500BC and 1350BC.

14.10 The Sea Peoples destroyed all the Bronze Age civilisations – except Egypt. The reason is that they had iron swords and daggers whilst their opponents only had bronze – a much softer metal. So, another oddity is Yahweh requesting all gold, silver, bronze and iron found in Jericho be set aside for him, supposedly around 3 centuries before the Sea Peoples had arrived in the Canaan. Likewise, the claim in Joshua 17:16 that all the Canaanites had chariots of iron is highly improbable and clearly confused with the Philistines who did have iron chariots – but they only arrived in Canaan in 1178BC – two or three centuries after Joshua's death. The command to collect up all the metal objects reflects the rarity and value of metals at that time.

The 50 cities razed and populations murdered in genocidal attacks

14.11 One thing is clear, it was obviously not our Creator God who ordered the genocidal destruction of 50 cities across Canaan.

14.12 If God had chosen the Israelites for a higher purpose, he would not have ordered all the adult men to mercilessly murder all the old, infirm, women young and old, and all the children – with blunt bronze weapons – upfront and personal. How traumatised would the Israelite men have been?? Why did Yahweh not simply send a plague? The whole idea is clearly ridiculous. And yet, many biblical apologists gamely try to analyse and justify such barbaric genocide:– forgetting that when you are in a hole – stop digging!

14.13 In fact, since Israel regained most of its historic lands after the Six Day War of 1973, Israeli archaeologists have identified 37 of the 50 cities mentioned in Joshua. Of these 37, only 3 show any signs of destruction by warfare. Jericho was destroyed in 1650BC (+/-20 years) [see new evidence in Chapter 18*bis*], when part of the Mitanni kingdom (a Hurrian people, i.e. of Japheth, and NOT Canaanite). The two other cities nearer the coast, show signs of destruction dated to around 1200BC. The more likely culprits for the destruction of the other two cities is either the Egyptians, perhaps after they failed to send the annual tribute to Egypt, or the Sea Peoples during their invasion during 1178BC. Certainly, Joshua's campaign did not last for 450 years!!

14.14 The Canaanites clearly survived, and thrived, known later as the Phoenicians (who gave the world its first alphabet, which was adopted by the Hebrews) and nowadays as the Lebanese. The Washington Post reported results from a large DNA sample of Lebanese collected during 2017 – which found 93% of modern-day Lebanese have inherited Canaanite DNA.

14.15 The good news for supporters of Yahweh – is that Joshua's description of the genocidal destruction of 50 cities and all their inhabitants is clearly all Fake News !! Biblical inerrantists face a stark choice – it is good news that they do not have to justify Yahweh's commands to commit genocide but bad news – as the bible is clearly not inerrant.

Military operations and international relations

14.16 There are numerous references in Joshua that betray much later authorship.

14.17 When attacking Jericho, Yahweh commands Joshua to collect all the gold, silver, bronze and iron – but iron was not in use at the time – it was introduced by the Sea Peoples, using iron weapons which were devastatingly effective against bronze weapons wielded by the bronze age cultures that they swept away as they advanced through what is now Turkey, Syria and into Israel in 1177BC. Jericho had long been prosperous, until it was devastated in 1650BC (+/-20), centuries before Joshua is supposed to have marched around its walls. Indeed, its destruction is more likely linked to the migration that saw the Hyksos arrive in Egypt than any much later Exodus from Egypt – for more detail see Chapter 18*bis*. During the 20th century, carbon dating had determined dates of 1617BC, 1573BC and 1530BC for Jericho's demise – all somewhat before the earliest dating claimed for the Exodus. Jericho then lay desolate until the 9th century BC (900BC to 800BC – a period in which the Israelites inhabited two separate kingdoms, Israel and Judah). All the dates indicated for the destruction of Jericho seem far too early for Joshua and any such destruction around these dates would most likely be by Egyptian arms. By 1530BC, the Egyptians were rapidly establishing their empire up towards the modern Turkish border and to the deserts east of the Jordan – whilst the proto Israelites, most likely as the Hyksos, had been chased across southern Israel and fled into Northern Arabia (Sinai), Moab and

Edom.

14.18 Joshua 10 relates that five Amorite armies from cities around Jerusalem attacked the Israelites – but these would have been Canaanites rather than Amorites, who inhabited areas of eastern Syria. The writers misled themselves thinking that Hittites had settled in parts of Israel – where there is no evidence they had and the whole of Canaan was a tribute land controlled by the Egyptians – whom Joshua never mentions!

14.19 Joshua 11:21 tells of the Israelites wiping out the Anakim and all their cities. In biblical commentary the Anakim tend to get conflated with the Nephalim, the Guardians and The Watchers – variously believed to be giants, aliens, or just the ungodly. However, other evidence and Egyptian records identify the Anakim as an Arab tribe who moved into the Negev c900BC and were known for smelting bronze. The Egyptian records tell of their demise at the hands of the Egyptians.

14.20 Joshua 13:2-3 tells of Joshua aging and Yahweh reminding him that he is yet to conquer the Philistines and their five cities in Gaza, the Pentapolis. However, these cities were only built by the Egyptians after they had defeated the Sea Peoples in 1177BC and established tutelage over them. 1177BC is far too late in biblical view of history to accommodate the period of the Judges leading up to Saul and David.

14.21 In Joshua 17:16 it is reported that Canaanites had iron chariots. But in 'The History of Iron Weapons & Chariots', Jerrod Thomas writes that the Hittites only started using iron weapons after 1300BC but the use of iron only reached Palestine with the invasion by the Sea Peoples in 1177BC.

14.22 Joshua 24:19 reveals Yahweh as incredibly jealous of other gods whom Israelites might worship. If Yahweh was the God who created the universe, it seems rather odd for him to be jealous of a few fake objects of worship – in fact such an emotion actually provides rather strong evidence that Yahweh was in fact another of the competing 'pagan' gods.

14.23 The priests writing Joshua were clearly confused without reliable records of history and relying on oral traditions and folklore – but they did have access and made accurate references to the books of the Pentateuch. Accordingly, the Book of Joshua is often considered as properly being part of the Pentateuch. As such it would have been written during the exile in

THE BOOK OF JOSHUA

Babylon in the 6th century BC.

14.24 An extraordinary detail appears in Joshua is 15:17, where Caleb gives his daughter Achsah to his own brother as his wife – a startling breach of Mosaic law! Maybe the Levite priests writing the various books lacked a degree of co-ordination.

14.25 Joshua promotes a racist theology: Joshua 23:12 – Yahweh commands that the Israelites shall not intermarry with other nations.

14.26 In Joshua 24, Yahweh again reveals his insecurity, threatening destruction of Israelites who worship other gods – so other gods (a) exist and (b) are likely to be thought of as worthy of worship, even by Israelites! This raises some interesting questions: Why would Yahweh be so jealous of other gods? If Yahweh was truly the Creator God – why would he be jealous of anything? If these other gods that Yahweh was jealous of are fake, idols without power or purpose – why would Yahweh be jealous. In fact, Yahweh was jealous precisely because he was just like the other gods – he was one of them and desperate to convince, bully and threaten the Israelites to worship him exclusively.

The sun stood still

14.27 This stands out. If you think this even remotely possible, just think about it. Firstly, it cannot be the sun standing still. The sun is travelling at c70,000kph – if it stopped and earth did not, we would at a minimum lose all our atmosphere and a big chunk of our oceans in very short order! The alternative view might be that it was the Earth that stopped still – so the sun appeared to remain stationary for the afternoon whilst Joshua slaughtered more armies. However, the Earth is orbiting at 107,000kph – so a sudden cessation of Earths spin would devastate the surface of the planet – an extinction level event accompanied by extreme volcanic activity. And then Joshua writes that the Earth suddenly starts forward motion again – clearly nonsense.

14.28 BUT – this mangled record is useful for dating the finalization of Joshua. Clearly, the sun cannot stand still – but the concept betrays the time when Joshua was written. The very idea stems from the belief that everything revolves around the Earth – a belief from Hellenistic period until Copernicus – a period when it was believed that the 'heavens' were a hemispherical dome above the Earth against which the sun and the

PART TWO: THE PROMISED LAND 2000 BC TO 1000 BC

planets moved – and so could possibly just stop. Whilst the Greeks had no tradition of astronomical observation, earlier cultures knew much more – certainly in Babylon (during the Exile, c600BC to 537BC) the locals knew the truth. The Babylonians still knew the knowledge developed by the Sumerians (pre 4000BC to c1960BC) that Earth was one of 9 planets orbiting the sun. According to Solomon Zeitlin in An Historical Study of the Canonization of the Hebrew Scriptures, Joshua was canonized (text locked and further editing disallowed) in the early Hellenistic period or possibly by Nehemiah c400BC.

14.29   In fact, the storyline of the sun standing still may just be yet another translation error! According to Colin Humphreys of Cambridge University Department of Materials Science & Metallurgy, "Modern English translations, which follow the King James translation of 1611, usually interpret the text to mean that the sun and moon stopped moving". Humphreys explains that reverting to the original Hebrew text, an alternative meaning could be that the sun and moon just stopped doing what they normally do: *they stopped shining.*

14.30   This may refer to an eclipse, an interpretation supported by the fact the Hebrew word translated as 'stand still' has the same root as a Sumerian word used in ancient astronomical texts to describe an eclipse. This explanation was in fact proposed by a certain Robert Wilson in 1918 – but he deferred from his conclusion because of "the laborious nature of the calculations required" to calculate the date. More recently, calculations found no total solar eclipse was visible in Israel between 1500BC and 1050BC the widest date range considered as the time when Joshua might have invaded Canaan. However, an annular eclipse, creating a 'ring of fire' did occur during the afternoon of 30 October 1207BC – a sight which would have terrified armies in battle as a sign of godly anger. This fits the description in Joshua – except that the Egyptian records show that the Israelites were defeated by the Egyptians who controlled the entire area of Israel, Jordan, Syria and Lebanon in this period.

14.31   The triumphant Egyptian pharaoh was Merneptah, who erected a stele in 1208BC near Hebron thanking God for his victory over forces including Israelites – which indeed is our earliest ever non-Biblical reference to Israelites. This stele can be seen in the Cairo Museum.

An interesting historical echo recorded in Joshua.

14.32 To commemorate crossing the Jordan, Joshua is recorded as constructing a temple comprising 12 pillars arranged in a circle. This is almost unique in Middle Eastern history – but the day on which this temple was consecrated, the tenth day of the first month, was also the day in 2130BC that the most spectacular temple constructed in Sumer was consecrated – that of Ninurta. The coincidence goes further, Ninurta's temple is the only other circular temple in the Middle East until the Crusaders church built in Jerusalem c1200AD

The story of Ruth

14.33 In this story, depicted events maybe a century after Joshua's supposed conquest, there is a famine in Israel and Elimelech takes his wife Naomi and their two sons to live in Moab. In the Book of Ruth, the two sons marry Moabite women, Orpah and Ruth. Later, Elimelech dies, followed by his two sons. The family now comprising three widows is in desperate circumstances. The two sons are called Mahlon and Chilion. Orpah returns to her Moabite family but Ruth stays with her mother in law and they return to Bethlehem where Naomi has a wealthy uncle, Boaz. Thence runs the biblical tale of loyalty leading to Ruth's redemption under Mosaic Law by Boaz. Boaz and Ruth the begat the grandfather of King David. This uplifting tale must have been handed down orally until David's time – as no Hebrew writing existed.

14.34 The names of Naomi's sons, Mahlon and Chilion, have various attributed meanings. Mainstream media such as encyclopedia.com suggest: 'Mahlon could be connected with root mahol, to dance, whereas Chilion is a word meaning completion'. A site guiding the naming of babies, 'she-knows', gives Mahlon as meaning infirmity, a harp or a pardon; whilst it gives Chilion the meaning finished, complete or perfect. So far, reasonable that parents might name their sons after dancing or a musical instrument and as complete or perfect. But a US Christian site, blogs.christian.com, states Mahlon derived from Machala, which means 'sickness or illness'; Chilion, spelt as Kilion derives from kelaya, which means 'extermination'. What kind of parents would name their sons as 'Illness' and "Extermination'! If blogs.christian.com is correct, it only undermines the credibility of the tale of Ruth – from factual history to an inspiring morality tale.

14.35 The Bible generally reports hostility towards the Moabites. The rationale may be traced through the supposed origin of the Moabites. According to the bible, the Moabites descended from the offspring of Lot (whose wife was turned into a pillar of salt) and his two daughters with whom he produced Ammon and Moab. It seems patriarchs could freely take multiple wives, servant girls and even widows of their deceased brothers – but their own daughters were deemed beyond the pale. Moab refers to an area on the east side of the Jordan, just south of the Dead Sea. Although closely related to the Israelites, the Moabites did not welcome those who arrived during the Exodus – hence the origin of enmity between Israel and Moab. Hence, in Deuteronomy 23:1–8, Yahweh declares that the sons of anyone who is (i) illegitimate, (ii) cuts off his penis, or (iii) is a Moabite, shall not enter the Temple for 10 generations. It goes on to exclude descendants of Egyptians and Edomites for a mere three generations. However, Solomon, who built and consecrated the Temple was only 4 generations descended from Ruth, a Moabite.

THE BOOK OF JOSHUA

15

The United Monarchy
– Saul, David & Solomon

15.1 Samuel is held to be one of the major prophets and, in the Old Testament story, is the one responsible for implementing Yahweh's decision to grant the Israelites their foolish desire for a king to supersede his appointment of judges to lead them. The two books of Samuel and the first half of 1 Kings (which covers similar ground) contain extraordinary details – many of which seriously undermine the idea that Yahweh is God – a even a worthy moral teacher. This chapter walks through these texts identifying some strange and ungodly happenings. The traditional view is that David and Solomon were beloved of God and were therefore showered with blessings. However, based solely on the biblical evidence (actually, none exists elsewhere), David is shown to be untrustworthy, bloodthirsty and immoral – indeed a very poor role model.

15.2 The tale starts with Elkanah, a man with two wives – one of whom had produced many offspring whilst the other, Hannah, was barren. This led to great taunting and jealousy. Hannah then prayed that if she was granted a son, she would give him away by dedicating him to serve Yahweh. As in 1 Samuel 1:11 "a razor shall never come on his head" – Samuel shall be a Nazirite.

15.3 Fulfilling her promise to dedicate her first born, immediately he had been weaned, Hannah gave Samuel over to the High Priest, Eli, and was then rewarded with five more children.

15.4 In 1 Samuel 2 we learn that Eli had two sons who also served in the temple but they behaved badly, demanding the choicest pieces of sacrificial meat and sleeping with the servant girls of the temple. This raised the wrath of Yahweh who promised an untimely and simultaneous end for Eli's sons.

15.5 In 1 Samuel 3:3, we learn that the young Samuel actually slept in the Holy of Holies next to the Ark – which must have seemed incredibly informal to the Israelites. However, this proto temple must have been a fairly humble abode compared with the temple that Solomon was instructed to build.

15.6 In 1 Samuel 4, we read that the Israelites lost 3,000 men in a battle against the Philistines. Following this, the Israelites decided to remedy their weakness by taking the Ark of the Covenant with them into the next battle – as they had always done whilst wandering Sinai. However, it seems that they did not seek prior permission from Yahweh – who is so put out by this lack of respect for due process, that Yahweh then allows the Philistines to slaughter 30,000 Israelites and take captive their Ark.

15.7 In chapter 5, we read the Philistines carry the Ark to a temple containing a statute of Dagon at Ashdod, one of the cities of the Pentapolis. Every night the statute of Dagon falls over and then the Philistines start experiencing painful tumours in their groins – from which large numbers then die. Dagon is the Canaanite and Amorite name for Ishkur (the Akkadian 'Adad' - see the family chart of deities in the appendix).

15.8 Many aspects of this behaviour appear odd. Firstly, from the perspective of the apparent strategy of the descendants of the pre flood civilisation. The background to the mission of Abraham and his descendants occupying the 'Promised Land' was for El Elyon (Sumerian, Enlil) to recover land wrongly colonised by Canaan and his descendants. Then, with the Burning Bush incident, it appears that one of Enlil's sons, Nannar (in Akkadian, Sin) takes over command of the mission. Ishkur was Nannar's younger brother and had been allocated land that is today Turkey, becoming the principal 'god' of the Hittites. Clearly, the Philistines, previously known as the Sea People, had adopted Ishkur after defeating the Hittites and occupying their land. The Sea People clearly continued worship of Ishkur as they swept southwards, their campaign ending with defeat by the Egyptians and absorption into their empire. The Sea People settled down forming the cities of the Pentapolis (today's Gaza Strip).

THE UNITED MONARCHY – SAUL, DAVID & SOLOMON

However, the following 150 years witnessed the slow decline of Egyptian power and, as Egypt's hold over its Asian possessions declined, the strength of what were now known as the Philistines grew. The Philistines gradually expanded over all the lowland areas of what is todays Israel, effectively isolating the Israelite tribes in two highland areas – the Judean Highlands and the Galilee Hills. So, one might conclude that Yahweh's younger brother had, to some extent, co-opted the invading Sea Peoples and had effectively turned them into a defensive bulwark on the southern flank against Egypt. At the same time, one might have thought that Yahweh/Nannar had enough on his plate dealing with the rise of Marduk/AmenRa based in Babylon. From this perspective it seems both brothers were still pursuing the objective of their father, El Elyon, to recapture the land promised to their family which had been seized by Canaan – so one might have thought that they would push the Israelites and the Philistines into a coalition.

15.9   Secondly, the overall impression we have is that 'gods' were regarded as very territorial. When people migrated or were moved into new territory, they then adopted the local god as the power whom they should obey. There are many examples of this throughout the Old Testament – David pleads with Saul that, being chased out of the Promised Land, he will be forced to worship another god. The Amorites, moved into Samaria by Ashurbanipal after he transported the Israelite tribes off to Nineveh, appealed for one of Yahweh's priests to teach them the rituals expected of Yahweh's people. Extensive archaeological shows that the Israelites themselves adopted worship of Ba'al (whom actually, I conclude is the same god as Nannar/Sin and Yahweh) and also Ashtoreth, Ba'al's consort who was adopted as Yahweh's consort. So, why did the Philistines not adopt Yahweh as a god that they should also worship – from the repeatedly fallen statute of Dagon, they might have also reached such a conclusion? Maybe, as Greeks, coming from outside the historical culture of the Middle East, they were not familiar with the local norms.

15.10 Thirdly, Yahweh's actions were also odd. Here was the chance to adopt a successful, warlike, people whose cousins would go on to flower as a dominant power spreading a powerful civilising culture right across the then known world. Despite claiming to be all powerful, Yahweh allowed his chosen people to be slaughtered in large numbers and then attacked the other side as well. Individuals, whether evil or righteous, counted for nothing in this strategy. When the golden opportunity presented itself,

PART TWO: THE PROMISED LAND 2000 BC TO 1000 BC

Yahweh made no attempt to appeal to the Philistines. Interestingly, the Israelite sources reporting on the terrible experiences of the Philistines, make no reference to Philistines getting electrocuted by touching the Ark.

15.11 However, Yahweh's behaviour soon resulted in the Philistines deciding they didn't want the Ark and in chapter 7 it is sent back to a border town of Beth Shemesh together with some tribute in gold. The Israelites celebrate the return of the Ark but 70 are struck dead because they 'looked into the Ark'. After this, with their enthusiasm dimmed, the Israelites decide to park the Ark in a remote village, Kiriath Jearim, 'consecrating' a young man (who was not even a Levite) to guard it – for no less than 20 years!

15.12 In 7:3, Samuel then warns the people to abandon 'foreign' gods and focus on Yahweh. Note: those gods they are to abandon are 'foreign', i.e. we are not told these gods are fake but that they do not have jurisdiction here – they are foreign.

15.13 Similarly, in 1 Kings 9:6, Yahweh says "but if you or your sons turn away…..and go and serve other gods and worship them..." Here, Yahweh seems to regard other gods as quite real and somehow very competitive with himself – no doubt because he was one of them – a descendant of the wise survivors of the Flood?

15.14 1 Samuel 10:1 states that Samuel took a flask of olive oil and poured it on Saul's head and kissed him, saying, "Has not the LORD anointed you ruler over his inheritance?" This echo's Deuteronomy 32:9 – The Lord's Portion is his people, Jacob his allotted inheritance. Meaning that Yahweh, being one of the 70 'sons' (descendants) of the Lord Almighty, El Elyon, was allotted the Israelites as his inheritance. Accordingly, the other 69 gods are just as real as Yahweh – with each inheriting different geographical territories.

15.15 In 1 Samuel 15, Samuel, acting as the senior Priestly Messiah, tells Saul that Yahweh wants Saul to attack the Amalekites, kill every man, woman and child, i.e. commit genocide and also kill all their livestock. Saul goes off and does this except he temporarily spares the king, Agag, and the choicest livestock to use as sacrifices to Yahweh. Yahweh then tells Samuel, that he regrets making Saul king as he has not carried out the letter of his instructions – and Samuel then tells Saul that he, Saul, has rebelled against the word of Yahweh, which is bizarrely equated to the sin of divination (using chance to make a decision); and he has been insubordinate, which is even more bizarrely judged as equivalent to the sin of idolatry – and, because of this, Yahweh has decided that Saul will be stripped of kingship!

15.16   The chapter described in previous paragraph is one of many in the Old Testament that causes apologists to tie themselves in knots attempting to justify Yahweh's behaviour as righteous and godly. No matter how you spin it, it is clear that Yahweh was just one of the 70 sons or descendants of the Most High 'god' and one of the least savoury characters at that.

Yahweh abandons Saul and turns to David

15.17   1 Samuel 16:7 sees Yahweh tasking Samuel to select Saul's successor from Jesse's sons – warning Samuel 'do not look at the appearance or stature because God sees not as man sees, for man looks at the outward appearance but the Lord looks at the heart'. This sounds very godly and righteous but bears no relation to Yahweh's own selection criteria – as set out in 1 Samuel itself! 1 Samuel 10:23 states "when Saul stood among the people, he was taller than any of the people from his shoulders upward" suggesting Saul was selected because of his outstanding stature amongst the people. However, this same Saul came undone because:

(i)   he was impatient to light the BBQ to feed his troops. After waiting seven days for Samuel to arrive at Gilgal (1 Samuel 13:8), Saul's troops were beginning to wander away. Saul then decided to light the alter fire himself, however this act was judged to be a heinous sin – because he usurped the priests right to light the BBQ;

(ii) delaying completion of the genocide of the Amalekites by saving their king for execution in front of the alter and keeping their choicest livestock for sacrifice to Yahweh

It seems rather capricious for Saul to be stripped of kingship and his family line to be destroyed by Yahweh based on such flimsy reasoning. The storyline resembles what authors of a soap opera might fabricate to get rid of one character to make way for the next hero.

15.18   So, checking back to 1 Samuel 16:7 – are we to conclude that Yahweh was misled by Saul's appearance and failed to check Saul's heart? Again, in 1 Samuel 16:12 when David is brought in "he was ruddy, with beautiful eyes and a handsome appearance" – tut tut!! Was it not outward appearance again misleading Yahweh's choice? However, for disobedience, apologists claim that Yahweh's actions against Saul are biblically justified – apparently by Deuteronomy 28:15 (disobedience brings down curses from Yahweh) and Deuteronomy 28:28 (Yahweh will smite you with madness and blindness).

15.19   As noted above, in 1 Samuel 13, although Saul waited seven days for the High Priest to arrive to preside over the ritual sacrifice, his temerity in lighting the BBQ himself resulted in Yahweh deciding to abandon him. In 1 Kings 3:3-4 we read that Solomon also made sacrifices to Yahweh himself, which the text notes was an exception from Solomon "showing his love for the Lord by following all his instructions". Yet, when Solomon usurped the role of the High Priest, Yahweh appeared to him in a dream and said "Ask for whatever you want me to give you". So, under Judaism, is one to conclude that there is no equality before the Law?

15.20   Further oddities continue. In 1 Samuel 17, the Israelites seemed to go along with the Philistine proposal to swap all-out battle for a combat between single champions to spare their armies – but when David won, we are told that the Israelites treacherously chased and cut down all of the Philistine army – a nice moral stance to take.

15.21   Saul is oddly described in 1 Samuel 17: David has been drafted in to the royal household to play the harp to soothe Saul's sore head. This is doubly weird – the mental anguish suffered by Saul is attributed to an evil spirit sent by Yahweh to terrorize Saul – what kind of God would do this? Secondly, if a shepherd became proficient with a musical instrument – a flute would be more plausible than a harp – can you imagine David lugging a harp around the hillsides, following after the sheep? Anyway, Saul would presumably be able to recognize his specialist harp player. Moreover, when David announces to Saul that he will have a go at fighting Goliath, Saul then ***personally*** tries to clothe David with his own armour, sword, etc. So, it is very odd that immediately after killing Goliath, David is brought before Saul who asks "who are you?" 1 Samuel 17:58.

15.22   In 1 Samuel 19:13 we learn that David and his first wife, Michal (a daughter of Saul) kept a household idol which was used to help David escape when Saul's men came to arrest him. Thus we learn that the royal households of both Saul and David maintained worship of multiple gods – and of course, Solomon built dozens of niches around the new Temple to accommodate many gods.

15.23 In 1 Samuel 22:10, we read that the High Priest, Ahimelek, uses divination (elsewhere described as a sin) to enquire (in Hebrew 'consult the oracle' by flipping the buttons Urim and Tummin) to ask Yahweh whether to give some stale shew-bread to David when he was sheltering from Saul's men. Flipping a coin to determine right from wrong is a quaint theology!

15.24 1 Samuel 25 relates the story of Nabel, a rich man who refuses gifts to David's men and whose wife, Abigail, then secretly helps David and ends up as being taken as another of David's wives. 'Nabel' means 'fool' – as in many 'stories' the names are descriptive – surely casting doubt on whether the story can be authentic.

15.25 1 Samuel 26:19 provides fascinating evidence of Yahweh being seen as just one of many gods and ruling only within his own territory – even by his own prophets. David asks Saul why he is hunting him down – is it because Yahweh has told Saul to do so or is it on the advice of men. If by men, then these should be cursed by Yahweh because they have driven David outside the lands forming the inheritance of the Lord, thereby saying "Go serve other gods". This seems to confirm the authors view that Yahweh's inheritance was the 'Promised Land' and outside this territory, lands belonged to other gods – who would have to be served if one lived there. 1 Samuel 27:7 states David lived for 1 year and 4 months in Philistine territory – it is silent as to which god David felt he had to worship during this period. Moab is another case: David took his parents to Mizpah to shelter with the king of Moab and, according to 1 Samuel 22:3-4, stayed with them for a while. According to Deuteronomy 29.1, Yahweh renewed his promise to the wandering Israelites in Moab, before they entered the Promised Land. Therefore, Moab was not part of Yahweh's inheritance – so, who did David worship when he was in Moab?

15.26 Imagine the scene for one moment. David turns up with his parents and a number of others at the home of the King of Moab. David would be relying on his kinship and reputation to gain an audience with the king, whilst the cultural norm was to welcome visitors and offer sustenance. Food and drink being offered first to god for blessing. So, as a supplicant and being outside the territory of Yahweh, does David participate in the worship of Chemosh (the biblical name of the Moabite god)? It would be extraordinary for David to abuse the kings hospitality whilst at the same time seeking shelter for his parents. Samuel is silent on this point.

15.27 1 Samuel 27:6 records David fleeing from Saul, taking 600 men and their families to the Philistine city of Gath. David then asks Achish, the Philistine 'king' of Gath for a small town to dwell in and is given Ziklag – verse 27:6 states that this Ziklag has belonged to the kings of Judah "until this day". This implies that Samuel was written long after the events described. It also indicates that the Philistines gave Ziklag to the Israelites – did it then become part of Yahweh's inheritance allowing David to exclusively worship Yahweh? According to Jewish tradition, the book was written by Samuel, with additions by the prophets Gad and Nathan. Modern scholarly thinking is that the entire Israelite history was composed in the period c. 630–540 BC by combining a number of independent texts of various ages.

15.28 Whilst David was living at Ziklag, under Philistine protection from Saul, he decided to while away his time by regular bouts of genocide – against the Geshurites, Girzites and Amelekites (again). Nice chap David, Yahweh seems good at selecting leaders with character!

The quest to house Yahweh's Shem

15.29 In 2 Samuel there are a number of references to the Name of the Lord, e.g. 6:2. These are translations of the word שם *'shem'* used in the Hebrew. *'Shem'* is not a Hebrew word and translators were at a loss how to translate it, eventually settling on 'name' – but this often reads oddly. It has been argued that *shem* is a loan word from Sumerian where it means a vessel – for crossing water or the skies. There are many references to the various ancient gods mastering flight – often they were depicted with feathered wings and many were described as flying in their aerial *shem*. What could be more natural than for the Israelites to want to build a place for the Name of their Lord, a place to park his *shem* – thereby tethering their Lord to a place of residence amongst his people?

15.30 No fewer than 34 references can be found in the Old Testament calling for there to be built a place for the *Name of the Lord* – https://bible.knowing-jesus.com/topics/A-Place-For-God~s-Name. Many of the most direct references are to be found in Deuteronomy, Kings and Jeremiah: 1 Kings 8:20 is as specific as any. This phenomena is something limited to the second millennium BC – from the Exodus to the establishment of the Monarchy, following which it is not mentioned. In 2 Samuel 7:13, apparently speaking of David, Yahweh states: "He is the one who will build a house for my Name, and I will establish the throne of his kingdom forever." Clearly the translation of "name" sounds odd, whereas "flying saucer" or "orbital lander" fits perfectly.

15.31 I give a few more examples to reinforce the point:

- Deuteronomy 12:11 – then it shall come about that the place in which the Lord your God will choose for His *shem* to dwell, there you shall bring all that I command you.

- Deuteronomy 12:21 – If the place which the Lord your God chooses to put His *shem* is too far from you.

- Deuteronomy 16:6 – at the place where the Lord your God chooses to establish His *shem*, you shall sacrifice the Passover.

- 1 Kings 14:21 – Rehoboam was forty-one years old when he became king, and he reigned seventeen years in Jerusalem, the city which the Lord had chosen from all the tribes of Israel to put His *shem* there.

- 1 Kings 5:3 – You know that David my father was unable to build a house for the *shem* of the Lord his God because of the wars which surrounded him

- 1 Kings 5:5 – Behold, I intend to build a house for the *shem* of the Lord my God, as the Lord spoke to David my father, saying, 'Your son, whom I will set on your throne in your place, he will build the house for My *shem*.'

- 1 Kings 8:44 – Solomon states: "the house that I built for Your *shem*" – why not say "the temple I built for You"?

- 1 Chronicles 22:7 – David said to Solomon 'I had intended to build a house for the *Shem* of the Lord'.

- 1 Chronicles 22:10 – The Lord speaking…'He shall build a house for My *Shem*,'

- 1 Chronicles 22:19 – build the sanctuary of the Lord…, so that you shall bring the ark and the holy vessels into the house that is to be built for the *Shem* of the Lord'

15.32 From the context, Yahweh's *shem* is clearly a personal possession and indeed the possession he cares most about. Hence, his people realised that if they built a fully equipped base for their god's *shem* – Yahweh would also stay there and they would feel secure under his protection. Yahweh, like all the ancient gods, had many names – which one do traditionalist believe all these references to building a house for his name refer to?

15.33 In 2 Samuel 6:6, we read the intriguing detail concerning the attempt to retrieve the Ark from Kiriath Jearim (see 15.11 above) in order to take it to Jerusalem. The Ark was placed on a newly built cart pulled by oxen but when the oxen stumbled, a man named Uzzah reached out to stop the Ark falling off the cart. His reward was to be struck down, seemingly electrocuted. David was so frightened that he decided to divert the Ark somewhere else – parking it with the household of Obed-Edom for three months.

15.34 In 2 Samuel 7:10-16 we read of Yahweh's promise to David and the nation of Israel as related by the prophet Nathan: "I will provide a place for my people Israel and will plant them so that they can have a home of their own and no longer be disturbed. Wicked people will not oppress them anymore, as they did at the beginning and have done ever since the time I appointed leaders over my people Israel. I will also give you rest from all your enemies. The Lord declares to you that the Lord himself will establish a house for you. When your days are over and you rest with your ancestors, I will raise up your offspring to succeed you, your own flesh and blood, and I will establish his kingdom. He is the one who will build a house for my Name, and I will establish the throne of his kingdom forever. I will be his father, and he will be my son. When he does wrong, I will punish him with a rod wielded by men, with floggings inflicted by human hands. But my love will never be taken away from him, as I took it away from Saul [because he only waited 7 days before lighting the BBQ], whom I removed from before you. Your house and your kingdom will endure forever before me; your throne will be established forever."

15.35 The promise in the paragraph above emphasises that it is to endure forever. The Israelites should have noted the fickleness of Yahweh's support for Saul and the extreme reaction to minor events that led to Saul's downfall (see 15.17 above). These promises made to David were equally worthless – the Bible claims that only one of David's descendants ever ruled over a united Israel whilst Abraham's seed has been subject to repeated genocidal campaigns ever since – Ashurbanipal, Nebuchadnezzar, Maccabean, Roman AD66-70 and AD140-144, Spanish, Polish, Russian pogroms, Holocaust, etc. Forever equates to c 40 years in 'Yahweh time' – maybe Yahweh died at this point or left the Israelites for good, as Ra left the Egyptians becoming AmenRa. It seems a bit odd to just disappear though, particularly after having waited so many centuries to get a proper parking place for his *shem*.

David's conquests and international reputation

15.36 Building on his genocidal sport of gratuitous murder whilst living under protection of the Philistine king, once becoming king himself, David then seeks to expand his kingdom further. No biblical justification is provided – there is no reference to occupying outstanding parts of the Promised Land nor is any mercy shown to kinsmen or those whose protection he enjoyed in his early years.

15.37 2 Samuel 8 describes David's military activities against the Philistines, the Arameans, the Moabites, Edom and Ammon. David's tactics are treacherous and immoral:

- the Philistines had sheltered David but he could have argued that they had spread out and occupied most of the lowlands of the 'Promised Land' – so perhaps he could claim that he was fulfilling a duty;

- the Arameans under king Hadadezer occupied the lands east of the Bekaa Valley as far as the Euphrates with Damascus as their capital – these lands were outside the area Promised so how was the warfare justified? David also mutilated thousands of their horses;

- the Moabites were his kinsmen, he had sheltered his own parents in the palace of the Moabite king and he himself was the great grandson of Ruth, the Moabite. David repays his kinsmen by lining them up and indiscriminately killing every 2nd and 3rd person. Moab was also outside the Promised Land.

- It seems that David might also have wondered about whether he should be waging war outside the Promised Land. In Psalm 2:8 (authorship attributed to David), he wonders aloud about waging war to **extend** the Lord's inheritance – asking Yahweh for direction on this point. Samuel concludes that Yahweh blessed David's actions 'by giving him victory wherever he went'.

15.38   Given his military prowess, as recorded in the Bible, it is surprising that no references to David's military actions have been found in any Egyptian, Phoenician, Philistine, Aramean or other records. Indeed, outside of the Bible, no direct evidence whatsoever for David has ever been found. The only historical pointer found so far is a fragment from a victory stele (known as the Tel Dan Stele) erected by King Hazael of the Arameans in 841BC which states as victor he had killed both King Jehoram of Israel and King Ahaziah of Judah – with additional partially damaged text which some interpret as describing Ahaziah as being "of the house of David" – from which one can surmise that there was an earlier King David.

15.39   David's affair with Bathsheba, wife of Uriah the Hittite whom David then arranged to die in battle, is well known. But Yahweh's treatment of the offspring of this union is weird: their first son is "struck down by the Lord" in 2 Samuel 12:15 but a few verses later, in 12:24 we learn that their second son, Solomon, is "loved by the Lord". If one believes that Yahweh is prescient and righteously makes such judgments – most of us could suggest a number of other candidates deserving of such preemptive action!

15.40   One might conclude that David also lacks parenting skills. In 2 Samuel 13, it records that Amnon, a son of David, rapes Tamar, one of David's daughters. In revenge another son, Absalom then kills Amnon. David is shocked by all this filial mayhem but Absalom becomes so popular that David's adviser switches over to support the usurper – whom David eventually defeats.

15.41   In 2 Samuel 24 provides further insight into the strange workings of Yahweh's mind. 24:1 reads "Again the anger of the Lord burned against Israel, and he incited David against them, saying, Go and take a census of Israel and Judah." For unspoken reasons, taking a census is regarded as a heinous crime and yet it is Yahweh himself who incites David to take a census? The reference to 'Israel and Judah' reveals the text was written sometime later – either after the kingdom had split into these two parts, or the authors knowledge that there had never been a united kingdom?

15.42 The census took nine months to complete and concluded that Israel could call upon 800,000 fighting men and Judah could call upon 500,000 fighting men. At this point, without explanation, David concluded that he had sinned. Yahweh came to the same conclusion and generously offered David a choice of three punishments: David could choose (i) his kingdom endure 3 years of famine; or (ii) he could be pursued by his enemies for 3 months; or (iii) or suffer 3 days of pestilence in his land? David chose option (iii) the three days of pestilence and the angel of the Lord struck down 70,000 people but as David saw the angel approach Jerusalem, the Lord stayed the angel's hand and David prayed for mercy. To atone, David purchased a threshing floor from Araunah and built an altar upon it to sacrifice many animals. One does wonder what the Israelites made of this strange saga?

Solomon – wives, concubines & sacrifices

15.43 The treatment of Solomon in the book of Kings seems highly fanciful. In 1 Kings 3:1 it is claimed that Solomon signs a treaty with Egypt and also gets the Pharaoh's daughter as part of the deal. This is culturally impossible and sets the tone for much of the legend of Solomon.

15.44 1 Kings 4 describes Solomon as ruling a substantial area from the Mediterranean to the Euphrates, which seems highly unlikely and is not recorded in the annals of any surrounding culture. Maybe, this description of a kingdom far exceeding the Promised Land became the basis for Solomon building niches in the new temple for the gods of these other lands that he ruled. According to verse 4:22, prodigious quantities of food were delivered daily to Solomon's household – including 5 tons of flour and 10 tons of meal – daily. This chapter concludes by extoling the great wisdom and cultural achievements of Solomon – the author of 3,000 proverbs and 1,005 songs, and claims that all the kings of the world sent people to listen to his wisdom.

15.45 The book of Kings seems to be propaganda prepared 350 years later, during the Exile, to bolster the spirits of the exiles by creating a myth of past national greatness comparable to or exceeding what surrounded them in Babylon.

15.46 Whilst it may be surprising to find all this obvious boasting and exaggeration in a biblical work, even more so is the description of Solomon's sexual prowess. The number of his wives and concubines is clearly set out to impress and reads as a great achievement and of favours bestowed by God. According to 1 Kings 11:3, Solomon had 700 wives (who were all royal princesses) and 300 concubines. The wives were described as foreign princesses, including a Pharaoh's daughter and princesses of Moab, Ammon, Sidon and of the Hittites. The only wife mentioned by name is Naamah, the mother of Solomon's successor, Rehoboam.

15.47 The number of wives has to be a wild exaggeration, there were unlikely 700 royal families in the entire world at that time. On the other hand, how many of these 700 foreign royal families recorded that a princess of theirs had married King Solomon – whom the story suggests would have been regarded as a big catch and which would have been cemented by an alliance or treaty? None.

15.48 Apart from the absurdly exaggerated numbers of female partners, two historical problems jump out from the biblical text. Firstly, the author of Kings was unaware that the Hittite kingdom had ceased to exist around 200 years before Solomon took the throne, having been destroyed by the Sea Peoples in 1179BC. This immediately confirms authorship long after the event. By the time of Solomon, the previous Hittite lands were carved up between the Phrygians, the Kaska and the expanding Assyrians. It is possible that the small city states that grew up, such as those listed in paragraph 4.7 above, were regarded as Hittite and daughters of a few city rulers were married to Solomon. Secondly, whilst the Bible records numerous references to the Pharaoh's daughter, indicating that such a wife was regarded as the ultimate trophy, Egyptian records are silent and culturally it would have contradicted a very strong Egyptian tradition. So, the author, writing long enough after the supposed events for the historical sequence to be blurred, had no knowledge of Egyptian culture – so remote and long after – again pointing to authorship during the Exile in Babylon.

15.49 Rabbinical sources identify the Pharaoh as Siamun but Egyptologists see a problem with the story of Solomon and Pharaoh's daughter. The issue lies in the fact that there is no record of Egyptian princesses around this time, or indeed at any time, being used to form alliances through marriage. As a British historian, Brian Roberts has argued: "the problem

THE UNITED MONARCHY – SAUL, DAVID & SOLOMON

is not with the synchronism of Solomon and Pharaoh Siamun per se, yet with the problems of attempting to fit the process of marrying out a daughter to a foreign leader. It is not a thing the ultra-orthodox Dynasty 21 would have done. We have an earlier example of the opposite, in fact. The king of the Mitanni had asked Amenhotep II for his daughter's hand in order to cement a political alliance. Amenhotep refused, offended by the suggestion that an Egyptian princess be submitted to ridicule from being married off to a foreign leader."

15.50 Another source points out that except for the story in the Hebrew scriptures there is no other claim that this happened. It states: "Royal women were married to their brothers or in some cases the father, to keep the throne in the family. Royal women were never married to foreign kings or princes. There is a written account that the King of Babylon sent a princess to King Amenhotep III to marry and requested an Egyptian princess be sent to Babylon to marry him. Amenhotep III turned down the request replying, 'That since the days of old no Egyptian king's daughter has been given to anyone.' Foreign princesses were welcomed to marry the Pharaoh but Egyptian princess did not marry foreign kings or princes. Any foreign princess that married the Pharaoh came with a large dowry and many attendants, she settled into life at the palace by taking an Egyptian name and becoming a minor (second line) wife.

15.51 Another illustration of rules to preserve the purity of the bloodline comes from the history of Queen Tiye (1398 – 1338 BC). Tiye was the daughter of a Semite, Yuya or Yusef, who was Prime Minister to both Thutmose IV who had a short reign and his son Amenhotep III who reigned from 1386BC to 1349BC. Interestingly, this was a period of great prosperity and artistic achievements. (Yusef is thought to have inspired the biblical story – but in the biblical story Yusef is confusingly combined with Joseph, the captive supposedly sold to Egypt some 400 years earlier.). Tiye was married to the young Amenhotep III when his official half-sister consort was too young to consummate. Initially, the priests ruled that any issue of Tiye could not inherit the throne nor could Tiye officiate at state functions – such a position must have reflected priestly fears that any son of Tiye might give prominence to a foreign god. However, Tiye became Amenhotep's favourite and one of her sons took the throne as Akhenaten. Akhenaten, was of course the pharaoh who introduced monotheism – thereby threatening the livelihood of 100% of the priesthood who failed to get a job with the new god – and fulfilling their worst fears.

15.52 As we have found in Chapter 3, there are many pointers suggesting the books of Samuel and Chronicles were written centuries after the periods described – it seems that apart from building the Temple, the wives, wealth, military and artistic accomplishments may all have been wildly exaggerated.

15.53 A final point from Kings further illustrates the extreme exaggeration employed in the work. 1 Kings 8:63 describes a massive sacrificial festival. It claims that Solomon sacrificed "22,000 oxen and 120,000 sheep". The festival went on for 7 days then he sent most people back to their tents/home before a further 7 days of festivities. Clearly this must be a gross exaggeration – even if the killing was evenly spread over the full 14 days, despite 'sending the people home after 7 days', and if sacrificing 24x7 non-stop – that would mean 422 oxen and sheep per hour day and night. How many could be put on the alter flame at any one time? How many priests would be committed to undertake the ritual butchery – maybe working in say 12 hour shifts? What to do with the vast piles of roast meat – particularly after the people were sent home? What would be the point of such wanton destruction? Estimates of the total Israelite population at this time are around 250,000 – suggesting a whole ox or sheep sacrificed for every adult of the entire population. Clearly this account is greatly exaggerated, another blow to the Biblical Inerrantists.

15.54 My own conclusion, from studying the biblical story and the historical record, is to question even the existence of the United Monarchy. The very small population of the Judean Highlands, maybe only c40,000, makes it unlikely that David could have carved out a substantial empire when surrounded by militarily competent Philistine forces. The adoption of Phoenician writing, the first alphabet invented c1050BC, for Hebrew around 1000BC would not have immediately produced the trained scribal class required to support administration of an empire nor the documentation of David's many thousands of songs and proverbs. It would be interesting to analyse Solomon's Proverbs and Song of Songs to determine whether these are predominantly written in Archaic or Classical Hebrew – if the latter, then authorship points to the time of the Exile in Babylon. In many places, details in Samuel, Kings and Chronicles indicate it was written many centuries after the supposed events occurred – which must cast doubt on many purported direct quotes of statements made by individuals. The frequent wild exaggerations are suggestive of post facto rationalisation – a story of past glories, weaved together during the depressed times in exile in Babylon.

15.55 If these three kings really existed, then it seems more likely to me that they were kings of Judah only. This would account for both their absence from any non-biblical records and the possible isolated development of the early Torah in Israel, from which the proto Deuteronomy is judged by some to have originated. After Israel rebelled against Assyria in 722BC, refugees fleeing from Assyrian retribution are understood to have brought a number of new traditions to Judah – including the novel idea that Yahweh was not only the most important god but that he was the only god to be worshipped. It was exactly 100 years after this, in 622BC that Hilkiah, high priest at the time, 'found' a copy of the Law in a dusty cupboard – generally believed to be an early version of Deuteronomy, and Mosaic Law was then adopted.

15.56 This 'rediscovery' of Deuteronomy in Judah in 622BC, explains two oddities of the Old Testament as presented. Firstly, the puzzling fact that the venerated lawgiver Moses disappears from the supposedly chronological record after Joshua invades the Promised Land – with not a single reference to such a towering figure throughout the period of the Judges, the United Monarchy or the period of two kingdoms up to 622BC! Secondly, it rather supports the idea that the Torah was mostly written in Babylon during the Exile and why the text is so full of factual errors of both history and geography.

Solomon's wealth and theological treatment

15.57 Before we dismiss David and Solomon completely, let's take a further look at the theological treatment, the possibility that David could have carved out a substantial empire and that Solomon did enjoy enormous wealth. Even the name Solomon, Shelomoh in Hebrew meaning peaceful, sounds suspect. It seems a slightly odd choice for a father engaged in incessant warfare, more likely a name created by literary types writing a story – in fact, the overwhelming majority of biblical names reflect the character of the person rather than a plausible parental choice of name.

15.58 The story of the kings David and Solomon forms a key part of the biblical story. David's line is seen as the ultimate ruling house blessed by God and genealogies in both Luke and Matthew seek to show Jesus was a descendant – and hence eligible to be a messiah. So, surely we should give these kings a second chance – let's see if we can redeem them. Solomon is painted as extraordinarily gifted, showing great wisdom and, as God's favourite, blessed with good fortune and great wealth. The biblical story of these three kings is recounted in the overlapping texts of Samuel, Kings and Chronicles.

15.59　Mainstream Christian teaching endorses the biblical construct that God so loved Solomon that he was endowed with great wisdom and extensive wealth. As noted in 15.39 above, let us recall that Solomon was born of the union of David and Bathsheba, the wife of a Hittite military leader in David's army that David had instructed be placed in pole position on a suicide mission in order that he, David, could take his then widowed wife, Bathsheba – whom he had already bedded. This makes it seem that David's lust for another man's wife and his role in arranging her husband's death was all part of God's great plan? Then we are asked to believe that God bestowed great wisdom upon Solomon and in addition he was showered with lavish wealth – described in 2 Chronicles 9:13-28 and 1 Kings 10:14-22. The biblical text claims that Solomon's mines yielded 25 tonnes of refined gold for every year of his 39 year reign, plus tributes from surrounding potentates and tariffs rendered on trade (1 Kings 10:14-15, 2 Chronicles 9:14). In addition there are various references to heavy taxation (1 Kings 12:4). Some enthusiasts have estimated his wealth in current terms as exceeding US$ 2 trillion.

15.60　The idea that Solomon enjoyed great wealth as a reward from God is quite bizarre. If one gives any credence to Solomon enjoying great wealth – then it came from being extracted as harsh taxation from his own citizens. Solomon imposed a Tenth Tax paid in flour, meal, cattle, sheep and other provisions; a separate poll tax on each family and the corvée (the old Egyptian system of forced labour). A force of 30,000 Israelite men according to 1 Kings 5:13 plus enslavement of all the descendants of peoples that David had conquered, per 2 Chronicles 8:8, who were used for logging and construction work. Solomon then treated all this wealth as his personal ill-gotten gains and spent it all on his own pleasures. Despite his supposed wisdom the biblical texts are silent concerning Solomon funding schools, the poor, the homeless, or the sick. Can one imagine Jesus echoing the lavish praise that the OT showers on Solomon?

15.61　Further, the more one tries to find information about the reigns of David and Solomon the more suspect the assertions become. When one

THE UNITED MONARCHY – SAUL, DAVID & SOLOMON

tries to evaluate the biblical story of a great kingdom and vast wealth it becomes an illusion. There is strong biblical and extra biblical evidence that the Philistines were powerful not only during the short period of the supposed United Monarchy (c1040BC to c930BC) but throughout the separate existence of the kingdoms of Israel and Judah. The biblical texts record Israelite forces claiming to have won some battles but also admit a number of defeats.

15.62 Unfortunately, the Philistines left no written records – as least none have been found yet. But, from contemporary Egyptian records, we find it was the Philistines who gradually displaced the Egyptians from the lowlands of Palestine – not the Israelites. Population estimates indicate the Jewish tribes in the Judean and Galilean Highlands were much smaller than the Philistines. The Philistines certainly started much better armed – they brought iron weapons and armour and were probably better fed from their control of more bountiful lowland areas. There is biblical reference to the Philistines banning the Israelites from even having blacksmiths – to prevent them from making iron weapons. The Israelites had to go to the Philistines even to mend their farming equipment (1 Samuel 13:19-22). Biblical references paint the Philistines as the main enemy through to the 7th century. As Assyria grew, they also recorded major battles with the Philistines hundreds of years after David's reign.

15.63 One text dating to the reign of Tiglath Pileser III (reign 745BC – 727BC) says that the Assyrian king had trouble finding a reliable vassal ruler who could control Ashkelon (which is biblically and independently described as a Philistine city). It goes on to report that Tiglath Pileser III was very angry that the "King of Ashkelon", named as Sidqia, "did not bow to my yoke" and as a consequence, Sidqia and his family were deported to Assyria.

15.64 Around 75 years later, another text records a treaty between the Assyrian ruler Esarhaddon (c681BC – 669BC) and the ruler of Tyre. In the treaty, Esarhaddon's control "of the land of Philistines" is acknowledged and the ruler of Tyre agrees that the cargo of any ships wrecked off this area belong to Esarhaddon. The Assyrian texts don't specify exactly what the "land of the Philistines" encompassed but it suggests that they regarded the Phoenicians and the Philistines as unified – for which there is no other evidence, but it does indicate that these two powers controlled the key Via Maris trading and military route along the entire coast from Gaza

PART TWO: THE PROMISED LAND 2000 BC TO 1000 BC

to Tyre. This suggests the kingdoms of Israel and Judah never actually gained direct access to the Mediterranean coast – check the map!

15.65 The Philistines disappear from written history during the 6th century BC after the Babylonian king Nebuchadnezzar II (reign ca. 605BC – c562BC) conquered the region and destroyed several cities, including Ashkelon and Jerusalem.

15.66 From the above, one might conclude that the Philistines constituted a continuing strong presence in Palestine even up to the rise of the Second Babylonian Empire and were only subdued in the same wars that ended with the exile to Babylon. Consequently, there seems to be little scope for a powerful United Monarchy. In fact, given that the Philistines would have continued to control the expansive lowlands between the Judean and Galilean Highlands, it seems unlikely that there ever was a contiguous United Monarchy. Archaeological evidence suggests that Jerusalem was a very small town during the time of Solomon – not the capital a large wealthy kingdom.

15.67 The incredible event where Hilkiah, the high priest, 'discovers' a scroll of (or part of?) the Torah in 622BC also points to almost watertight parallel theological development in Israel and Judah. Scholars suggest the scroll discovered was an early form of part of Deuteronomy – perhaps derived from Psalm 78. This Psalm reads like an executive summary of the Exodus – however in this version, God named as El Elyon (sometimes as El Shaddai) makes the running with his name appearing more than 100 times as the senior god; Yahweh (as a junior god) is referred to only twice; Jacob twice and Joseph once – but the supposed star of the whole story, Moses, is glaringly absent !! How could David have written a Psalm describing the whole Exodus and forgotten about Moses? The obvious conclusion is that 'Moses' had not yet been invented – Moses was an embellishment added during the Babylonian Exile – four centuries after David wrote Psalm 78.

15.68 There is a complete absence of any non-biblical evidence for Saul, David or Solomon from any other source. The absence of these monarchs may be considered alongside circumstantial evidence from a number of sources that there was no geographical space for the expansive and wealthy United Monarchy during this period. The inevitable conclusion points to the tales of David and Solomon having been embroidered during the

THE UNITED MONARCHY – SAUL, DAVID & SOLOMON

Exile to create a Golden Age element of the foundation myth to lift the spirits of the exiles and burnish the stature of the Levite priests. Leading Israeli archaeologists find the earliest non-biblical reference to the Kingdom of Israel dates to c890BC, whilst that for the Kingdom of Judah dates to c750BC – Israel Finkelstein and Neil Silberman.

15.69   As always there is likely to be some kernels of truth upon which the myths were fabricated:

- The stories of great wealth, gold, abundant food, concubines, etc may reflect oral traditions of the Egyptian court – the Egyptians had access to plenty of gold they mined in Sinai but these deposits had been exhausted by around 1150BC;

- The control of major trading roots may reflect knowledge of Phoenician business – at the time Solomon ascended the throne, the Phoenicians had established ports, warehouses, markets, and settlements all across the Mediterranean and up to the southern Black Sea. Led by Tyre, colonies were established on Cyprus, Sardinia, the Balearic Islands, Sicily, and Malta, as well as the fertile coasts of North Africa, including Carthage c800BC and along the Mediterranean and Atlantic coasts of the mineral rich Iberian Peninsula. Trading by Judah may have included a role in the spice trade from Arabia, particularly if my linkage of the expelled Hyksos to the People of 'Ad, forerunners to the Nabateans just across the Jordan from Judah, has some foundation.

- Likewise there may have been tribal chieftains of Judah bearing the names David and Solomon whose small fiefdom devoted its resources to fighting Philistines, with a modest degree of success, although some biblical records of overwhelming Israelite victories sometimes blatantly contradict hard archaeological evidence of abject defeats – e.g. against Moab (the Mesha stele 840BC) and against the Egyptians on "the day the sun stood still" (when the Israelites seem to have even forgotten whom they were fighting) per the Merneptah stele 1208BC;

- As tribal chief of Judah, Solomon may have built a small three-room temple – upon massive ancient foundations discovered when taking Jerusalem. It is interesting to note that these circumstances foreshadow a similar occurrence at Baalbek, where the Romans built a huge temple to Jupiter upon massive and far more ancient foundations.

16

The stunning implications of the name Elizabeth

16.1   The first clue that there is something interesting is in the first syllable "el" meaning "god".

16.2   If one researches the origin of the name Elizabeth, one finds the Hebrew name Elisheba – the name of the mother of John the Baptist and also the wife of Aaron, from whom the entire Levite priesthood descended – two highly significant people in Biblical terms.

16.3   But what does Elisheba mean? The Hebrew root is of two parts: 'el' and 'sheba'. El means 'god' and appears in numerous Hebrew words. 'Sheba' comes from either עבש *(sheba)*, meaning seven, or עבש *(shaba)*, meaning oath or swear. So, literally Elisheba means "god of seven". Given the post Exilic Jews were trying to be strictly monotheistic, the idea of 'god is seven' or 'god of seven' sounds inappropriate.

16.4   According to Abarim Publications' online Biblical Hebrew Dictionary, there are two distinct roots of the form עבש *(sb')* in the Jewish scripture. However, when the Masoretes began to mark the Old Testament texts with vowel notations (diacritics) around AD800, some 1000 years after much of the individual books had been canonised (text locked), they made one group of עבש *(sb')* words sound like sh- words, and the other group sound like s- words.

16.5   The result is one group of words that are related to the verb עבשׁ *(shaba';* dot to the right), and one group of words that are related to the verb

שבע (sabe'a; dot to the left). However, for the scribes writing the original texts and copying them long after the texts were canonised, there was no difference between the two.

16.6   So, in writing with a diacritic dot above the name, Elisheba became Elishaba and nowadays it is often explained as 'god of oath' – which does sounds rather peculiar.

16.7   The oldest original texts we have are the Dead Sea Scrolls – which only use Elisheba.

16.8   Having named my own daughter Elizabeth, the origin intrigued me. In Portuguese the spelling is Elisabete, clearly linked to 'sete' meaning 'seven'. Why might Portuguese be especially relevant – because the main influence on their pre-Roman, but later Latinised language, was Phoenician from whence the Portuguese obtained their first written language. And the Phoenicians were descendants of the Canaanites.

16.9   By now you might be wondering where this is going? What might God of Seven refer to? God of Seven or Lord of Seven was an epithet of Enlil, aka El Elyon – the chief god of the Canaanites (according to the tablets found at Ugarit) and also of the Israelites – according to Genesis.

16.10 But that still does not explain why God of Seven? According to the Sumerian records, Enlil was the ruler of Earth, Earth is the seventh planet you come across as you fly *into* our solar system from the outside. Hence Enlil was Lord of (planet) Seven.

16.11 This also provides an interesting new explanation for the Queen of Seven, the Queen of Sheba. Described as a wealthy, beautiful and powerful woman who came out of nowhere and seduced Solomon, there have been numerous theories as to where the Queen of Sheba came from. As a consort or sister of a ruler of Earth, or perhaps just wielding powers or using similar transportation to the Lord of the Planet, such a woman could easily claim, or be assumed by simple Israelites to be, Queen of Seven.

16.12 1 Kings 10 describes the quest of the Queen of Sheba to meet the fabled source of wisdom and her amazement at Solomon's wealth and organisation – apparently, she also showered him with gifts of gold and rare spices. This royal visit must have made a lasting impression – even Jesus made reference to the Queen of Sheba, recorded in Matthew 12:42, noting that the Queen travelled far to hear the wisdom of Solomon, but greater wisdom can be found in Jesus.

16.13 The Sumerian records relate that Inanna, granddaughter of Enlil, was the one who selected Etana, a handsome shepherd boy, to be the first fully human king of Sumer, c 3760BC. Given that Genesis states that the Lord Most High, El Elyon, was the one who instructed Abraham to ride off to re-capture the Promised Land from the descendants of Ham, it is quite reasonable to think Inanna (known as Astoreth to Canaanites and Israelites) popped in to check on how Abraham's descendants were doing after Solomon dedicated the new Temple.

16.14 Finally, it might seem odd to name a girl 'King of the World' but it would be more troublesome for a son to grow up having to identify himself as 'God of the Planet' whilst such a name for a daughter was presumably seen as a dedication and as a mark of respect.

16.15 The fundamental conclusion is that the fact this name, Elisheva, was the name of such venerable Israelites as Aaron's wife (the mother of every priest of Yahweh) and of John the Baptist's mother, indicates clearly that the Lord Most High of the Israelites was indeed Enlil and that the gods of the Old Testament were the same gods that conventional historians have labelled the pagan gods of Sumer, Egypt and Babylon.

17

Cyrus conquest of Babylon – aided by Yahweh or by Marduk?

17.1 This chapter goes somewhat beyond the scope of the title of this Part Two – moving forward in time to the middle of the first millennium BC – to examine key events around the ending of the Babylonian Exile. But, given the wealth of evidence indicating much of the Old Testament was probably written during the Exile in Babylon, I think this the issues surrounding the treatment of Cyrus conquest is informative.

17.2 The main focus is to compare the Judaic scribes adoption of Emperor Cyrus as Yahweh's anointed, even as a messiah, to bring about the restoration of the Israelites to Jerusalem – with the historical evidence which explains the same events as the end game event in the long struggle for supremacy between Enlil's son, Nannar (aka Sin), and Enki's foremost son, Ra (aka Marduk).

17.3 Most Christian scholarship has long considered the Book of Isaiah to be an anthology, the two principal compositions of which are the Book of Isaiah proper (chapters 1-39), with some exceptions containing the words of the prophet Isaiah himself, dating from the time of the First Temple, around 700 BC, and Second Isaiah (Deutero-Isaiah, chapters 40-66), comprising the words of an anonymous prophet, who lived some one hundred and fifty years later, around the end of the Babylonian exile or even later during the restoration of the Temple under Nehemiah around 440BC. By around 150BC, the date of the "Isaiah Scroll" found at Qumran, Isaiah was already regarded as a single composition.

17.4 The use of the term 'Tartan' in Isaiah 20:1 shows at least this section of Isaiah was written early, prior to 600BC. Tartan is a military term in the Assyrian Army and is the highest position in the Army under the King himself. There would typically be one Tartan controlling the left side of the battlefield and another controlling the right side, and the King controlling the central deployment. The Assyrian Army ceased to exist when the Assyrian Empire ceased in 609BC, when it was destroyed by the Babylonians. The language fell into decay and its military terms would have fallen more quickly into oblivion, seeing as there was no longer any Assyrian Army after 609BC.

17.5 Furthermore, there is historical information in Isaiah chapters 1 to 39 which has been confirmed from other sources. Most experts accept this section was written when it claims to have been written, soon after 700 BC.

17.6 *Carelink Ministries – Bible Lives*, writes: Whilst the application of the whole of Isaiah to the times of Hezekiah is sound, the evident reference of Isaiah 40-66 to the returning exiles implies that this section of Scripture, along with many other prophecies, was re-written under inspiration by the Jewish prophets in Babylon and applied to their own times. Isaiah has so many detailed allusions to Babylonian life and beliefs that it's impossible to think that it was all written in Hezekiah's time, with no reference to the Babylonians. We find the specific names of Babylonian idols (Isaiah 46:1, 2), ceremonies and processions known only in Babylon (Isaiah 46:7), omens (Isaiah 44:25), magic and astrology (Isaiah 47:1, 2, 12, 13). Time and again there is specific reference to leaving Babylon and returning to Judah (Isaiah 40:3-11; Isaiah 42:15, 16; Isaiah 48:20-22; 49:9-12; 52:11, 12).

17.7 The idea of prophecies being re-written shouldn't come as strange to us. Many of the Psalms are clearly relevant to David, and yet just as clearly relevant to Hezekiah and other Kings. Thus Psalm 41 is David's reflection on the situation of 2 Samuel 15 – but evidently it has been re-written with reference to Hezekiah, also afflicted with an "evil disease"; and Ahithophel's part in David's life was played out in Hezekiah's life by Shebna (Isaiah 22:15). It seems apparent they were re-written over time, and hence have relevance to various historical settings. As an example, consider Psalm 51, which down to v. 17 is clearly relevant to David's sin with Bathsheba. But then, in order to make the entire Psalm an acrostic, we find verses apparently 'added', referring to God building the walls of Jerusalem and acceptable sacrifice being offered again in the temple *(which didn't exist in David's time)*. David's sin and restoration was evidently understood by some inspired scribe or prophet at the time of the exile to speak to Judah's sin, punishment and restoration. Hence the apparent changes of some passages from "I" to "we". Psalm 137 speaks of Judah in captivity, apparently initially as a result of Sennacherib's invasion as recorded in 2 Kings 18:13. And yet it seems to have been re-written with reference to Judah's captivity at the hands of the Babylonians more than a century later.

17.8   The liberal application of redacting to make scripture relevant to contemporary audiences was regular practice and extended to the revision of whole books. J.W. Thirtle claims that the original manuscripts of most Old Testament books were sealed with Hezekiah's seal, as they had been re-written and edited during his time. Scripture itself testifies to him and his men re-organizing the writings of David. Isaiah, with its initial application to Hezekiah, and then it's obvious reference to the captivity and restoration after the Babylonian exile, is another example. Isaiah 14, an oracle against the King of Babylon, goes on to speak of him within the same chapter as the King of Assyria (Isaiah 14:4, 22, 25). What seems to have happened is that a prophecy relevant to the Assyrian invasion under Hezekiah has been re-written, under inspiration, with reference to the pomp of Babylon being cast down as well.

17.9   Any serious student of Job will have observed the huge number of links and verbal similarities to the restoration prophecies of Isaiah 40-66. Job lost his family as a result of God's hand, endured the silence of God for a period, and then the Lord 'restored his captivity' (Job 42:10) and he received a new family even more numerous than the old one, and great wealth. Clearly, the story of Job was re-written as encouragement to the exiles to endure the apparent silence of God, and to believe in their ultimate restoration – as well as an exhortation to pray for their captors, as Job prayed for his friends. The same could even be said of parts of the Genesis record concerning Jacob, who figures so widely in Isaiah as an encouragement to the exiles – for he too went into exile and returned.

17.10 2 Maccabees 2:13 speaks of Nehemiah collecting the writings of David and editing them, and it has been suggested that Ezra and Nehemiah may have been responsible for this inspired re-writing of various Old

Testament books at the time of the exile. There are several references within the historical books that appear to be notes added during the exile – e.g. Judges 18:30 refers to a situation being ongoing until the time of the deportation to Babylon. Clearly an inspired editor was at work in Judges at some date after the exile.

17.11 Many theological academics, such as Whittaker and Thirtle, find it problematic that Messianic language be applied to a pagan king like Cyrus? Rather than run a red line through the text and disregard it as uninspired, can there be an explanation?

17.12 Firstly, it should be noted that Isaiah 40-55 especially is packed full with allusion to the Marduk cult. Marduk was the Babylonian name given to Enki's firstborn son, Ra. All that Marduk claimed to do and be, Isaiah explained as actually true, and solely true, of Yahweh, God of Israel. The descriptions of Cyrus as having been anointed, etc., are allusions to the way Cyrus was held to have been anointed and raised up by Marduk. Yahweh is saying that actually he, and not Marduk, had done this. The Abu-Habba collection in the British museum actually has an inscription that claims Nabonidus dreamt that Marduk raised up Cyrus. Isaiah's point is that actually it was the God of Judah who had done this. The references to Yahweh taking Cyrus by the hand, anointing him, pronouncing his name and giving him a throne (Isaiah 45:1, 8) are almost word-for-word what Cyrus claimed about Marduk in his 'Cyrus Cylinder'.

17.13 This is dynamite. It indicates that Cyrus, known to be a strict Zoroastrian believer in monotheism, did not regard Marduk as a god but as a super intelligent teacher/guide. This suggests the "mythological pagan hero's" were not 'gods' but super intelligent and powerful leaders who were worshipped as hero's and lived like 'gods' in temples built for them by grateful communities.

17.14 But secondly and more importantly in our context, Cyrus was identified as the Messiah by none other than Yahweh. Cyrus was the anointed one, the 'Christ' of God (Isaiah 45:1). Such anointing is associated with being anointed as a king in the Davidic line, as it seems very unlikely the anointing was intended to be as priestly messiah. (1 Samuel 2:10,35; 2 Samuel 22:51; 2 Samuel 23:1; Psalm 2:2). Could it be that Yahweh considered appointing Cyrus as Judah's King?

17.15 The Jews of Isaiah's day would have had big problems with this idea of

CYRUS CONQUEST OF BABYLON – AIDED BY YAHWEH OR BY MARDUK?

a Persian king becoming the king messiah of Judah and being Yahweh's special "servant". But passages like Isaiah 45:9-13, Isaiah 48:14-16 and much of the material that follows the servant songs, are in fact seeking to answer objections to this – e.g. by saying that God is the potter and men are mere clay, and He will raise up precisely *whom He wishes* – even Cyrus – to be His man. And everyone (except Daniel it seems!) would have known Cyrus religious beliefs were strictly monotheistic – so he was not all bad!!

17.16 There is of course a far more plausible explanation. Cyrus enjoyed the patronage of Ra/Marduk who had lost patience with the Babylonian monarchs after they turned back to the Enlilite descendants. As recorded on original tablets recovered from excavations, Marduk marched with Cyrus at the head of the Persian army and when the Babylonian forces saw the founder and city god approaching – they threw down their weapons and flung open the city gates. Cyrus immediate grant of religious and personal freedom would have been seen as deliverance by the exiles. Who would deliver them from captivity? It could only be Yahweh. None of the exiles would have seen Yahweh since the capture and destruction of Jerusalem – so none of the exiles then alive in Babylon could recognise him. But, this powerful god who captured Babylon without a fight and gave them freedom must therefore be Yahweh.

17.17 Deutero-Isaiah was accordingly written up to reflect this view of Marduk as Yahweh and Cyrus as king messiah. Upon taking over the Babylonian empire, Cyrus became king of Judah – so better to claim this was Yahweh's plan than the more tortured explanation that Yahweh had got rid of one tyrant but allowed another to immediately succeed him.

17.18 If one thinks about it, Marduk must have been rather touched to hear the Judean prayers being dedicated to his Egyptian alter ego – Amen Ra.

Why power passed from Babylon to Persia:

17.19 At this point you may think it rather far fectched that my explanation involves a 'pagan' god acting as a real force to change history. Is it more fanciful than believing Yahweh used the Persian king to release the exiled Jews? Let's look at the explanation provided by the historical records.

17.20 Nabonidus was the last king of the Neo-Babylonian Empire, reigning from 556–539 BC. He seized power in a coup, toppling King Labashi-Marduk. As his throne name indicates, Labashi-Marduk was loyal to the traditional god of Babylon, Marduk (né Ra). Nabonidus went on to anger the priests and commoners of Babylon by neglecting the city's chief god, Marduk, and elevating the status of his great rival, Sin (aka Nannar), the city god of both Ur and Harran (of Abrahamic fame) Sin, associated with the Moon.

17.21   Nabonidus took an interest in Babylon's past, excavating ancient buildings and displaying his archaeological discoveries in a museum. In most ancient accounts, he is depicted as a royal anomaly. Nabonidus is supposed to have worshipped the god Sin beyond all the other gods, to have paid special devotion to Sin's temple in Harran, where his mother was a priestess, and which he extensively restored, and to have neglected the primary Babylonian god Marduk. He left the capital and travelled to the desert city of Tayma in Arabia early in his reign, from which he only returned after many years. In the meantime, his son Belshazzar ruled in Babylon.

17.22   It is not clear yet why Nabonidus stayed in Tayma for so long. His reason for going there seems clear: Tayma was an important oasis, from where lucrative Arabian trade routes could be controlled. The Assyrians before him had already attempted to do the same. However, why Nabonidus stayed for so long (probably about ten years, perhaps from 553–543 BC) and why he returned when he did remain unresolved. It has been proposed that this was because he did not feel at home in Babylon, which was opposed to his emphasis on Sin. We have previously identified, in Part One, that at this time Tayma was a cult centre for Yahweh, located in the middle of the area originally named Sinai (land belonging to Sin). Does the decade long residence of Nabonidus lend further weight to the idea that Yahweh was just the Hebrew name for Sin?

17.23   Nabonidus return to Babylon may have been due to do with the mounting threat of Cyrus and growing disagreements with Belshazzar, who was relieved of his command directly after Nabonidus had come back, along with a number of administrators. During his stay, Nabonidus adorned Tayma with a complex of royal buildings, most of which have come to light during recent excavations.

17.24   Faced with mounting opposition, Nabonidus brought many statutes of Sumerian and Akkadian gods to Babylon (relations of Sin) to help guard it against Marduk and his forces. Marduk later returned all these statutes to their original cities. This is corroborated by records of both Cyrus and Nabonidus found in Babylon: in the words of Cyrus himself, as recorded on the Cyrus Cylinder, found in Babylon in 1879:

"As for the gods of Sumer and Akkad which Nabonidus, to the wrath of the lord of the gods, brought to Babylon, at the command of Marduk, the great lord, I (Cyrus) caused them to dwell in peace in their sanctuaries, (in) pleasing dwellings. May all the gods I brought (back) to their sanctuaries plead daily before Bel and Nabu for the lengthening of my days, may they intercede favorably on my behalf." Cyrus Cylinder, 30-34

And in the Babylonian Chronicles:

"From the month of Kislîmu to the month of Addaru, the gods of Akkad which Nabonidus had made come down to Babylon, were returned to their sacred cities." Babylonian Chronicles on the 17th year of the reign of Nabonidus.

17.25 Nabonidus attempt to displace Marduk explains why it was claimed that Marduk led the Persian forces and why the Babylonian army would not fight the Persians but opened the way for Cyrus to enter Babylon in 539BC. King Cyrus became popular among the residents of Babylon by restoring Marduk to his rightful place in the city.

17.26 Modern perceptions of Nabonidus' reign have been heavily coloured by accounts written well after his reign, most notably by the Persians and the Greeks. As a result, Nabonidus has often been described in very negative terms in both modern and contemporaneous scholarship. However, an accumulation of evidence and a reassessment of existing material has caused opinions on Nabonidus and the events that happened during his reign to alter significantly in recent decades.

Hebrew offertory laws, probably written in Babylon and borrowed/influenced by local customs

17.27 Jo Scurlock has researched details of animal sacrifices in Mesopotamia. She identified records from Babylon showing that Marduk expected to be fed with offerings twice a day without fail. Nebuchadnezzar II boasted that he had increased the level of daily offerings – which comprised an ungelded bull, fattened long hair sheep, fish, birds, bandicoot rats, eggs, honey, butter, milk, finest oil, sweet beer and pure wine. Other gods required different diets.

17.28　In some cities, gods gathered in one temple to receive daily offerings. In Uruk, food for Anu and Antu and their offspring Nannar and Ishtar had to be provided four times a day. This gathering of the most closely related gods for daily meals gives a very human flavour to the lifestyle practises of the gods.

CYRUS CONQUEST OF BABYLON – AIDED BY YAHWEH OR BY MARDUK?

18

Biblical Inerrancy and its threat to the Christian faith

18.1 Before we get deeply into this subject, I quote one supporter of inerrancy and invite readers to contemplate what they have read so far. In his 'Biblical Revelation', Pinnock argues strongly against what he describes as a puerile maxim: 'To err is human – scripture is written by humans – therefore scripture errs'. Pinnock goes on to propose an amended maxim "to err is human – ergo, God gave the scripture by inspiration – so that it does not err". I leave readers to judge whether or not the preceding chapters show conclusively that the scriptures are full of errors.

18.2 A number of readers of Part One responded to me that their beliefs were anchored in their view of the Bible – that it recorded God's Word, written by persons inspired by God (or his Spirit). From this perspective, many are drawn to conclude that, inspired or even 'breathed' by God, the Bible must be free from error – hence the label "inerrant". Whatever one's views about Yahweh, Moses, Joshua and Daniel (just as examples), inerrancy is an unnecessarily extreme position to take – and sets up the argument for easy demolition. This position is similar to the arguably extreme, but certainly majority, Muslim position that holds that the Qur'an is an exact copy of the original Qur'an held by Allah in heaven – err, would that be with, or perhaps without, the diacritics?

18.3 Having never once myself considered the Bible could be inerrant, I nevertheless felt duty bound to read texts championed by believers in biblical inerrancy to ensure I had made a rounded assessment. I have been stunned by the lengths to which inerrancy believers have gone to argue their point – including, so called, Young Earth Creationists, who argue that rock formations containing fossilised dinosaur skeletons cannot be older than 4004BC (Bishop Ussher's calculation of the age of the universe) and must be some kind of prank devised by our Creator to amuse us! There are a number of colleges in the US whose teaching staff adhere to the idea of Biblical inerrancy and even 'Creation Museums' in Kentucky and Montana!

18.4 Let us look at a few arguments put forward by the Inerrant camp.

18.5 I have read papers by a number of leading academic evangelicals who argue that the Bible is the inerrant word of God, written by authors inspired by God and thereby 'God breathed', at least in their original autographia – i.e. before any subsequent edits made by men. I recommend the following theological academics for those wanting to study the point in detail – Gleason Archer, Barton Payne, Walter Kaiser and Greg Bahnsen. Here, I will draw out a few points advanced by Greg.

18.6 "Throughout its record, the Bible presupposes its own authority." Ok, that's certainly true!! Greg writes that the Old Testament ("OT") is frequently cited in the New Testament ("NT") using the formula "God says". For that reason, all theological arguments are settled decisively by the inherent authority signified in the formula "it stands written". The same authority attaches to the writings of the apostles since these writings are placed on a par with the OT scriptures. Therefore, the OT and NT are presented in the Bible itself as the authoritative, written, Word of God. This is purely circular logic – the Bible is the word of God because it says so!! The trap appears to be that once one decides that any part of the Bible was written by an inspired author, that text assumes the status of being the Word of God rather than of man, this logic is then applied to the entire Bible without any distinction, blithely labelling any 'difficult passages' as 'beyond our ken, but still inerrant'!!

18.7 The Westminster Confession of Faith (WCoF) goes further, calling all the books of the OT and NT, in their entirety, the Word of God written, all of which are given by the inspiration of God who is the author thereof. The WCoF goes on to assert that these books are, in their entirety, of infallible truth and divine authority. According to this grand confession of the Church, no error can be attributed to the Bible at any place. However, some slack should be given to the WCoF – it was drafted in 1646 by the young Anglican Church keen to establish its doctrinal purity amongst the English following, what for many, was the deeply troubling rupture with Rome – and at that time the Bible presented the only accessible written history prior to the Alexander the Great – and no one could read hieroglyphs or cuneiform.

18.8 At this point the Inerrancy belief starts to reveal its internal logic – "After all, if God sets forth false assertions in minor areas where our research can check His accuracy (such as in historical or geographical details), how do we know that He does not err in major concerns like theology?" Such writers (Archibald Alexander, Charles Hodge, B.B. Warfield) assert that the Bible is free from all error whether of doctrine, fact or precept; inspiration not being confined to moral or religious truths but extending to all statements of facts – whether scientific, historical or geographical. These writers maintain that the Bible is absolutely errorless in all the subjects it touches upon – including history, natural history, ethnology, archaeology, geography, natural science, physical and historical facts, philosophical principles and spiritual doctrine.

18.9 One might well wonder at the rationale for such extreme belief. But, then comes the underlying logic – trusting in the inerrancy of the Word of God is the basis for our assurance of salvation, without the doctrine of inerrancy our faith in the Gospel message rests on the minimal and fallible authority of men.

18.10 This is really pitiful – that we have to accept the Bible as entirely inerrant in order to have faith in our redemption? This comes back to a statement that I made in Part One, which I learned shocked a few readers, namely that for many the Bible had itself become a crutch for their beliefs. I do not write to shock people but to set you free by illuminating the truth. Search your soul (an interesting statement), we are wonderfully made with incredibly powerful and creative minds – we are equipped to think rationally and (particularly nowadays) provided with access to vast knowledge. Remember the adage, "ignorance of the law is no defence". Today, we are given the opportunity to search out and find the real truth – when you get to the Pearly Gates you cannot just say I was taught to believe in the Bible at Sunday School – no more than others might say I was told to believe Mein Kampf or Mao's Little Red Book. It is clear that the intelligence that created our universe and wrote the complex rules that govern its evolution is a vastly superior being, far beyond our comprehension – unlike Yahweh, who was a surprisingly human character filled with hatred for those who failed to follow all his rules, and who suffered from a raging blood lust whilst craving roast meat and – surprisingly for a god – was very allergic to yeast!

18.11   Reading the arguments made by 'Inerrants' about biblical infallibility, one is left concluding the motivation is fear rather than faith. 'Inerrants' belief in salvation is predicated by belief that the Bible texts have been inspired or breathed by God – so that it can be claimed that the Bible is the 'Word of God'. This concept is advanced as the basis for belief in the Gospel message and as that it is the inerrant Word of God, one must then extend the same aura to the rest of Bible – whilst ignoring totally the very shameful way that the present constituent books came to be selected; how Judaism itself views their books that Christians have appropriated as the OT and numerous glaring factual errors scattered throughout the Bible.

18.12   Yet again, Gordon R. Lewis (a faculty member of Denver Seminary for 35 years) makes further extraordinary claims: *"The fact that God knows all temporal things simultaneously does not rule out the significant and real succession of events. God knows the entire sweep of history simultaneously and yet carries out his activities of creation and providence successively in accordance with his changeless plans."* This is an amazing assertion, clearly devoid of any evidence!! The statement cries out for revision, how about: *"Whilst all available evidence shows time results in events occurring in a chronological sequence, it may be suggested that an intelligence of such power to have created our universe might enjoy some degree of awareness outside of our understanding of time"*. There is far more circumstantial evidence that our creator either does not monitor events on Earth on a continuous basis and cannot *"know all temporal things simultaneously"* – how else can one attempt to explain the 300 million year reign of the dinosaurs brought to an end by a meteorite hitting the Yucatan peninsula – did God make a mistake, puzzle how to correct it for 300 million years and then send an meteorite to do the job? And what of the Holocaust – was that known in advance and all part of *"God's changeless plans"*? Again, Gordon Lewis states the same logic that belief in absolute inerrancy is required to have belief in the Gospel message: *'if one's view of eternity does not allow for inerrant information then sooner or later he will see his view of eternity also rules out incarnation at a specific time and place. The concern many have for inerrancy is not merely for the integrity of the scriptures themselves but for the reliability of the Gospel message and for the integrity of Jesus claims of salvation'*. As this series will address, in Part Four, the gospel message reflected in biblical texts appears to be significantly different from what Jesus actually taught. The Church itself has already worked to distort the original autographia of the NT to the extent that Jesus original teaching is significantly misrepresented in the Bible.

18.13   Another inerrancy academic, Paul D. Feinberg (of Dallas Seminary, et al), argues that although it is a "heavy burden" to defend the Bible on all points – "it is nevertheless necessary". Feinberg sees it as simply impossible to separate the historical and scientific from the theological, fearing the consequences of divorcing the historical and factual from the doctrinal and theological. He posits an unbeliever responding to acknowledgement that the Bible has numerous inaccuracies of a historic, scientific and even ethical nature but is absolutely without error in all those wonderful, "unbelievable" things about God and heaven. He fears "the unbeliever would not view it as credible if asked to believe all these things that I have no possible way of confirming whilst at the same time allowing that there are numerous errors in areas that I can confirm". That's all right then, Feinberg is happy to insist on the inerrancy of historical claims in the Bible, denying overwhelmingly proven historical facts (as in chapters 1 to 17 herein) in order to be consistent in insisting on the accuracy of the unknowable and unverifiable claims in the Bible.

18.14   Paul Feinberg's argument is actually quite important – if, as can easily be shown, on 'historic, scientific and even ethical' matters the Bible is full of inaccuracies then how can we have assurance that its theology is not equally riddled with errors. As I have explored elsewhere, the facts seem to strongly suggest that Yahweh was just one of the pre Christian pantheon of 'pagan' gods whilst Jesus rejected most of the key tenets of Judaism. Moreover, it can be shown that the OT prophesies had nothing whatsoever to do with Jesus. Furthermore, study of the earliest Christian writings reveals sharp differences between Jesus original Nazarene theology and later Pauline theology – and that's before Rome started developing concepts of the Trinity and evolving the role of Jesus' mother and of Mary Magdalene. As Spinoza, a Dutch Sephardic philosopher of the 17th century, wrote 'it is scarcely credible that God purposely set out to narrate the life of Christ four times over' let alone breathe direct contradictions into the different versions. (See Part Three for analysis of the direct contradictions in Gospel descriptions of the nativity.)

18.15 Norman Geisler (of Dallas Theological Seminary) wrote (in 1970's) "that new discoveries in science and archaeology have not prompted new departures from the orthodox (inerrant) view of Scripture, indeed the factual evidence is more supportive of inerrancy than ever before". The basis of this extraordinary statement was not explained.

18.16 On close examination, the very idea that the Bible could be inerrant is by definition impossible. Advancing a position that claims that there are no errors in the Bible is utterly untenable. Furthermore, the vast majority of such claimants start with one or other English translations – of which there are hundreds in circulation – so which version is believed to be inerrant? The confusion over the Greek translations of the Hebrew texts used in Israel during Jesus life led to the Gospels recording Jesus, who probably preached in Greek, as quoting from the Septuagint which, when reading the Bible today, appears to record Jesus Himself as frequently misquoting scripture! The OT texts we use today are from more accurate translations of the Hebrew Masoretic text which have replaced earlier translations based upon the Septuagint – at least in all second millennium bibles. So, which is correct, post Roman translations of Hebrew Masoretic text underlying our OT today or quotes by Jesus himself – whose text where different is derived from mistranslations by the 70 translators in Hellenistic Alexandria? In fact, translation errors and changes from interpretation are relatively unimportant – but do involve errors that have long been cherished as facts – such as Eve being made from Adam's "rib".

18.17 Most Inerrants try to avoid mistranslation errors by fixating upon the original autographia – the original written texts of each author. The only problem is that we do not have a single original of any biblical text. The oldest incomplete copies of OT texts date from the Dead Sea Scrolls – which depending upon your belief, were already copies of copies made over a period of up to c1,500 years. The overwhelming majority of OT scholars agree that OT texts were regularly "updated" over the centuries to make their messages more relevent to contemporaries – before being canonised (text sealed) – and only the five books of the Torah were canonised as far back as 444BC. The NT texts are no better, the further back we go, the greater the variations in the surviving early texts and it appears all texts dating prior to cAD200 were destroyed – mainly by the Church. Therefore, as no original autographia actually exist – it is a moot point whether they were divinely inspired or not – we do not have any!

18.18 We do have enormous volumes of early manuscripts of New Testament texts – many incomplete. Catalogues of manuscripts now identify over 5,800 complete or fragmented Greek manuscripts, more than 10,000 Latin manuscripts and over 9,300 manuscripts in other languages of the earliest churches – including Syriac, Slavic, Gothic, Ethiopic, Coptic and Armenian. Biblical apologists focus on the sheer volume to claim originality for modern bible texts – but gloss over the facts that research shows that no two copies are identical.

18.19 Textual comparison of the surviving 5,800 odd Greek manuscripts has revealed over 400,000 variations – which is somewhat concerning given that the entire New Testament comprises only 139,000 words. The vast majority of the variations are unimportant, many appear to be from sloppy copying (lines repeated or omitted) and frequent spelling mistakes. There also seems to have been a common practice of copying into new texts additional words that were previously margin notes – particularly where the extra text reinforced a doctrinal message or seemed to add useful detail. However, there are also many changes which indicate the earliest versions were changed to suppress views which came to be regarded as heretical (or gnostic) and/or to promote views which came to be regarded as orthodox. The earliest manuscripts refer to Jesus being adopted as a Son of God only at his baptism when aged c30 or at his resurrection. Indeed, on the single most important gospel message – it is only Mark who refers to Jesus death as an atonement for human sin. Early versions of the gospels all fail to mention Jesus appearing to anyone after his resurrection. These early texts do not support the orthodox dogma on fundamental issues. Similarly, the only two biblical verses directly supporting the core concept of a trinity (see Part One and in more detail Part Three, plus 18.22 below) are clearly late additions.

18.20 The idea that belief of inerrancy is fundamental to belief in Jesus death being required to atone for our sins and thereby for our salvation. This is an extraordinary construct and maybe wishful thinking. As in the paragraph above, biblical evidence is built on shaky foundations. It sits uncomfortably with other dogma – if Jesus is God, then surely God cannot die? So, under the Trinity, Jesus as God cannot die but the death of the man in which Jesus, as God, dwelt for a short while paid for all human sin for all time? This sounds unlikely. To my simple mind, the Creator

God would hardly submit to death on an obscure planet, Earth, on the outer edge of a smallish galaxy. And, if God 'died' but was able to resurrect himself – he didn't die – so maybe no sins were absolved. A far more elegant and plausible answer may be found in Part Four of this series!

18.21 Inerrancy doctrine ties itself in knots trying to make squares out of circles – apparently, all redactions and subsequent edits may also be inspired by God. The well documented facts (Rabbinical records) concerning the canonisation of the OT texts – a process of accepting modified drafts that took place over many centuries, suggests that either the original authors made numerous errors (due to weak inspiration or poor hearing perhaps?) or that God kept wanting to edit his word?

18.22 I wait to read an argument from the Inerrancy clique that the Matthew 28:19 and the Comma Johannine (two well documented edits made to those Gospels around 250AD and 1500AD(*) respectively) were inspired by God – because Jesus had forgotten to mention the idea of the Trinity whilst on Earth – so God had to inspire individuals to 'correct' the original text of some Gospels in order to make it clear!!

(*) In 1522, Erasmus included the revised text for the 3rd edition of his Greek New Testament only after the Vatican had managed to produce a version of a Greek NT including the revised phrase. A few 4th and 5th century Latin manuscripts (i.e. translations from Greek) include the revised text - but as a margin note.

18.23 To me, it seems illogical and also pointless to argue inerrancy – given the huge number of indefensible issues that arise – why bother? The concern of many sincere Christians is understandable, if you accept the Bible contains errors – where do you stop – will the entire theological edifice fall apart? Yes, lots of encrusted dogma may be cast aside but surely the imperative must be to find the Truth – not cling to discredited dogma !

18.24 The key question inerrancy raises must be – what is the value of the Bible and what role should the Bible have in Christian belief? WWJD? Rather, what did Jesus do – He wrote nothing that has survived (as far as we know) – Why? Maybe because His message, in essence, was quite simple: "Love others as you love yourself, and in doing so you show your love for God, whose spirit inhabits all of us". If you adopt this command, everything else follows.

18.25 Jesus is quoted in the NT as making numerous references to Jewish scripture but given the focus of NT writers to prove Jesus was a Jewish Messiah and given the manifest errors and changes made to the Gospels (covered in Parts Three and Four) – how can we have confidence that these quotations are accurate? Remember, in reality, the Bible is very far removed from inerrancy!

18.26 My findings are that much of the OT is fiction, partly derived from ancient half remembered oral traditions blended with popular historical writings traced back to Sumerian times, mixed into an Israelite foundation myth mainly concocted during the Exile in Babylon to sustain the Levite priesthood. Taking the 3 divisions of the Hebrew scriptures: the Torah and the Writings are totally discredited as historically accurate whilst much of the Prophets is highly suspect. The prophesies in the OT, supposedly linked to Jesus actions in the Gospels are uniformly weak and show Gospel writers, three of whom who were not eyewitnesses and, writing up to 70 years after the event, are struggling to convince Jewish audiences that Jesus must be a Messiah because he fulfilled hundreds of prophesies.

18.27 Inerrancy enthusiasts defend claims that Moses wrote the entire Pentateuch – because the bible says so! Such a claim flies in the face of many major problems – there is not a shred of evidence that Moses ever existed but is a composite fictional character developed in Babylon during the Exile; there is no historical timeframe for an exodus, for the plagues nor any evidence or period when Israelites conquered the Promised Land; if Moses had existed, he could only have written in Egyptian or cuneiform Akkadian – as Hebrew had no written form until c1000BC when it adopted the new Phoenician alphabet which emerged around 1050BC – and what priest would have dared to translate such precious texts?

18.28 According to the pseudo historical texts of the OT, God decided to reveal his personal name of Yahweh to Moses during the burning bush incident – and the rest of the Torah follows this change of name. However, we are then led to consider Judges, Kings, Chronicles, Proverbs, Ezekiel and others as covering the period from settlement in the Promised Land up to the Exile to Babylon – so why do all these books revert to use of the earlier traditional names of God as being El Elyon or El Shaddai? Yahweh is mentioned in these 'prophetic' books but far less frequently – and maybe the inclusion of Yahweh reflects redactions, of which there is plenty of evidence, during or following the Exile

18.29 Inerrant proponents base their arguments solely on biblical claims that it is 'breathed' or 'inspired' by God guiding its author what to write and therefore cannot contain any errors. When discrepancies are pointed out, extreme contortions follow to 'prove' that the text is consistent. The incredibly weak arguments outlined in Kitchen's book, referred to in sections 7.23 to 7.26 above, seeking to 'prove' the Sinai covenants during the Exodus were of a format used in the mid 2nd millennium BC is a good example. Very suspect logic of comparing a tiny sample, of which only a sole example is quoted, is taken by an Inerrancy disciple, J Barton Payne, to "prove" the Torah was written around 1400BC. In an essay entitled "Biblical Criticism and Biblical Inerrancy", Payne claims that the structure of the Egyptian Hittite Treaty of Kadesh 1258BC reflects "the form-critical study of Deuteronomy as a 1400BC type of Hittite suzerainty testament has done much both for the understanding of the book and for its *authentication to this very period.*" This is an extraordinary claim based entirely on thin air!! Presumably the arbitrary date 1400BC is chosen to "fit" with estimated dating of Mosaic wanderings – 1258BC being rather late to be used as an exemplar for Moses drafting! One wonders why the Treaty of Mitanni c1380BC was not chosen – maybe the structure differs too markedly from the model used in Deuteronomy? Kitchen has obviously no grasp of the history of the Levant during these centuries!

18.30 Another typical Inerrancy argument, by Greg Bahnsen, is that the Book of the Law found by Hilkiah in the Temple (622BC) during the reign of Josiah was the original autographia written by Moses! Such an assertion is utterly farcical – on many grounds:

- Given the supposed prominence of Moses in Hebrew belief, how could the Temple lose the only extant scroll of the Mosaic Law and its sacred contents then have been totally forgotten by the priests?

- The Temple was only built c 950BC – so where had the scroll been for the many centuries prior to that?

- Until around 200BC, the Torah was always a single scroll – so how come Hilkiah found only a small section of one modern book?

- The Hebrew language had no written form in say 1400BC – the date

Bahnsen puts Moses supposed time.

- Papyrus would not be very good condition after c800 years.

- There is no shred of evidence that Moses ever existed or that any exodus actually occurred.

18.31 During my research, I came across a new book, published in 2015 by Walter Kaiser entitled "Tough Questions about Yahweh and his actions in the OT" which quickly raised my interest when flicking through and discovering references to 'rakia' and 'Tiamat' plus questions such as "Can the God of Peace order genocide?" Kaiser identifies many "difficult" passages in the OT as questions to be addressed – so I was highly expectant when starting to read. However, for most of the headline questions, his responses defending the OT do not really address the questions, indeed they raise further questions.

18.32 Kaiser asserts that "God's (Yahweh's) name, character, reputation, works and purposes were beautiful, righteous, just, fair and upright" – therefore any difficulties arise from our "poor readings and interpretations of difficult passages" whilst requiring a "sympathetic approach as it is nonetheless God's Word". Starting from this position tightly inhibits debate!

18.33 Kaiser lists reasons why 'modern' readers may feel distance from the OT – it is not as familiar as the NT; some complain about its antiquity, its culture is too far removed; its books too long. Given that most of the OT is only 25% older than the NT these arguments hold no water. Kaiser justifies the retention of the OT in the Bible by questioning whether God would dispose of 75% of his revelation by discarding the OT. This overlooks the fact that the Chosen People have never regarded the "Writings" as divine at all. 'My Jewish Learning' states: "Unlike the Torah and the books of Prophets *(Nevi'im)*, the works found in *Ketuvim* (the Writings) *do not present themselves as the fruits of direct divine inspiration."* On this basis, Inerrants should drop Psalms, Proverbs, Job, Song of Songs, Ruth, Lamentations, Ecclesiastes, Esther, Daniel, Ezra, Nehemiah and Chronicles – as all these texts have never been regarded as inspired by Judaism – and they should know!

18.34 However, our Christian OT omits some key texts highly regarded by Jesus and by early Christians. Besides the 100+ early Christian texts ruthlessly hunted and destroyed by the Roman Church, there are others which one would have expected to be included in the OT. The Book of Enoch was clearly familiar to Jesus and to his brothers, James and Jude, who all quoted from 1 Enoch, yet Kaiser does not suggest it should be canon. Michael Knibb states: In the case of 1 Enoch, evidence exists for the view that the early Enochic writings (the *Astronomical Book* and the *Book of Watchers*, the *Book of Dreams and the Epistle*) were regarded as authoritative by the community at Qumran and by other Jews. The fact that the early Enochic writings were translated into Greek, and that they spawned other writings linked to the figure of Enoch, particularly the *Book of Parables* and *2 Enoch*, is further evidence of the authority they enjoyed.

18.35 Kaiser asserts people focus on NT and do not understand the context and culture of the OT – yet his defence of Yahweh's anger flounders in his own ignorance about the cultural significance of the golden calf and his acceptance of the whole Moses story as factual. No one can produce any factual evidence to support any part of the Moses story but, on the contrary, every detail when examined can be seen as fictional. The whole point of the Exodus story, written in Babylon during the Exile, was to rededicate the dispirited Jews after Yahweh's dwelling place, Solomon's Temple (housing his *shem*), had been destroyed. The intention was to develop an epic foundational myth of being a special chosen people protected by a loving Yahweh, who equally vented his anger upon them when they disobeyed his intricate legal system but eventually repented and forgave them. The promise being that they would eventually be freed and rise up again, returning to dwell in the Holy City for ever – except that the Jews in Jerusalem were then subjected to regular massacres and excluded entirely from entering, on pain of death, for 470 years from 140AD to 610AD.

18.36 The writers of the Torah sought to project a redemptive cycle: the people sinned, had to repent, provide sacrifices (i.e. food and wine for the priests) and then be forgiven. To ensure everybody sinned regularly, the rules had to be complex and transgressions almost impossible to avoid – otherwise there would have been a vicious cycle of less sinning, less repentance, less sacrifices – resulting in poor prospects for the priests. The control of the temple bureaucrats was enhanced during the Exile by the creation of hundreds of rules to be observed by the Israelites. The priesthood established increasing control over the lives of the people by greatly extending the Ten Commandments into no fewer than 613 Mitzvot laws.

18.37 By attributing all good things to Yahweh, he seems loving and bountiful. Yet he is feared and his anger knows no bounds – he commands the brutal massacre of countless peoples and "allows/arranges" brutal massacres of his Chosen People from time to time. Kaiser posits that Yahweh's love is enduring but he has to react to sinning – being holy he cannot tolerate sin but must display anger, however, his wrath is always short lived. However, Kaiser's logic is so pedestrian it can barely claim to be civilised – an intelligence that designed the rules controlling atoms and DNA does not exhibit anger or wrath.

18.38 Kaiser overlooks the more likely explanation that the OT is not written by Yahweh but written by men talking about Yahweh – and by persons with a vested interest. Kaiser refers to Canaanite writing from 1400BC to 1200BC recovered from Ugarit from which we get our alphabetic script. I am surprised he does not claim or infer that the Canaanites/Phoenicians got their idea of an alphabet from Moses!! Of course, Kaiser's timing is easily shown to be wrong. The extensive records recovered from Ugarit, the Canaanite capital, covering a broader period than that quoted by Kaiser, are all in cuneiform, and all are written in Akkadian. Our alphabet, and the Hebrew alphabet were derived from Phoenician, with the earliest fragments of Hebrew writing yet found date to c1020 BC. It is unfortunate that when Kaiser does consult extra-biblical information, he gets facts and dates significantly wrong.

18.39 Kaiser ventures that the OT text may exaggerate what ills befell the Canaanites! "Even though the language of the Israelite conquest sounds like a total 'eradication' of the Canaanite population including all men, women and children, it is important to allow for the presence of traditional Middle Eastern hyperbole in their 'war-talk'." It seems Kaiser is delicately stating that the OT exaggerated what happened, it wasn't really genocide – but surely his adding in this excuse for hyperbole sits rather awkwardly alongside his claims every word is God breathed. Kaiser describes Yahweh's patience, waiting 400 years for their sin to build up and reach its limit. By comparison, it seems the citizens of Sodom and Gomorrah had maxed out their sinning allowance a few centuries earlier.

18.40 Kaiser writes that one might object that the Canaanites should not be blamed for what they were practising since they were perhaps untaught? "Perhaps" seems an understatement!! The reason given for "divine" genocide of the Canaanites was that their sins had reached a full measure. But there is no evidence that Yahweh had ever tried to teach them what was sinful, they had not been Chosen! There is no evidence Canaanites were given the 10 Commandments or any other rules to live by from Yahweh. Kaiser parries accusations that the biblical destruction of Canaanite cities was not ethnic cleansing or genocide – because there is no evidence that Israel's conquest was stirred up by racial hatred, nor that the Israelites "relished" raping and pillaging. So, if you believe your raping and pillaging is your religious duty – that's OK according to Kaiser! To prove the Israelites were not racist, Kaiser recalls Abraham sharing his war booty with the Canaanite king Melchizedek and Moses second wife being a Cushite (negress). This **misses the point** completely, the charges of racism and genocide are directed at Yahweh, **not** those Yahweh is ordering about.

18.41 Let us consider for a moment what Abraham sharing his booty with Melchizedek was really about. In Hebrew, Melchizedek is described as king of Jerusalem and High Priest there to El Elyon – the same god that Abraham worshipped – so it is hardly surprising Abraham shared his loot. Furthermore, we now know that Abraham and his small military force of 600 naar had 'invaded' Egyptian territory, engaged four peripheral forces and captured lots of flocks and valuables. Abraham was on his way to see the Pharaoh, so pacifying the local centre of Egyptian power, the military garrison of Uru-salem and its local king cum high priest, Melchizedek, was an obvious move.

18.42 If Yahweh is God and as God had obliterated Sodom, Gomorrah and 3 other cities around the Dead Sea, deploying what seems like tactical nuclear weapons *, why not use similar surgical devices against the Canaanite cities as well – after all, the order was to exterminate every man, women and child.

> * There are many reports of geologists discovering tektites around the Dead Sea and evidence of ancient structures seemingly destroyed by a unidirectional force, indicative of a very powerful explosion. *See new information concerning this destruction now included as a new chpater, 18 bis, at the end of this chapter.*

18.43 Surely, if the real God had destroyed these cities, he would have done so clinically rather than brutalise generations of his chosen people – surely Yahweh would know the psychological impact on Israelite soldiers methodically killing young and old, men and women, upfront and very personally with blunt metal swords and spears. Remember, iron swords and armour came with the Sea Peoples in 1177BC – the Israelite soldiers were commanded to commit genocide using bronze weapons – soft and blunt by comparison. All this leads inevitably to the conclusion Yahweh is not God.

18.44 But the irony is that biblical Inerrants set themselves the hopeless task of trying defend genocide as godly and holy because they insist the Bible is inerrant – when in truth the evidence indicates that there was no genocide. An interesting YouTube video reports on Israeli archaeologists uncovering a majority of the 50 cities of Canaan. Only 3 of the 31 cities reported as destroyed by Joshua show any signs of warfare – Jericho, Hazor and ??(difficult to hear the name on the video). The same video also gives estimates of the early Israelite population. These archeologists suggest that there were c25 settlements in the Canaan hill country with pop c 5000 around 1200BC, by 1000BC these settlements had spread south with c250 settlements and a population of c50,000. These numbers are consistent with the estimates by McNutt (see section 6.8) and with Israel Finkelstein (section 6.7). These estimates are in stark contrast with claims in Exodus of an army of 603,000, within an Israelite population exceeding 2 million.

18.45 Kaiser's apologetic analysis of Genesis shows zero comprehension of astronomy, even of Earth and its moon!! Kaiser's analysis is bound totally to the Genesis text, having Earth created first, then the Sun and Moon – and seemingly, he dismisses the rest of the universe as background light!! Kaiser's knowledge of astronomy and the creation of the universe is clearly non-existent.

18.46 Surprisingly, Kaiser does make reference to the link between the Hebrew 'tehom' and 'Babylonian' Taimat – thinking both mean 'deep'. 'Taimat' was the Sumerian name for a planet existing between Jupiter and Mars, so called because it was mostly covered in water, which had a catastrophic collision early in the history of the solar system resulting in the largest fragment forming into a new planet closer to the sun – Earth, uniquely in our system, tilted at 23° inclination to the solar plane. The shattered remnants still circulate in Tiamat's orbit, known to us as the asteroid belt and to the Sumerians as the 'hammered bracelet' – the same word 'rakia' (referred to by Kaiser) is used to describe a flat hammered bracelet in

PART TWO: THE PROMISED LAND 2000 BC TO 1000 BC

Akkadian, Aramaic and even modern Arabic. Today, mainstream astronomers have mostly concluded that the Sumerian story of the creation of Earth may in fact be correct as it explains so much. Kaiser confuses hammered bracelet with hammered dome of a hemisphere over the earth containing all the heavenly objects fixed to its surface – beliefs only starting with the Romans, the Romans having lost the knowledge of the Sumerians and succeeding Mesopotamian empires.

18.47 Kaiser identifies 'raqia' as meaning to "beat out/to spread out" and the misleading Vulgate translation as a 'firmament' – concluding 'expanse' is more appropriate. Kaiser gets close to the Sumerian and Aramaic (hence also Qur'anic) description of 'hammered bracelet' meaning the asteroid belt constituting the remains of Tiamat after the catastrophic collision that likely created the Earth. Surprisingly, Kaiser then states: "Those who render raqia as a 'dome' are more influenced by Near Eastern myths than they are guided by the revelation of God". Actually, it was the Greeks and Romans (not Near Eastern people), whose astronomy had regressed so far that they saw the heavens as a dome over the Earth – hence the descriptions in Revelations about God hurling stars from the canopy "down" on to Earth!!

18.48 The most surprising aspect of Inerrancy is the unshakeable belief that human authors were so guided by God's spirit when writing those texts that have become canon – that the resulting texts constitute the inerrant 'Word of God'. This despite multitudinous errors both material and immaterial. A final quote from an Inerrant writer, Henry Krabbendam, whose CV states he is an ordained minister (Canadian Reformed church and Orthodox Presbyterian) and an associate professor (Covenant College, Tennessee) *'those that reject Biblical inerrancy suffer from a rebellious heart and some other form of deficiency in their lives – they must address a fundamental problem which arises from apostasy and can arise only from apostasy. The grip of apostasy can only be broken by repentance'*. Reading this left me speechless!

18.49 The puzzle to me is not whether the 'Inerrancy' position has any merit – when it tries to deny most knowledge mankind has painfully accumulated over centuries across a very wide range of disciplines – for unverifiable assertions in a single book. My interest is to try to understand the motivation of those with such beliefs. To argue inerrancy requires a certain sufficiency in literacy, but to brush aside all evidence from all other sources than the Bible suggests education took place in a Christian equivalent of a madrassa. So, what is the objective? The arguments propounded by the 'Inerrants' have an 'other worldly' air about them. Is 'Inerrancy' actually a Fifth Column seeking to destroy Christianity from within? On balance, I conclude 'Inerrants' really see themselves as true Christians but it seems they have faith only in a book but not in God – surely this is a very bad call !!

18.50 As readers of Part One may have agreed, there is ample evidence that our Universe was designed rather than a spontaneous happening – design is predicated by there being a designer – and something as awesome as the designer of our universe deserves the title 'God'. In the absence of any known writings by Jesus himself, what reliable records do we have of Jesus teaching? This is something which is addressed more fully in Part Four – leading to surprising and delightful conclusions.

18.51 Within the existing canon, it appears to me that the earliest canonised writings, Acts, and the epistles written by Paul may be the most authentic and reliable. We understand that following his conversion cAD34, Paul regularly visited Jerusalem and acknowledged James (Jesus brother) as head of the Nazarene Church headquartered there. However, around 15 years later when Paul started writing his Epistles, maybe with Galatians in AD49, Paul begun to greatly develop his Christology – and references to differences in theological beliefs and teachings start to arise. Paul's writings are somewhat divergent from the original beliefs of the Nazarene followers of Jesus, many of whom became known as the Nestorians, founding the Churches in Syria and Egypt. The Nazarene Church flourished in southern France, northern Portugal and north west Spain. Surprisingly, the Nazarenes became so strongly established in Ireland that it took the Vatican almost a thousand years to stamp out their 'divergent' views and ensure strict compliance with Vatican dogma. As late as AD754, the Celtic Church continued in what may have been a fairly pure form of Nazarene faith – Irish churches celebrated the Judaic Sabbath, Judaic Passover and ritual killing of animal sacrifices – as well as denying the Trinity and Jesus virgin birth. The Vatican had no political or military reach into Ireland and so had to play a long game of quiet subjugation whenever the chance to appoint outside bishops arose.

18.52 Examination of Paul's writings does illuminate significant differences with the Gospel writers, particularly the linked synoptic Gospels. Once one understands the difference between Paul who worked closely with

Jesus family members and others who had known Jesus during his ministry – and the writers of the synoptic Gospels, at least two of whom had never met Jesus – it becomes clear that the synoptic Gospels contain much elaborative embellishment which was invented to try to sell Jesus message to Jewish and Gentile audiences.

18 *bis*

New evidence concerning the destruction of Sodom & Gomorrah and Jericho

18.53 New archaeological evidence points to a strong probability of a far-reaching biblical inaccuracy. The new evidence appears to merge together two events that traditionally are regarded as very distinct and very far apart in time. Whilst the information laid out in the rest of this chapter is new, the detail and accuracy is very convincing.

18.54 Recent analysis of soil and rock samples from Jericho, and from extensive ruins of a large city in the suspected location of Sodom &/or Gomorrah, has yielded additional information confirming their destruction as being attributable to a meteor strike.

18.55 We have long had clear archaeological evidence that Jericho suffered devasting destruction. The earliest permanent settlement at Jericho, known as Tell es-Sultan, has been dated to 9600BC, the end of the Younger Dryas period. The city location may have been initially chosen because of the number of fresh water springs in the area. It grew in importance due to its location on the key connecting road between the ancient highways – the Way of Horus (later known as the Via Maris) and Kings Highway. As referred to in paragraph 14.17 above, efforts to date the destruction of Jericho by various archaeologists during the 20th century have provided arrange of dates – 1617BC, 1573BC and 1530BC. But all agree that the destruction was not limited to the city walls falling down – devastation was such that the entire city was abandoned for many centuries, with limited reoccupation from around 850BC – it remained derelict for around 700 years.

18.56 Excavations since 2006, at a site known as Tell el-Hammam, 10km east of the River Jordan and 10km north of the northern boundary of the Dead Sea, have uncovered a vast ancient urban site five times the area of ancient Jericho. The city contained a number of multi-storey buildings but the whole area appears to have been flattened by a devastating explosion. Unlike the impact of earthquakes or warfare, the excavations indicate a different cause for the destruction. Pottery sherds have outer surfaces melted into glass, mudbricks and building plaster appearing to have boiled, bubbled and melted whilst human and animal bones were shattered into tiny fragments. Other evidence, including shocked quartz, iron and silica rich micro-sphericals and nano diamonds, indicates temperatures of 2000C to 2500C – which only arises from a meteor impact or airburst. Some have speculated that the same by-products are formed by a nuclear detonation.

18.57 Professor James Kennett of UC Santa Barbara, compares the destruction seen at Tell el-Hammam with the Tunguska event of 1908 when a meteor estimated at 60m diameter exploded about 2 miles above the Siberian forest with an explosive force estimated at 12 megatons (c1000 times the power of the Hiroshima bomb). The Tunguska explosion felled all trees for 40km in every direction.

18.58 Tell el-Hammam is a mere 15 km east of Jericho, hence the force shown to have destroyed the former would equally have devastated the latter at the same time. The city was devasted from above and, over the millennia, a hilltop formed over the rubble – which is now being excavated. This points to a meteor lacking a solid metal core making it susceptible to gravitational stresses as it entered earth atmosphere, resulting in an explosive air burst and the absence of an impact crater at ground level.

18.59 Tell el-Hammam, at 5 times the size of the then contemporary Jericho, was clearly a major city and many conclude that it must have been the city which became infamous in the biblical story of Sodom – even Google Maps now gives it the secondary name of Sodom! Most academics believe Sodom and Gomorrah comprised a single city. Given its size, it must have existed for some centuries prior to its demise, so far excavations have uncovered evidence of occupation back to 4700BC. Considering its location beside the Kings Highway, it must have traded with Egypt in the centuries prior to the Hyksos occupation of Lower Egypt. So, there must be references to the city but with a name we have never been able to place.

18.60   The new excavations have arrived at a date of 1650BC (+/- 20) for the destruction of Tell el-Hammam, which is close to the earlier estimates for the destruction of Jericho – which, being so close, must have happened at the same time from the same cause.

18.61   Such an explosion, a few miles up in the atmosphere, would have been both heard and seen throughout the ancient Middle East. (Note: the Tunguska event in 1908 was heard in London, more than 8000km away.) Early Canaanites living between 50 and 200 kms away from the epi-centre would have been terrified by this awesome display of divine wrath and likely have fled – maybe this event triggered the Hyksos flight into Egypt. The best date for the Hyksos take-over of Lower Egypt is 1655BC – spot on for the newly estimated date of the meteor event.

18.62   The fact that both Jericho and Sodom were subsequently abandoned for many centuries is somewhat puzzling. As we have examined, Egypt controlled the Levant for most of the Second Millennium BC. Tell el-Hammam is close to the ancient Kings Highway and Jericho is on the main link from the Kings Highway to the Way of Horus. These two roads formed the key trunk routes for trade and military operations across the Egyptian possessions in Asia. Such was their importance that military garrisons were maintained at intervals along both roads. So, after Pharaoh Ahmose, expelled the Hyksos from Lower Egypt around 1550BC and Egyptian rule was progressively re-established over what is now Israel and the areas north and east of modern Israel, why did these former trade centres remain abandoned until long after the Egyptians retreated in the 11th century.

18.63   The reason appears to lie in the high concentration of salts found samples from the ruins, ranging from 4% to as high as 25%. Tell el-Hammam and Jericho both lie only 10km north of the current shore of the Dead Sea, indicating that the explosion would have evaporated large volumes of the very salty Dead Sea waters and debris falling back to the ground depositing a layer of material with salt concentrations so high as to make the soil infertile. The excessive salt in ground deposits may have also contaminated the natural springs for a long time. The extremely high temperatures recorded in the destruction of the urban areas would also have rendered the soil under the airburst brittle and probably un-

The destruction of these cities is immortalized in biblical accounts

18.64   We have previously found evidence of the extraordinary historicity truly ancient myths have been found to be derived from – see the Prequel to this series (7.47 and 7.48) which point to tribal memories of catastrophic events dating back to c6,000BC and c35,000BC respectively. It has been estimated that we have around 500 tribal myths which seem to relate to a global inundation, ceaseless rains and great famines – which relate ancient memories of the Younger Dryas meteor impact c10,765BC. Therefore, it would hardly be surprising to find references to the cataclysmic destruction of great cities which occurred around 3700 years ago also featuring in tribal myths.

18.65   The biblical story of its location and of its destruction certainly fits well with the site of Tell el-Hammam and its fate. One can readily appreciate how the fabled stories of the destruction of the Sodom and Jericho become woven into the oral tribal myths handed down over the centuries. Outside of the bible, there are no references to the Hebrew names of Sodom and Gomorrah, these names probably reflect the general biblical practice of naming places and people according to their character. In Judaism, Sodom and Gomorrah are often referred to as a twin city. The meaning of the name Gomorrah, formed from two words, carries meanings of tyranny, binding and people to be feared. Furthermore, these Hebrew names were not even recorded until 975BC at the earliest, when Hebrew writing emerged, and maybe much later when much of the Torah was written during the Babylonian captivity in the 6th century BC. Therefore, it is hardly surprising that the names Sodom and Gomorrah do not appear in any then contemporary Egyptian or Babylonian records.

18.66   But now we know the date it should be relatively easy for historians to identify the original name of Tell el-Hamman as its destruction must have been a major event. Unfortunately, surviving records of the ruling pharaoh, Merkheperre, are sparse as Egypt was suffering from dynastic feuds and the influx of the Hyksos, probably fleeing from the catastrophic event. Babylonian records should be more promising, given the relative proximity and its stable rule under the Amorite dynasty of the First Babylonian Empire. It is estimated that Ammi-Ditana, grandson of

Hammurabi, ruled 1683BC to 1647BC and was followed by two further descendants until Babylon was attacked and largely destroyed by the Hittites under Mursilis I in 1595BC. Amongst the hundreds of thousands of cuneiform tablets sitting in the store rooms of museums in Berlin, London and Philadelphia probably lies a description of the destruction of Jericho and what we know as Tell el-Hamman, revealing its original name.

18.67 The biblical account in Genesis places the destruction of Sodom and Gomorrah contemporary with Abraham, after departing from Egypt where he had stayed with Pharaoh Senusret I (1971BC to 1926BC), so maybe around 1950BC. But, Jericho's destruction is biblically linked with the entry to the Promised Land under Joshua, soon after Moses died, maybe 400 years later. Tribal memory of stories relating to the destruction of the two cities may have originated from two different eyewitness accounts that later seemed to fit naturally into different parts of the national foundation myth as it evolved. Thus we might appreciate popular tribal myths as important conveyors of kernels of historical information about major events – but inerrant they surely are not!

19

An alternative view of our creation

19.1 And now to something completely different. I received much comment on the 'scientific' explanation in Part One of proof of the existence of a divine intelligence behind the design of our universe. Because of the apparent popularity, I now go one step further to consider features that suggest our universe might be an artificial creation – a simulation rather like the Matrix, as presented in the film trilogy.

19.2 Reasons to believe that the universe is a simulation include the fact that it behaves mathematically and is broken up into pieces (subatomic particles) like a pixelated video game. According to Rich Terrile, a scientist at Nasa's Jet Propulsion Laboratory "Even things that we think of as continuous – time, energy, space, volume – all have a finite limit to their size. If that's the case, then our universe is both computable and finite. Those properties allow the universe to be simulated. Quite frankly, if we are not living in a simulation, it is an extraordinarily unlikely circumstance".

19.3 Is it logically possible that we are in a simulation? According to Max Tegmark, a professor of physics at MIT, "yes, but in order to make the argument in the first place, we need to know what the fundamental laws of physics are where the simulations are being made. And if we are in a simulation then we have no clue what the laws of physics are. What I teach at MIT would be the simulated laws of physics".

19.4 That we might be in a simulation is, Terrile argues, a simpler explanation for our existence than the idea that we are descendants of the first generation to rise up from primordial ooze and evolve into molecules, biology and eventually intelligence and self-awareness. The simulation hypothesis also accounts for peculiarities in quantum mechanics, particularly the measurement problem, whereby things only become defined when they are observed.

19.5   Fundamental physics is in a metaphysical mess and needs help. The attempt to reconcile its two big theories, general relativity and quantum mechanics, has stalled for nearly 40 years. Efforts to unite them, such as string theory, are mathematically ingenious but incomprehensible even for many who work with them. This is well known. A better-kept secret is that at the heart of quantum mechanics is a disturbing paradox – the so-called measurement problem, arising ultimately out of the Uncertainty Principle – which apparently demonstrates that the very measurements that have established and confirmed quantum theory should be impossible. Oxford philosopher of physics David Wallace has argued that this threatens to make quantum mechanics incoherent – the only known remedy being to vastly multiply the number of universes.

19.6   Beyond these domestic problems there is the failure of physics to accommodate conscious beings. The attempt to fit consciousness into the material world, usually by identifying it with activity in the brain, has failed dismally, if only because there is no way of accounting for the fact that certain nerve impulses are supposed to be conscious (of themselves or of the world) while the overwhelming majority (physically essentially the same) are not. In short, physics does not allow for the strange fact that matter reveals itself to material objects (such as physicists).

19.7   And then there is the mishandling of time. The physicist Lee Smolin's recent book, Time Reborn, links the crisis in physics with its failure to acknowledge the fundamental reality of time. Physics is predisposed to lose time because its mathematical gaze freezes change. Tensed time, the difference between a remembered or regretted past and an anticipated or feared future, is particularly elusive. This worried Einstein: in a famous conversation, he mourned the fact that the present tense, "now", lay "just outside of the realm of science".

19.8   Recent attempts to explain how the universe came out of nothing, which rely on questionable notions such as spontaneous fluctuations in a quantum vacuum, the notion of gravity as negative energy, and the inexplicable free gift of the laws of nature waiting in the wings for the moment of creation, reveal conceptual confusion beneath mathematical sophistication. They demonstrate the urgent need for a radical re-examination of the invisible frameworks within which scientific investigations are conducted. We need to step back from the mathematics to see how we got to where we are now. In short, to un-take much that is taken for granted.

19.9 Perhaps even more important, we should reflect on how a scientific image of the world that relies on up to 10 dimensions of space and rests on ideas, such as fundamental particles, that have neither identity nor location, connects with our everyday experience. This should open up larger questions, such as the extent to which mathematical portraits capture the reality of our world – and what we mean by "reality". The dismissive "Just shut up and calculate!" to those who are dissatisfied with the incomprehensibility of the physicists' picture of the universe is simply inadequate. "It is time" physicist Neil Turok has said, "to connect our science to our humanity, and in doing so to raise the sights of both".

19.10 So who has created this simulation? According to Terrile it is our future selves – but I think more credibly it could be our Creator. At least the idea makes you think, and in 2017 there was news indicating that Elon Musk has invested heavily in a secret project to prove or disprove whether we are just software in a program!!

20

Conclusions of Part Two

20.1 Personally, I am convinced that a supreme intelligence triggered the creation of our universe – from evidence buried in the Periodic Table of Elements and the exquisiteness of many physical laws governing the interaction of atoms. That these atoms carry the characteristics to enable combination under defined conditions that leads to the precursors to living organisms and thence to life itself is astonishing. I also wonder at the design of DNA which, whilst it may have been a natural outcome of the predestined evolutionary process, also exhibits impossibly complex features suggestive of intervention by a divine creator.

20.2 At the same time, there appears to be overwhelming evidence that the two main gods of Judaism – Abraham's god (named El Elyon in Hebrew) and Yahweh (initially most likely to have been Nannar/Sin and later identified as Shamash, as in Psalm 84) – belong to the well tabulated pantheon of 'pagan gods' of the Middle Eastern, Greek and Roman empires – and played no role whatsoever in the creation of our solar system let alone the universe as a whole. All of these gods may have been descendants of a few elite survivors of the Flood resulting from the Hiawatha Glacier meteor impact – as described in the Prequel to his series.

20.3 Moreover, the biblically derived belief that humans were made in the image of the gods may have a factual basis. The original account, from which we see a garbled summary at the beginning of the Book of Genesis, does suggest that El Elyon's half-brother and half-sister (Enki and Ninharsag) may have carried out genetic modifications that created homo sapiens sapiens from more primitive Earthly primates. Hence one may explain that those more advanced human survivors led to a tiny band of rulers, who became known as 'gods' did indeed make man in their own image.

20.4 Whilst containing some great moral teaching, the Old Testament of adopted Jewish scripture is really all about a dynasty of humans who became referred to as gods – Enlil (the Lord Most High), Enlil's son Nannar (Sin in Akkadian and Semitic) and Enlil's grandson through Ninurta, Shamash (aka Yahweh). According to Sumerian records, Enlil appointed Shamash controller of Ur-Shulim (Jerusalem) – tantalizing evidence indeed! Note: Jesus is never recorded as referring to Yahweh, Sin or El Elyon.

20.5 The Torah + Joshua (often grouped together by academics) has little of factual or historical value. If one seeks a more accurate account of the formation of Earth, in the early period of our solar system, then the Emuna Elish (with original source documents up to c6,000 years old) is a better bet. The base case now agreed by the many astronomers is that account of the history of our planet contained in the Enuma Elish is highly plausible: it accounts well for our unique axial tilt; our precessional and nutational wobbling; and, our oversized moon. Moreover, we continue to find plentiful water existing inside and beyond the asteroid belt – these are quite literally the 'waters above and below the firmament'. The theology contained in the Torah is largely based on ancient, recognizably 'pagan', gods – as the Israelite god is progressively linked down the generations of the Sumerian supreme god, Enlil, to his son Ninurta and then to his grandson Shamash – one psalm even states unequivocally in Hebrew "Yahweh is Shamash; Shamash is Yahweh"!!

20.6 The Prophets (the 2nd division of the Jewish bible) has better theology but also suffers from widespread historical errors indicating much later authorship. This surely brings into question the accuracy of the frequent and voluminous quotations generally treated as accurate contemporaneous recordings. Critically, internal biblical evidence suggests Saul was never king whilst other biblical evidence indicates David was the first king. Further, it is surprising that, outside of the Bible, no direct evidence whatsoever for Saul, David or Solomon has ever been found. The only historical evidence is a fragment from a victory stele found at Tel Dan erected by the Aramean king, Hazael, in 842BC which states as victor

CONCLUSIONS OF PART TWO

he had killed both King Jehoram of Israel and King Ahaziah of Judah – with a fragmentary character remaining, which some interpret as meaning "of the house of David" – from which it is deduced that there was an earlier King David. Tenuous indeed!

20.7 According to the Bible, Solomon had 700 wives and 300 concubines. The wives were described as foreign princesses, including a Pharaoh's daughter and princesses of Moab, Ammon, Sidon and of the Hittites. The only wife mentioned by name is Naamah, the mother of Solomon's successor, Rehoboam. This has got to be a wild exaggeration, there were unlikely 700 royal families in the entire world at that time. On the other hand, how many of these 700 foreign royal families recorded that a princess of theirs had married King Solomon? None!

20.8 Apart from the absurdly exaggerated numbers, two historical problems jump out: (i) the Hittites had ceased to exist in 1178BC, some two hundred years earlier, and (ii) as a major principle, no Egyptian princesses were ever married out – being reserved for their brothers or father to preserve the purity of the royal bloodline and to avoid claimants from arising.

20.9 The level of historical inaccuracies is indicative of both oral traditions being written up long after the events supposedly took place and of earnest efforts to develop a tradition of a glorious heritage for a Chosen People blessed by God. Typically, newly written or redacted versions were introduced during periods of great sinning or subsequent retribution having been visited upon Israel – so past glories and past victories provided the incentive to repent and to be raised up once more.

20.10 The big breakthrough from my research for this booklet is, as set out in chapter 2, is that the origin of descriptions of the slavery under the Egyptians can be attributed to the pre-monarchical centuries living in Canaan. After the Egyptians defeated the Hyksos occupying Lower Egypt and expelled them, there is evidence that remnants ended up east of the Jordan. Gradually, these nomadic tribes started trickling back into Egyptian territory from across the Jordan and moved into the Judean Highlands, the Samarian Highlands and possibly Amurru. From these territories they raided towns and caravans moving between garrisons along the Kings Highway – posing a nuisance value that led to punitive action by the Egyptians, and enslavement when captured alive. Those that settled in Egyptian controlled towns in the lowlands or along the coast or in the dozens of Canaanite towns owned by Egyptian temples, would have prime targets for selection for the corvée and for the annual slave quotas sent to Egypt.

20.11 Israelite memories of slavery under Egyptian control would have arisen from events between c1500BC and the demise of direct Egyptian rule over Canaan circa 1130BC, when the Philistines spread out from the Pentapolis (the five walled cities in modern day Gaza, built by Egypt in 1175BC for their defeated army) up the coast and across the lowlands surrounding the Judean Highlands and the area south of the Sea of Galilee. Thus, instead of the biblical tale of slavery in Egypt followed by a glorious exodus to the Promised Land, the reality was an inglorious expulsion from Egypt, followed later by enslavement under Egyptian masters from which there was no escape – until Egyptian power waned during the century leading to the Israelite capture of Jerusalem c1000BC.

20.12 Theologians maintain there is continuity from the Old Testament through to the Gospel message and conclude the purpose of the OT was to presage the New Testament. It is clear that the various writers of OT scripture were inspired by a love of their creator but if The creator had an influence – it must have been tenuous at best. Why? Let us paraphrase the argument of one of the Biblical Inerrants – those believing the Bible conveys the very words of God and therefore contains no errors. Paul Feinberg, of the Dallas Seminary, says it is simply impossible to separate the historical and scientific content of the Bible from the doctrinal and theological. Those who seek the truth find the Old Testament is riddled with inaccuracies of a historic, scientific and even ethical nature – so, is it credible that the theology contained in the Old Testament remains absolutely without error when telling of all those wonderful, "unbelievable", things about God and heaven? Is it credible to believe all these things that there is no possible way of confirming whilst at the same time allowing that there are numerous errors in areas that can be confirmed?

CONCLUSIONS OF PART TWO

Key – colours indicate name of each 'god' in principal languages:
Sumerian; *Akkadian*; Egyptian; Hebrew

* Until Moses met the Burning Bush, the god of Genesis was named El Elyon, the Canaanite name for Enlil. From Moses up to Saul, the Hebrew deity appears to have Nannar but by the Psalms of David the title had passed to Shamash. In all translations of Jewish scripture into Greek, Latin, English, etc., all names of 'god' are assumed to refer to a single entity.

Appendix

Selected family members of ruling elite – survivors of 'the Flood' or perhaps ET's?

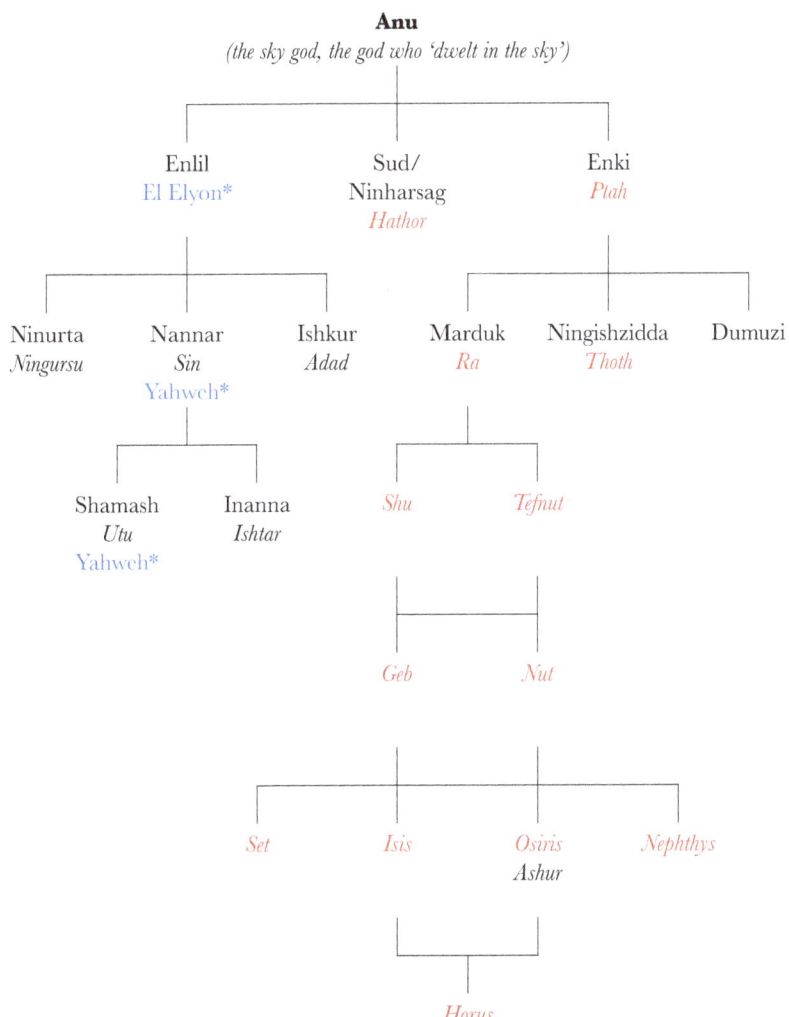

Index

Abdi-Heba, *governor*	4.13
Abraham	1.6, 1.10, 2.9, 2.12, 2.19, 2.29, 3.1, 3.8, 3.10, 3.18, 3.19, 6.3, 6.4, 7.1, 7.2, 7.9, 7.22, 7.25, 7.27, 7.31, 7.34, 8.1, 8.2, 8.6, 8.9, 8.10, 8.24, 8.25, 9.4, 10.12-14, 10.20, 10.21, 12 *passim*, 13.1, 13.6, 14.6, 16.13, 18.40, 18.67, 20.2
'Ad, People of	2.23, 3.32, 6.2, 7.3, 15.69
Agag, Amalekite *king*	15.15
Ahaziah, *king of* Judah	2.29, 15.38, 20.6
Ahimelek, *high priest* YHWH	15.23
Ahmose, *pharaoh*	3.30, 3.34, 3.38, 5.2, 7.2, 18.62
Akhenaten, *pharaoh*	5.18, 15.51
Akkadian, *language & people*	1.8, 2.5, 2.6, 2.12, 2.14, 3.11, 3.13, 3.18, 3.31, 3.42, 3.47, 5.18, 5.20, 6.18, 7.20, 7.24, 10.14, 11 *passim*, 12.20, 12.21, 13.4, 15.7, 18.27, 18.38, 18.46
Alalakh	3.36, 5.20
Aleppo – *see Yamkhad*	
Alexander, Archibald	18.8
Alexander III, *the Great*	12.28
Amarna, inc Letters	3.42, 5.12, 5.13, 5.15, 5.18
Amelekites	3.18, 4.15, 6.14, 7.17, 7.18, 15.15, 15.28
Amenemhat II, *pharaoh*	3.20
Amenhotep II, *pharaoh*	15.49
Amenhotep III, *pharaoh*	15.50, 15.51
Amenophis II, *pharaoh*	3.41
Amenophis III, *pharaoh*	5.18
Ammi-Ditana, *Amorite king*	18.66
Ammon	15.37, 15.46, 20.7
Amorites	2.23, 3.3, 3.5, 3.26, 3.27, 3.37, 3.42, 12.21, 14.18, 15.7, 15.9

Amurru	2.23, 3.42, 3.45, 3.47, 3.54, 6.2, 7.5, 7.29, 7.30, 20.10
Apophis, *pharaoh*	3.28, 3.29
Aramaic	12.20, 18.46, 18.47
Arameans	2.23, 2.29, 7.15, 9.3, 12 *passim*, 13.2, 15.37, 15.38
Archer, Gleason, *theologian*	18.5
Ark of the Covenant	10.7-9, 15.5-7, 15.10, 15.11, 15.33
Aryan	12.22
Ashkelon	15.63, 15.65
Ashtoreth/Asherah	1.10, 7.20, 7.21, 8.2, 8.16, 8.21, 10.3, 15.9, 16.13, 20.3
Ashurbanipal, *Assyrian king*	7.25, 9.6, 15.9, 15.35
Assyrians	2.30, 3.27, 3.34, 4.15, 8.21, 9.4, 9.6, 9.10, 10.14, 11.3, 12.19, 12.20, 12.28, 12.32, 12.33, 12.37, 13.4, 13.5, 15.48, 15.55, 15.62-64, 17.4
Avaris	3.22, 3.24, 3.25, 3.29
Ba'al	1.10, 7.20, 15.9
Baalbek	7.33, 10.10, 10.11, 15.69
Babylon, *originally Dingir-Ra*	1.4, 1.8, 2.12, 2.16, 2.26, 3.34-36, 6.12, 6.13, 6.18, 7.25-27, 8.21, 8.22, 9.6, 10.14, 12.15, 12.19, 12.20, 12.25, 12.28, 12.29, 12.34, 13.5, 14.1-3, 14.23, 14.28, 15.45, 15.48, 15.50, 15.54, 15.56, 16.15, 17 *passim*, 18.27
Bahnsen, Greg, *theologian*	18.5, 18.6, 18.30
Bathsheba	15.39, 15.59, 17.7
Beersheba	12.11
Behistun Inscription	2.5
Beirut	7.14
Berossus, *c3ʳᵈBC historian*	3.18
Beth Shean	4.3, 4.4, 5.2, 5.13, 5.15
Byblos	3.35, 3.39, 3.40, 4.8, 5.12, 5.15, 7.14
Canaan, *son of Ham*	8.3-5, 8.9, 9.3, 9.5, 14.5
Canaanites	12.5, 12.17, 12.21, 12.26

Carchemish, *R. Euphrates*	3.36, 3.40, 3.54, 4.7, 7.30
Carduchi, *proto-Kurds*	12.28
Carthage	15.69
Celtic church	18.51
Chaldeans	8.21, 8.22, 9.10, 12 *passim*
Chemosh, *god of Ammon & Moab*	15.26
Cimmerians	9.3, 9.4
Copernicus, *astronomer*	14.28
Corvée	2.20. 2.24, 5.6, 6.3
Cyprus	3.35, 3.49, 3.50, 3.52, 3.54, 5.8, 15.69
Cyrus I, *Persian emperor*	1.4, 2.12, 2.16, 2.17, 8.22, 10.22, 14.2, 14.3, 17.2, 17.11-17, 17.24, 17.25
Cyrus Cylinder	17.12, 17.24
Dagon – *see Ishkur*	
Damascus – *aka Upe*	3.41, 3.43, 5.13, 7.15, 7.33, 12.17, 12.20, 14.7, 15.37
David, *king*	2.9, 2.29-31, 4.10-14, 6.1, 6.8, 6.9, 7.9, 7.11, 7.12, 10.1, 10.6, 10.8, 10.16, 10.17, 12.37, 14.20, 14.33, 15 *passim*, 17.7, 20.6
Dedu-mose, *pharaoh*	3.23
DNA	1.2, 20.1
Dumuzid, *aka Tammuz*	1.5, 10.19
Edom	7.3, 7.5, 7.6, 7.34, 14.17, 14.35, 15.37
Egyptian Book of the Dead	2.14, 6.18
Einstein	19.7
El Elyon *(aka Enlil)*	1.10, 2.12, 3.8. 3.10, 7.1, 7.25, 8.3, 8.9, 8.15, 8.20, 8.21, 8.23, 10.3, 10.10, 11.1, 12.6, 12.12, 12.17, 14.6, 15.8, 15.14, 16.9-11, 16.13, 16.15, 17.2, 18.28, 18.40, 20.2-5
El Shaddai	18.28
Elam	9.6
Eli, *Jewish high priest*	15.3, 15.4
Elisheba/Elisheva	16.2, 16.3, 16.6, 16.7, 16.15
Enuma Elish	1.7, 2.12, 7.25, 8.6, 20.4, 20.5
Enki – *see Ptah*	

Esarhaddon, *king*	15.64
Esau, *son of Isaac*	12.13, 12.24
Etana, *Sumerian king*	10.1-6, 10.14, 10.16, 16.13
Ezra, *prophet*	17.10
Feinberg, Paul D, *theologian*	18.13, 18.14, 20.12
Finkelstein, Israel, *archaeologist*	6.7, 6.8, 7.16, 15.68, 18.44
Geisler, Norman, *theologian*	18.15
General relativity	19.5
Gibson, Dan, *historian*	7.3
Göbekli Tepe	7.33, 7.37, 8.11, 10.18, 10.21
Goliath	15.21
Goshen	9.9
Gutenberg	2.3
Habiru	4.13
Hagar, *aka Keturah*	12.23, 12.24
Ham, *son of Noah*	3.37, 8.2, 8.4, 8.5, 9.5, 12.26, 14.5, 16.13
Hammurabi, *king & Code*	3.31
Hathor – *see Isis*	
Harappa	8.2
Harran	2.19, 3.8, 7.2, 7.27, 7.34, 7.37, 8.6, 8.25, 10.13, 10.20, 10.21, 12.16, 12.18, 12.25, 12.27-29, 17.20, 17.21
Hattsua, *Hittite capital*	3.5, 3.54, 5.18, 5.20
Hattusilis I, *Hittite king*	3.36
Hattusilis II, *Hittite king*	3.46, 3.47
Hattusilis III, *Hittite king*	5.13
Hazael, *Aramean king*	15.38, 20.6
Hazor	3.30-32, 3.34, 6.6, 7.3, 7.29, 18.44
Hebron	12.4, 12.7, 12.8, 12.10, 12.11, 14.31
Hezekiah, *king of Judah*	17.6-8
Hiawatha meteor impact	20.2
Hilkiah, *high priest*	2.13, 2.30, 12.8, 12.30, 15.55, 15.67, 18.30
Hittites	1.15, 2.18, 3.1, 3.5, 3.27, 3.35, 3.37, 3.42, 3.44, 3.49-52, 3.54, 4.1, 4.7, 5.9, 5.20, 7.5,

	7.15, 7.29, 7.30, 12 *passim*, 14.4, 14.8, 14.9, 14.18, 14.21, 15.8, 15.46, 15.48, 18.66, 20.7, 20.8
Hodge, Charles, *theologian*	18.8
Hoshea, *king of Judah*	6.4
Hurrians	3.5, 3.6, 3.18, 3.35-37, 3.42, 5.9, 8.21, 14.13
Hyksos	2.20, 2.22, 2.23, 3.1, 3.2, 3.4-6, 3.19-34, 3.36, 3.38, 3.43, 5.1, 5.10, 6.2, 6.4, 6.18, 7.2-4, 7.17, 7.28, 7.31, 7.35, 10.12, 10.20, 12.26, 13.5, 14.17, 15.69, 18.59, 18.61, 18.66, 20.10
Inanna, Ishtar, Isis – *see Asherah*	
Isaac	3.20, 12 *passim*, 13.1, 13.6
Ishkur *(aka Adad, Dagon)*	15.7-9, 12.17
Ishmael, *son of Abraham*	12.23, 12.24
Jacob, *son of Isaac*	3.20, 12 *passim*, 13.1, 13.2, 13.6, 15.14, 15.67
Japheth, *son of Noah*	3.37, 8.2, 9.3, 9.4, 12.22, 14.5, 14.13
Jebusites	4.11-13
Jehoram, *king of Israel*	2.29, 15.38, 20.6
Jericho	7.33, 14.10, 14.13, 14.17, 18.44, 18.54-67
Jerusalem, *aka Uru-salem*	2.9, 2.20, 2.30, 2.31, 3.43, 4.8, 4.11-13, 5.15, 6.2, 6.8, 6.13, 6.17, 7.5, 7.13, 7.16, 7.20, 7.26, 10.8, 10.9, 10.11, 10.12, 12.7, 14.1-3, 14.18, 14.32, 15.33, 15.42, 15.65, 15.66, 15.69, 17.2, 17.7, 18.35, 18.40, 18.51, 20.4
Joseph, *son of Jacob*	13.1-5, 15.67
Josephus, Flavius, *historian*	3.18, 3.19, 4.9, 7.4
Joshua, *patriarch*	2.27, 6.6, 6.11-13, 12.35, 14 *passim*, 15.56, 18.44, 18.67, 20.5
Josiah, *king of Judah*	2.13, 6.13, 12.30, 12.33
Jubilees, *book of*	8.4, 14.5
Kadesh, *& battle of 1258BC*	3.39, 3.41, 3.42, 3.44, 3.45, 3.47, 3.48, 7.29, 12.8, 12.11, 18.29
Kaiser, Walter, *theologian*	18.5, 18.31-40, 18.45-47

Kamose, *pharaoh*	3.23, 3.25, 3.28, 3.29
Kassites	3.35, 3.36
Kings Highway	2.20, 3.43, 5.2, 5.15, 6.16, 7.30, 7.32-35, 14.7, 18.55, 18.59, 18.62, 20.10
Kiriath Jearim	15.11, 15.33
Kish	10.2, 10.4, 10.15
Kitchen, K. A., *theologian*	7.23-26, 18.29
Krabbendam, Henry, *theologian*	18.48
Labashi-Marduk, *king of Babylon*	17.20
Libyans	3.22, 3.52, 3.53, 9.5
Leah, *wife of Jacob*	12.24
Lewis, Gordon R., *philosopher*	18.12
Maccabean	15.35
Macedonia	12.28
Malta	15.69
Mantheo, *Egyptian priest c3rd BC*	3.5, 3.19, 3.21, 3.23
Marduk – *see Ra*	
McNutt, Paula, *historian*	6.8, 7.8, 18.44
Mediggo, *battle of 1482BC*	3.39, 5.2
Melchizedek	18.40, 18.41
Menuhotep II, *pharaoh*	3.1, 12.5, 12.10
Merneptah, *pharaoh, stele*	3.51, 3.53, 6.10, 7.8, 7.14, 7.17, 14.31, 15.69
Merkheperre, *pharaoh* 1663-1649BC	18.66
Mesha, *king of Moab, stele*	7.12
Midian	7.34
Midrash	12.23
Mitanni, *and Treaty 1380BC*	3.5, 3.37, 3.40-42, 3.46, 7.30, 14.13, 15.49, 18.29
Moab	7.3, 7.5, 7.6, 7.9-12, 7.34, 14.17, 14.33, 14.35, 15.25, 15.26, 15.37, 15.46, 20.7
Mohenjo-Daro	8.2
Moses	1.6, 1.13, 2.9, 2.14, 2.29, 6.2, 6.6, 7.22, 7.34, 12.30, 12.31, 12.35-37, 15.56, 15.67,

	18.27, 18.28, 18.30, 18.35, 18.40, 18.67
Mursilis I, *Hittite king*	3.36, 18.66
Mursilis II, *Hittite king*	3.44
Musk, Elon	19.10
Muwatallis, *Hittite king*	3.44-46
Mycenae	1.15, 3.1, 3.52, 5.8
Naar, Ish.nar, Lu.nar	3.18, 7.2
Nabateans	2.23, 3.32, 7.3, 15.69
Nabonidus, *king of Babylon*	17.12, 17.20-26
Nannar, *aka Sin*	1.10, 8.25, 10.10, 10.12, 10.13, 12.17, 14.6, 15.8, 15.9, 17.2, 17.20-22, 20.2, 20.4
Nathan, *prophet*	15.34
Nazarite	15.2
Nazarenes	18.51
Nebuchadnezzar II, *king*	1.8, 7.12, 8.6, 8.25, 9.7, 12.15, 15.35, 15.65, 17.27
Necho II, *pharaoh*	9.9, 13.7
Nehemiah, *prophet*	14.28, 17.10
Nelson, Richard, *historian*	6.11
Nestorians	12.29
Nineveh	1.8, 2.17, 15.9
Ninharsag – *see also Isis*	
Ninurta	14.32, 20.4, 20.5
Nippur	3.10, 3.11, 3.14-17, 7.1, 7.25, 8.17, 8.21
Noah – *see Ziusudra*	
Noth, Martin, *historian*	6.12
Nubians	3.22-24, 3.30, 3.32, 4.1, 4.16, 5.2, 5.3, 6.4, 6.18, 9.5
Onomasticon of Amenemope	4.5
Osiris	6.19
Palmyra	7.33
Paran	7.34
Payne, Barton, *theologian*	18.5, 18.29
	15.27, 15.28, 15.36-38, 15.54, 15.61-66,

	15.69, 20.11
Phoenicians	2.13, 2.31, 3.39, 4.14, 7.14, 7.15, 7.25, 12.21, 14.14, 15.38, 15.54, 15.64, 15.69, 16.8, 18.27, 18.38
Piankhy, *pharaoh*	6.18
Pinnock, Clark, *theologian*	18.1
Pithom	13.7
Pressler, Carolyn, *theologian*	6.11
Promised Land	7.34, 8 *passim*
Ptah – *aka Enki*	5.5, 6.19, 8.2, 8.3, 8.15, 8.16, 8.18, 8.20, 8.21, 8.23, 10.10, 17.2, 17.12, 20.3
Puduhepa, *Hittite queen*	3.51
Qatna	3.1, 3.34, 12.5, 12.10
Qode	3.54, 7.30
Quantum mechanics	19.5
Qumran	2.7, 17.3, 18.17
Qur'an	18.2, 18.47
Pithom	13.7
Ra/Marduk, *inc Amun Ra*	4.2, 5.5, 6.18, 6.19, 7.25, 8.21, 8.22, 10.10, 14.2, 15.8, 15.35, 17 *passim*.
Rachel, *wife of Jacob*	12.24
Rakia	18.31, 18.46, 18.47
Ramesses I, *pharaoh*	3.43, 3.44
Ramesses II, *pharaoh*	3.44-48, 3.52, 3.53, 4.13, 5.13, 5.18, 6.4, 6.6, 9.9, 13.7
Ramesses III, *pharaoh*	3.53-55, 4.1, 4.3
Ramesses XI, *pharaoh*	4.2
Rawlinson, Sir Henry *(1810-1895)*	2.5
Rebekah, *wife of Isaac*	12.16
Rehoboam, *king of Judah*	6.17, 15.46, 20.7
Rosetta Stone	2.4
Ruth, *great grandmother of King David*	14.33-35, 15.37
Sabians	8.25, 10.21-23
Samaria, Samaritans	12.34

Sarai, *aka Sarah*	3.13, 12.4, 12.7, 12.8, 12.12, 12.23
Sargon. II, *Assyrian king*	9.4
Saul	2.30, 4.8, 6.1, 6.4, 7.11, 10.16, 14.20, 15 *passim*, 20.6
Se'ir	7.6
Sea Peoples *(Greek)*	1.15, 2.25, 3.1, 3.31, 3.48, 3.52-55, 4.3, 4.7, 5.5, 5.10, 5.20, 6.7, 12.10, 13.5, 14.8, 14.10, 14.13, 14.20, 14.21, 15.8, 15.48, 18.43
Semite, Semitic	12.21-26
Sennacherib, *Assyrian king*	17.7
Senusret I, *pharaoh*	18.67
Seqenenre, *pharaoh*	3.29, 3.30
Seti, *pharaoh*	3.44, 4.13, 6.6
Shabtake, *pharaoh*	6.4, 9.5
Shamash	20.2, 20.4, 20.5
Sharuhen	3.30, 5.15, 7.2
Sheba, *queen of*	16.11, 16.12
Shechem	3.1, 7.5, 7.13, 12.5, 12.10, 12.34
Shem, *Name of Yahweh*	10.8-10, 15.29-32, 15.34, 15.35
Shem, *son of Noah*	3.37, 8.2-5, 8.9, 9.3, 9.4, 9.6, 12.22, 12.26, 14.5, 14.6
Sherley, Sir Robert, *adventurer*	2.5
Sheshonq I, *pharaoh*	6.17, 7.18
Sheshy, *pharaoh*	3.23, 6.4
Siamun, *pharaoh*	15.49
Sidon	4.8, 6.14, 7.14, 9.7, 15.46, 20.7
Sin – *see Nannar*	
Smolin, Lee, *physicist*	19.7
Sodom and Gomorrah	18.39, 18.42, 18.54-67
Solomon, *king*	1.3, 2.29, 2.31, 3.41, 4.10-12, 6.6, 6.9, 6.17, 7.22, 8.8, 10.1, 10.14, 10.15, 10.18, 10.19, 14.35, 15 *passim*, 16.12, 16.13, 20.6, 20.7
Spinoza, Baruch, *philosopher*	18.14

Sumerians	8.1, 8.2, 8.6-8, 8.10, 8.16, 8.19, 8.24, 10.2, 10.6, 10.19, 10.20, 11.2, 12.21-24, 14.6, 15.29, 16.13, 17.24, 18.47
Suppuliuma, *Hittite king*	12.8
Table of Elements	1.1
Tadmor, *aka Palmyra*	7.32
Taharqa, *pharaoh*	4.16
Talmud	12.23
Tammuz – *see Dumuzid*	
Tanis	4.9, 9.9
Tayma, Teman	10.12, 17.21-23
Tegmark, Max, *physicist*	19.3
Tell el-Hamman - *see Sodom & Gomorrah*	
Terah, *father of Abraham*	3.10, 7.9, 10.10
Terrile, Rich, *astronomer*	19.2, 19.4, 19.10
Thebes, *city of Amun-Ra*	2.24, 3.23, 3.28, 3.30, 3.32, 4.2, 4.9, 6.18
Tiamat, Tehom, *Asteroid Belt*	18.31, 18.46
Tiglath Pileser I, *king*	13.2
Tiglath Pileser III, *king*	15.63
Tiye, *wife of Amenhotep III*	15.51
Thoth	6.19
Thutmose III, *pharaoh*	3.38-40, 3.43
Thutmose IV, *pharaoh*	3.41
Toba mega volcano	1.9
Tower of Babel	11 *passim*
Trajan, *emperor AD98-117*	7.35
Tudkhaliyas, *Hittite king*	3.52
Tungusha event 1908	18.57, 18.61
Turin List	3.21
Turok, Neil, *physicist*	19.9
Tutankhamun, *pharaoh*	3.43, 5.18
Tyre	4.8, 4.9, 5.15, 6.14, 7.14, 9.7, 15.64, 15.69
Ugarit	3.1, 3.47, 3.54, 4.7, 5.2, 5.15, 5.20, 7.5, 12.5, 12.10, 16.9, 18.38

Ulun Buru	5.8
Ullaza	3.39, 5.15
United Monarchy	15 *passim*
Upe – *see Damascus*	
Ur	2.12, 2.19, 3.12-15, 7.1, 7.27, 7.34, 8.17, 8.24, 8.25, 10.10, 10.21, 12 *passim*, 17.20
Ur Kasdim, *aka Ura, Urfa*	12.28
Uriah, *the Hittite*	15.39
Uruk	17.28
Ussher, *bishop*	18.3
Vatican	18.51
Via Maris – *see Way of Horus*	
Wallace, David, *philosopher*	19.5
Warfield, B.B., *theologian*	18.8
Way of Horus *(aka Via Maris)*	2.20, 3.43, 4.4, 4.5, 5.2, 5.13, 7.7, 7.32, 7.35, 12.6, 14.7, 15.64, 18.55, 18.62
Westminster Confession of Faith	18.7
Woolley, Charles, *archaeologist*	12.27
Xenophon, 431-354BC, *historian*	12.28
Yahweh, YHWH, YWH	*passim*
Yamkhad (Aleppo)	3.34, 3.36, 3.40, 4.7
Younger Dryas Period	8.11, 18.64
Yusef *(aka Joseph)*	15.51
Zedekiah, *king of Judah*	4.11
Ziklag	15.27, 15.28
Ziusudra *(aka Utnapištim, Noah)*	1.9, 8.2, 8.3, 8.5, 8.6, 9.3, 12.22
Zoroastrian	17.13

Biblical References

Chronicles	18.28, 18.33
1 Chronicles 2:21-22	13.2
1 Chronicles 4:22	7.12
1 Chronicles 7:14	13.2
1 Chronicles 18:2	7.12
1 Chronicles 22:7	15.31
1 Chronicles 22:10	15.31
1 Chronicles 22:19	15.31
2 Chronicles 8:8	15.60
2 Chronicles 9:13-28	15.59
2 Chronicles 34, 35	2.13
Daniel	18.33
Deuteronomy	12.31-33, 15.67
Deuteronomy 5-26	12.33
Deuteronomy 12:11	10.9, 15.31
Deuteronomy 12:21	15.31
Deuteronomy 16:6	15.31
Deuteronomy 23:1-8	14.35
Deuteronomy 28:15	15.18
Deuteronomy 28:28	15.18
Deuteronomy 29:1	15.25
Deuteronomy 32:9	1.11, 8.9, 15.14
Deuteronomy 33:2	7.6
Enoch	18.34
Exodus 1:11	13.7
Exodus 16:3	2.22, 6.2
Ezekiel	18.28
Ezekiel 8:14-15	10.19
Ezekiel 16:3	3.27

Genesis 9:25-26	8.3
Genesis 10	1.12, 8.9, 9 passim, 12.1, 12.12, 12.22
Genesis 10:7	6.4
Genesis 11	9.4
Genesis 14	7.34
Genesis 20	12.12, 12.13
Genesis 23	12 passim
Genesis 24	12.24
Genesis 25:20	12.16
Genesis 26	12.13
Genesis 26:34	12.11
Genesis 28:5	12.16
Genesis 28:9	12.24
Genesis 37-46	13.1
Genesis 37:36	13.4
Genesis 41:34	13.4
Genesis 42:7	13.5
Genesis 42:9	13.5
Genesis 45:11	13.2
Genesis 46:12	13.2
Genesis 47:11	13.6
Hosea	12.32, 12.36
Isaiah	12.22, 17.3, 17.5, 17.6, 17.9, 17.12
Isaiah 14:4, 22, 25	17.8
Isaiah 20:1	17.4
Isaiah 22:15	17.7
Isaiah 40:3-11	17.6
Isaiah 42:15, 16	17.6
Isaiah 44:25	17.6
Isaiah 45:1, 8	1.4, 14.2, 17.12, 17.14
Isaiah 45:9-13	17.15
Isaiah 45:14	10.22
Isaiah 46:1, 2, 7	17.6

Isaiah 47:1, 2, 12, 13	17.6
Isaiah 48:14-16	17.15
Isaiah 48:20-22	17.6
Isaiah 49:9-12	17.6
Isaiah 52:11, 12	17.6
Job	17.9, 18.33
1 John 5:6-8	18.22
Joshua 10	14.18
Joshua 11:3	14.9
Joshua 11:21	14.19
Joshua 13:2-3	14.9, 14.20
Joshua 15:17	14.24
Joshua 17:16	14.10, 14.21
Joshua 19:6	3.30
Joshua 23:12	14.25
Joshua 24	14.26
Joshua 24:2-3	12.28
Joshua 24:19	14.22
Joshua 24:29	6.6
Judges	18.28
Judges 1:19	6.14
Judges 2:12-30	6.14
Judges 4:3	6.14
Judges 5	6.4
Judges 5:4	7.6
Judges 6:5	6.14
Judges 7:12	6.14
Judges 8:21-26	6.14
Judges 11:13	6.14
Judges 11:25	6.14
Judges 13	6.14
Judges 18:30	17.10
Kings	18.28

1 Kings 3	10.14, 15.43
1 Kings 3:3-4	15.19
1 Kings 4	15.44
1 Kings 5:3	15.31
1 Kings 5:5	15.31
1 Kings 5:13	15.60
1 Kings 6:1	6.5
1 Kings 8:20	15.30
1 Kings 8:44	15.31
1 Kings 8:63	15.53
1 Kings 9:6	15.13
1 Kings 10	16.12
1 Kings 10:14-22	15.59
1 Kings 11:3	15.46
1 Kings 12:4	15.59
1 Kings 14:21	15.31
1 Kings 14:26	6.17
2 Kings 17:4	6.4
2 Kings 18:13	17.7
2 Kings 22:8	2.13, 12.30
Luke	15.58
2 Maccabees 2:13	17.10
Matthew	15.58
Matthew 12:42	16.12
Matthew 28:19	18.22
Numbers 13:22	6.4
Proverbs	15.54
Psalm 2:2	17.14
Psalm 2:8	15.37
Psalm 41	17.7
Psalm 51	17.7
Psalm 78	12.37, 15.67
Psalm 82	1.12, 8.21

Psalm 84	20.2
Psalm 137	17.7
Revelations	18.47
Ruth	14.33-35, 18.33
Samuel	12.32, 15 passim
1 Samuel 1:11	15.2
1 Samuel 2	15.4
1 Samuel 2:10, 35	17.14
1 Samuel 3:3	15.5
1 Samuel 4	15.6
1 Samuel 5	15.7
1 Samuel 7	15.11-12
1 Samuel 10:1	15.14
1 Samuel 10:23	15.17
1 Samuel 13:5	4.15
1 Samuel 13:8	15.17, 15.19
1 Samuel 13:19-22	6.14, 15.62
1 Samuel 13:21	4.15
1 Samuel 15	15.15
1 Samuel 16:7	15.17, 15.18
1 Samuel 16:12	15.18
1 Samuel 17	15.20, 15.21
1 Samuel 17:4-7	4.15
1 Samuel 17:38-39	4.15
1 Samuel 17:58	15.21
1 Samuel 19:13	15.22
1 Samuel 22:3-4	7.11, 15.25
1 Samuel 22:10	15.23
1 Samuel 25	15.24
1 Samuel 25:13	4.15
1 Samuel 26:19	15.25
1 Samuel 27:6	15.27
1 Samuel 27:7	15.25

1 Samuel 30:17	3.18, 4.15
2 Samuel 1:6	4.15
2 Samuel 5:2	10.6
2 Samuel 6:2	15.29
2 Samuel 6:6	15.33
2 Samuel 7:10-16	15.30, 15.34
2 Samuel 8	15.37
2 Samuel 8:2	7.12
2 Samuel 12:15	15.39
2 Samuel 12:24	15.39
2 Samuel 13	15.40
2 Samuel 15	17.7
2 Samuel 20:15	4.15
2 Samuel 22:51	17.14
2 Samuel 23:1	17.14
2 Samuel 24:1	15.41
2 Samuel 31:10	4.5
Song of Songs	15.54, 18.33

Bibliography

Asad, Muhammad. *The Message of the Qur'an.* The Book Foundation, 2003

Barnes, William H. *Studies in the Chronology of the Divided Monarchy of Israel.* Atlanta: Scholars Press, 1991

Bunch, T.E. et al. *A Tunguska sized airburst destroyed Tall el-Hammam a Middle Bronze Age city in the Jordan Valley near the Dead Sea.* Science Report, 29 September 2021

Bray, Dr Gerald. *Biblical Interpretation: Past & Present. InterVarsity.* Press, Illinois, 1996

Brown, Raymond. *An Adult Christ at Christmas.* Liturgical Press, Minnesota, 1978

Cline, Eric. *1177BC The year civilization collapsed.* Princeton University 2014

Creach, Jerome F.D. *Joshua.* Westminster John Knox Press, 2003

Dever, William G. *Did God Have a Wife? Archaeology and Folk Religion in Ancient Israel.* William B Eerdmans, Grand Rapids, 2005

Finkelstein, I. *The Archaeology of the Israelite Settlement Jerusalem.* Tel Aviv University, 1988

Finkelstein, Israel; Silberman, Neil Asher. *David and Solomon: In Search of the Bible's Sacred Kings and the Roots of Western Tradition.* New York: Simon and Schuster, New York, 2007

Gibson, Dan. *Quaranic Geography.* CanBooks, 2011

Heaster, Duncan. I*saiah 40- 66 New European Christadelphian Commentary.* Carelinks, Australia, 2018

Humphreys, Colin and Waddington, Graeme. *Solar eclipse of 1207BC helps to date pharaohs.* Astronomy & Geophysics, University of Cambridge, 2017

Kaiser, Walter. *Tough Questions about God and his actions in the Old Testament.* Kregal Publications, Grand Rapids, 2015

Kee, Alastair. *Constantine v Christ.* Trinity Press International, 1982

Kitchen, K. A. *Ancient Orient and Old Testament.* Chicago, InterVarsity 1966

Manning, Sturt et al. Severe multi-year drought coincident with Hittite collapse around 1198–1196BC. Nature, 8 February 2023

McNutt, Paula. *Reconstructing the Society of Ancient Israel.* Westminster John Knox Press, 1999

Murphy-O'Connor, Jerome. *Keys to Jerusalem: Collected Essays.* Oxford University Press, 2012

Payne, J Barton. *The Nature of Biblical Criticism.* Louisville, Kentucky: Westminster John Knox, 2007

Pines, Shlomo. *The Jewish Christians of the Early Centuries of Christianity.* Bible Society, 1996

Pinnock, Clark H. *Biblical Revelation.* Moody Press, 1971

Redford, Donald B. *Egypt, Canaan and Israel in Ancient Times.* Princeton University Press, 1992

Said, Rushdi. *The River Nile: Geology, Hydrology and Utilization.* Pergamon Press, 1993

Scurlock, Jo Ann. *A History of Animal Sacrifice in Ancient Near East.* Brill, 2001

Seely, Paul. *Westminster Theological Journal No. 63.* Westminster Theological Seminary, 2001

Sitchin, Zecharia. *When Time Began.* Bear & Company, 1994

Smolin, Lee. *Time Reborn.* Houghton Mifflin Harcourt, 2013

Velikovsky, Immanuel. *Ages in Chaos.* Doubleday, 1952

Vermes, Geza. *The Complete Dead Sea Scrolls in English.* Penguin, 2004

Yadin, Yigael. *Hazor, Schweich Lectures of the British Academy, 1970.* Oxford University Press, 1970

Zeitlin, Solomon. *An Historical Study of the Canonization of the Hebrew Scriptures.* The American Academy for Jewish Research, 1933

The Truth Will Set You Free – Series

Prequel: Younger Dryas meteor impacts, The Flood & Atlantis

As we evolved, humanity experienced periodic climate swings from ice ages to warmer periods over 100,000 and 40,000 year cycles. After the last ice age maxima, this pattern was disrupted by a series of events causing abrupt global warming and cooling – periods known as the Dryas Periods. Evidence is now emerging of the cause of some of these events – meteor impacts which decimated human societies at that time. Tribal memories passed down over millennia, originally dismissed as myths, are now being reassessed as oral history. We are now beginning to understand details of the what, when and where of events immortalised as Noah's Flood and the destruction of Atlantis. Second Edition due 2024.

Part One: God, Enki, Ra/Marduk & Yahweh

Proof of a divine Creator is not to be found in the Bible. However, the real identity of Yahweh may be discerned from biblical texts. The most memorable figures from the Old Testament include Noah, Abraham, Moses and kings David & Solomon – one might expect these find international recognition, with references to their exceptional feats in the historical record of surrounding affected cultures. But only one of these hero's has been verified, one appears to be adopted from another culture, one surprises by his total invisibility and the kings are acknowledged only by an isolated and obscure fragment. Third Edition published September 2023.

Part Two: The Promised Land, 2000 BC to 1000 BC

The Old Testament books covering the time of Abraham to David (c2000 BC to c1000 BC) tell of the Israelites led from slavery to conquer the Promised Land. However, clear evidence reveals these books were largely written during the Babylonian captivity, after 596BC, by priests with only hazy notions of geography and history. The biblical story overlooks the fact that the entire area of the Promised Land formed part of the Egyptian Empire for the greater part of the entire millennia. Third Edition published March 2024.

Part Three: Jesus, the Nazarene

Arguably, Jesus has had the most formative impact on humankind. Today, the New Testament stands as the only authoritative source of his life and teaching – but almost all of the books written about him in the first century have been destroyed. How authentic and reliable are those texts selected for the New Testament? The Old Testament is reputed to contain hundreds of prophesies concerning Jesus – are they credible? We name him Christ, meaning Messiah, a term the church has allowed to be widely misunderstood. Is Jesus part of a Trinity? Second Edition published in July 2022.

Part Four: Truth Revealed – What Jesus Really Taught

This final work identifies many significant changes made to the Gospels to mould Christian beliefs in line with Church dogma. The majority of early Christian texts were ruthlessly destroyed by the Roman Church – why? What did they say? Aided by the earliest uncorrupted manuscripts and the few surviving examples of texts declared heretical, we can piece together Jesus original teaching. What is revealed dovetails well with ancient belief systems, explaining why Nazarene teaching spread like wildfire in the first century. Many of the difficult to grasp elements of conventional Christianity are exposed as being man-made. Many clues have survived, even in the New Testament, which support these findings. First Edition published August 2022.

Documents available for download from the Series website:
www.quintologypublications.com

Texts ruled heretical by the Roman Church

Truth Series Master Index of Issues

Thomasine Creed - a radical update of the Nicaean Creed

Symbols used on covers in this series

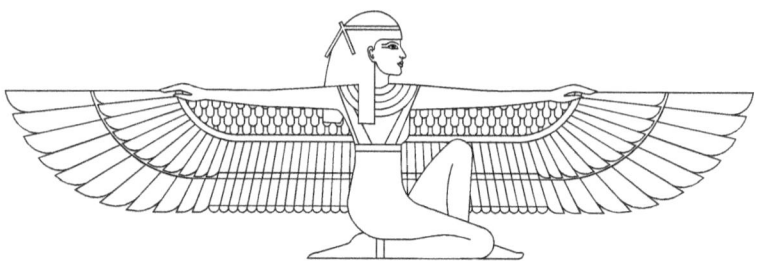

Prequel: Winged Isis

The goddess Isis was immensely popular from very ancient times. The sister and wife of Osiris, their only son was fathered after Osiris was killed and had ascended to heaven. This conception led to their son, Horus, being acclaimed as born of a perpetual virgin – and possibly an inspiration for the conception story in the gospels of Matthew and Luke. Ancient references associate Horus with the Giza pyramids and with Baalbek Terrace which are geometrically aligned to each other. The 'Winged Isis' symbolises her ability to fly, albeit with mechanical aids. Worship of Isis endured many millennia – growing to become the most popular god across the Roman Empire at the time of Jesus visit.

Part One: The Ankh

The Ankh symbolises the unity of Osiris and Isis. Osiris was murdered and rose to heaven. As a god in heaven, Osiris miraculously impregnated his wife, Isis, who gave birth to Horus. The manner of Isis conception led to her being described as a perpetual virgin, the Isis Mery. Ancient Egyptians believed that when Osiris returned to rule the Earth, he would resurrect the bodies of the dead and they would be reunited with their souls. Elements of these, already ancient, beliefs may have influenced gospel writers in the 1st Century AD.

Part Two: The Eye of Ra

Not to be confused with the eye of Horus. The Eye of Ra represents the power of the sun and the protection of Egyptian royalty. The symbol is used for this book to represent Egyptian suzerainty over the entire Promise Land for almost the entire 2nd Millennium BC.

Part Three: The Ichthys

The sign of the fish adopted by early Christians referring to the dawning of the new age of Pieces. The symbol served as a secret identification, Christians would scratch it on the ground to identify themselves to fellow believers. ΧΘΥΣ (IKhThUS) is an acronym or acrostic for the Greek phrase "'Ιησοῦς Χρῖστός Θεοῦ Υἱός Σωτήρ", which translates into English as 'Jesus Christ, Son of God, Saviour'.

Part Four: Templar symbol of two men riding one horse

Representation of the ancient belief of our binary spiritual nature. The two men represent the Spirit and the Soul riding in unity on a mortal body. Riding in unity parallels the yoked oxen, another parable denoting unity of Soul and Spirit – described by Jesus as the qualification to enter the kingdom of heaven.

www.ingramcontent.com/pod-product-compliance
Lightning Source LLC
Chambersburg PA
CBHW042322090526
44585CB00025BA/2808